LAW, MORALITY AND VIETNAM

The Peace Militants and the Courts

LAW, MORALITY AND VIETNAM

---

*The Peace Militants
and the Courts*

John F. and Rosemary S. Bannan

Indiana University Press   Bloomington & London

Published in Canada by Fitzhenry & Whiteside Limited,
Don Mills, Ontario
Manufactured in the United States of America

Library of Congress Cataloging in Publication Data

Bannan, John F
  Law, morality, and Vietnam; the peace militants and the courts.
  Includes bibliographical references.
  1. Trials (Political crimes and offenses)—United States.   2. Vietnamese Conflict, 1961–
    —Protest movements—United States.   I. Bannan, Rosemary S., 1925–   joint au-
    thor.   II. Title.   III. Title: Peace militants and the courts.
KF221.P6B3   345'.73'0231   73–16522
                              ISBN 0–253–14732–8

To Denyse and Eric

CONTENTS

ACKNOWLEDGMENTS

The authors wish to acknowledge the support of the National Institute of Mental Health, whose Research Grant—RO 16554—to Rosemary S. Bannan was indispensable in the investigation upon which this book is based. We wish to acknowledge also the assistance of the Russell Sage Foundation for its Summer Fellowship. Our thanks also to Vernell Woods and to Mary King, who typed our difficult manuscript.

LAW, MORALITY AND VIETNAM

The Peace Militants and the Courts

INTRODUCTION

Chapter One

Justice and Jeopardy

Between 1965 and 1969, the American peace movement tried to draw the nation's legal system into the struggle against the Vietnam war. Peace militants prompted arrest by deliberately breaking the law and used their trials as forums in which to challenge both the morality and the legality of the government's military policy. The result of these attempts was courtroom drama, often of the highest order, and profound crises for each of the parties involved.

For the peace movement it was a moment of greatest opportunity: perhaps a way had been found to bring hitherto undreamed-of pressure, constitutionally sanctioned and law supported pressure, against the continuation of the war. For the legal system it meant a dilemma of the most serious proportions. To accept the challenge of the peace militant would be to risk a destructive conflict with the President and Congress, each of which was committed to the war. To refuse the challenge would risk a serious failure in the courts' deeply felt responsibility to society: the responsibility of being the place where justice is available.

Our purpose is to explore this conflict of law and morality. To do this we shall describe and evaluate several cases where the judiciary had to respond to the peace movement's attempt to translate its moral convictions into legal instruments. Most of this book is devoted to an analysis of a series of trials where the legality of the war and of the

3

government's war-supporting policies was challenged. We do this to present the legal process in some detail, its characteristic behaviors, its own moral commitments, and its implications for our national life. We have also tried to convey a sense of the actual courtroom situation, of the give and take, the complexities, the compromises, the magnanimities and pettinesses of courts and defendants.

We have not limited ourselves to the trials, however, but have also interviewed both peace militants and judges. We are interested in the initiative of the peace movement and in its striking moral figures, about whom so much has been said in recent years. We have spoken to them, and their responses to our questions will be found here. But we are no less interested in the judicial response. The story which the judges have to tell is at least as important, though we have heard it less often. Their views on this period of dramatic confrontation are an essential part of this work.

THE EXPECTATIONS OF JUSTICE: CONFLICTING PATTERNS

When we speak of the legal system, we mean the courts, judges, juries, prosecuting and defense attorneys, their practices, interrelationships, administrative agencies, and personnel. The Constitution of the United States established the legal system and distinguished it from the other two fundamental branches of government, the legislative and the executive. Each of these three branches is most familiarly defined by its relation to law. The legislative makes laws; the executive attends to their being carried out; the legal system, or judiciary, is that complex of persons, procedures, and institutions from which society expects justice when it is claimed that the law has been broken or equity violated.

Break the law was precisely what certain peace militants did. If this lawbreaking was not ultimately to be reckoned a crime and if, by refusing induction, burning his draft card, or raiding a selective service office, the peace militant became a moral hero rather than a criminal, it was because, paradoxically, his illegal behavior had advanced a moral value: life, for example, or peace or justice.

The paradox of morality in the guise of illegality is rooted in a rich and familiar tradition. It has furnished our imaginations with those powerful scenes in which moral heroes defy law and society in the name of conscience. Socrates and Jesus played such roles and helped to establish them among the patterns for our expectations of justice. According to these patterns, justice lies not with the society accusing, nor with its judges and juries, but with the accused. The appearance of the moral hero threatens to undercut the court, to reveal it as impotent or, worse, as malicious.

The question is not, of course, that of the court's doing justice to this particular individual, though the unusual personal force of the moral hero might prompt one to think that the hero himself is the only issue. But he speaks for other men, for victims who cannot speak for themselves. He demands for them something that they have been denied—life, peace, justice: basic values in which virtually everyone says he believes. It is because we all say that we believe in such values that the moral hero is able to grip our imagination and that we are vulnerable to him. And it is because society is committed to these values that his appearance can set society at odds with itself. In the terms of this tradition, the peace militant of the 1960s burned his draft card or raided a selective service office in the name of the people of Vietnam as well as of all Americans called on to fight there. If his society threatened him personally, it was because it threatened their life, their peace; it was because it denied them justice. If he defied his society, it was to force it to do justice to those whom it had violated. When he appeared in court, he evoked the presence and the suffering of those victims and demanded a verdict in that place where society makes its most deliberate moral judgments and where it goes to its greatest lengths to assure itself that it has acted justly.

It was a rare court that did not respond with warnings of the chaos awaiting a society that tolerates defiance of the law. Of course the imagination dominated by the trials of Socrates and Jesus is not disposed to sympathy with judges and juries and is therefore quite ready to ridicule these warnings of disaster. But the law is also a work of conscience. The judge who presides over the trial of the defiant peace militant and the jury that finds him guilty or innocent speak for fellow citizens who have called on them to act in their name and to affirm the moral values to which their society's conscience is attached. Society has its own allegiance to life, peace, and justice; this is what opens its conscience to the challenge of the peace militant. But this is also why it has established courts and a legal system. Society, though it is committed to a complex of values, sees justice as a special key to all the rest. The expectation that justice is available is indispensable to society's spiritual well-being, and the judiciary is the institutional guarantee that this expectation is being met.

Under the impact of the peace militant, the legal system had to face the question of whether it could offer the justice that it was designed to provide and that it holds itself responsible for providing. If the question deeply moved the judges—and it did—it stirred also in the mind of a public that knew of legal systems which had ceased to be dispensers of justice to become accomplices in oppression. The spectre of chaos which was so often evoked by judges as they faced lawbreaking by peace militants is doubtless rooted in the quite understandable fear that society might lose confidence in the courts and be left with no place to go to find justice.

SITUATION OF THE PEACE MOVEMENT

The American peace movement had often enough encountered the law during its history, but had not traditionally sought it out in the interest of advancing its cause. When, during the 1960s, it did begin to seek out the law, the character of the movement changed markedly.

The peace militants who had protested hydrogen bomb tests, the Polaris submarine, and civil defense air raid drills during the nuclear arms controversies of the 1950s had broken laws. They were duly arrested at the scene of their "crimes," tried, convicted, and served their terms in jail. Their action from initial protest to release from prison can best be described as providing *witness,* announcing the message of resistance to whoever would hear and attempting to influence these hearers as individuals. It was, to put it another way, a technique of sensitization. If there was to be any impact on government policy or institutions, it was expected to be distant and indirect: these would change when the message of peace reached the hearts and minds of those responsible for them.

This was the approach of civil disobedience. It reflected the attitudes and practices of the radical pacifists, like A. J. Muste, Dorothy Day, and David Dellinger, who led the peace movement at the time. Though they broke one law or another, they respected law as an institution and submitted without resistance to its processes. Though they were in conflict with many people, they respected their opponents—and everyone else; they would attempt only to persuade, and this only by appeal to individual conscience. Thus they rejected not only physical violence but also moral or psychological force. Passive, non-violent witness was the distinctive character of this approach of radical pacifism.

The change which occurred in the 1960s resulted to an important degree from the experience of the civil rights movement, in which, incidentally, many peace militants had worked. A new generation of civil rights leaders had awakened to the Constitution and the courts and had discovered in them the possibility of directly changing the nation's institutions. Specifically, they discovered that principle of the American doctrine of judicial review according to which a person tried for breaking a law achieves by this fact a position from which he can challenge that law's constitutionality. Segregation, they saw quite correctly, could be made illegal, and the practices which had institutionalized this injustice could be outlawed by court decision. There was no need for the detour through the hearts and minds of men. These could catch up at their own pace.

Perhaps even the Vietnam war could be attacked in court. Perhaps one need only break a law—burn a draft card, refuse induction, raid a draft board office, etc.—and then demand vindication by invoking the nation's most fundamental legal principles. This approach did involve coercion by law—moral and psychological force —and for this reason it was rejected by some of the radical pacifists, Dorothy Day, for example. Others long associated with the peace movement, like David Dellinger, accepted it. More important, however, was the fact that this approach attracted many who were not pacifists at all. The ranks of the peace movement were increased spectacularly by people moved to join it by their moral objection to the Vietnam war in particular and in most cases also by moral objections to the general state of American society. Most of the war resisters with whom this book is concerned fall into this category. In them, respect for law and for those who opposed them had to compete with mistrust and condemnation of the social system of which the law and the opposition were part: the rules, the procedures, and the functionaries which oppress the poor, draft the young, conduct imperialistic wars, etc. For these war resisters, non-violent protest was a tactic dictated less by a commitment to non-violence than by

the circumstances in which the peace movement found itself. It was
an articulate minority, the object of growing interest and sympathy,
but without the power to move the establishment in conventional
ways.

Because of the highly visible features which the tactics of these
peace militants shared with the approach of the radical pacifists—
the avoidance of physical violence, the acceptance or even courting
of arrest, and the deliberately public style of the witness—the public
and the news media saw no reason to find a new name for this conscientious law violation of the 1960s. They continued to call it *civil
disobedience*. But the shift from moral witness to legal confrontation
did make for some changes which should be noted. We have already
seen that the aim of this lawbreaking was no longer to sensitize individuals, but to change government policy. In addition, the laws violated were invalid, according to the peace militants. Thus what they
did was not illegal, but legal, and from the courts they expected not
a sentence, the acceptance of which would allow them to prove their
sincerity, but vindication.

The fact that the laws broken were considered invalid moved
some peace militants to refuse to call what they did civil disobedience. David Mitchell III, one of the earlier resisters, said that this
was not the correct term for his refusal to be inducted, for example.
He suggested another term, *civil challenge,* as more appropriate.[1]
The American Civil Liberties Union, whose lawyers had defended a
number of peace militants, also felt that this legal confrontation
should not be called civil disobedience. They attacked the confusion
in terminology by offering a definition which excluded legal confrontation. Civil disobedience, they said, was "the wilful, non-
violent and public violation of valid laws. . . ."[2] Like Mitchell's
choice of terms, this definition turns on whether or not the law
broken is valid. It has the merit of distinguishing those conscientious
law violations which can be defended on constitutional grounds from
those which cannot. Civil disobedience, as they define it, cannot.

But both the A.C.L.U. definition and David Mitchell's suggested
terminology are at odds with the more frequent usage not only
among the public but also in the peace movement and even among
lawyers and legal authorities. As will be evident when we turn to
our interviews with peace militants and with judges, both groups

were aware of the distinction based on the validity or invalidity of the law violated, but with few exceptions the members of neither group were disposed to restrict their use of "civil disobedience" accordingly. It was the fact that the behavior of the peace militant was wilful, non-violent, and public, not the validity of the law violated, which prompted them to call an action civil disobedience.

Legal authorities who wrote on the topic at the time were apparently guided by the same themes. Thus, Associate Supreme Court Justice Abe Fortas, in his influential *Concerning Dissent and Civil Disobedience,*[3] applied the term civil disobedience to the conscientious violation of valid laws (citing Gandhi as his example) *and* to the conscientious violation of invalid or unjust laws. He cited John Milton's defiance of England's censorship laws and Martin Luther King's refusal to obey what he considered unjust segregation laws as examples of the second type, which he called "civil disobedience in a great tradition."[4] Fortas also said that such civil disobedience "may sometimes be a means, even an essential means, of testing the constitutionality of the law."[5]

All of the cases which we analyze are instances of legal confrontation. When we can avoid the term civil disobedience without harm to the narrative, we will do so in the interest of clarity. When we do use the term, it will be in the broader and more common acceptance, that is, *inclusive* of the violation of invalid laws.

PATTERNS OF POLITICAL POWER—
SOME ELEMENTARY BUT IMPORTANT CIVICS

To appreciate the way in which these peace movement attempts to move the establishment developed, it is necessary to remind ourselves of the patterns in which political power is exercised in the United States. We speak of these patterns in their most fundamental terms. These, like all fundamental terms, are quite simple. But the issues raised by the militants of the peace movement and by the judicial response to them go precisely to these fundamentals.

According to the United States Constitution, the power of the government is exercised by three branches of government, legislative, executive, and judiciary, each with its own area of responsibility. One of the ways of changing a policy which issues from any of these branches is to change the minds—to reach the consciences—

of those who make the decisions there. This approach by direct appeal is particularly valued by the radical pacifists. There are two other approaches, more clearly political in nature: one is geared to the relation of the various branches to the people, and the other to the relations between branches. The first of these is the elective process, the classical direct political approach. The second operates by calling into play the system of checks and balances by which the various branches of government reciprocally limit each other.

During the period in question, the peace movement was constantly urged to carry its case to the people, to prove itself by becoming a force in electoral politics. In such an approach they could take advantage of the constitutional guarantees aimed at protecting the political initiative of the people: free speech, which allows a person to attempt to reach the minds of others; and free assembly, which protects his gathering with those who think as he does and his forming with them a political force. It was true, of course, that such an effort would encounter two political parties already established in the American scene and in the habits of the electorate. But perhaps one or both of these established forces could be moved. Certainly, if the war issue could be turned into a strong current of popular opinion with a definite direction, then the established parties might willingly seize upon it. If they did not, a third party might.

As events proved, however, the issue generated no such strong current. An increasing number of Americans were convinced that the Vietnam venture was immoral. An even greater number sensed that it was impractical, that there were no stakes in Southeast Asia worth the terrible loss of life and the massive expenditure of material. But all this uneasiness in the nation's conscience generated no clearly defined collective urge to strike out in another direction. During the period in question it produced only indecision. "Peace candidates" were rarely supported by a major party and even more rarely elected. Only Eugene McCarthy in 1968 managed to generate real excitement. This was already very late—and he lost.

This failure of the elective process as an avenue of appeal against the war left only the system of checks and balances. The intent of the system is that each branch of government, out of concern for its own integrity and for an appropriate equilibrium among the wielders of official power, will act to restrain unwarranted expansion of the other branches. We see it operating when the President vetoes an act of Congress, and when Congress refuses to fund a project requested by the President. We have also seen it in the Supreme Court's prerogative of reviewing the acts of both President and Congress to rule upon their constitutionality. Tensions among these branches are inevitable, of course, but in the process of resolving them important problems can be solved. There are those who have maintained that the Supreme Court's power of judicial review gives the judiciary a priority in the scheme of checks and balances—a sort of unchallengeable veto over the other branches. They are usually reminded, however, that the Supreme Court must depend on the other branches for enforcement of its rulings, and that it lacks a supportive constituency.

The American military venture in Vietnam had raised the possibility of a classic confrontation between legislative and executive power. Perhaps Congress would oppose the President's decision to make war, maintaining that it (Congress) alone had the right to do this. The general lines of this confrontation—which had also arisen at previous periods in our history—are set forth in the Constitution itself. On the one hand, the Constitution asserts that it is within the power of Congress alone to declare war, to make rules to govern the armed forces, and to appropriate governmental funds. On the other hand, conduct of our affairs with foreign governments is the responsibility of the President, who is also charged with seeing that the laws are faithfully executed and with overseeing the conduct of the armed forces as Commander-in-Chief. By historical development, the President's prerogatives have come to include the dispatching of troops to any location where he feels that they are needed in order to repel an attack or invasion, prepare for defense of the nation, protect American lives or interests abroad, or fulfill treaty obligations. As a result, the President's power to dispatch troops has sometimes meant that he could involve the nation in actual hostilities. If critics of this role point to the fact that the Constitution reserves to Congress the right to declare war, its defenders note that military actions can take a form other than a formally declared war and sometimes should.

In practice presidential decision has been responsible for the entry of the nation into military hostilities more often than congressional declaration. In addition to this extremely important precedent—or rather, as part of it—one finds congressional endorsement of the President's power: when the latter has acted in this way, Congress has supported his initiative both by formal resolution and by providing the economic means for conducting the military operations. Like the rest of the nation, the branches of government tend to close ranks in time of danger—real or imagined—from without. This was quite clearly the case with Vietnam when, in August 1964, Congress passed the Gulf of Tonkin Resolution authorizing the President to take the action needed to protect American armed forces and to prevent future aggression. Congress then provided money, in very large amounts, for the military operations in Southeast Asia, which, many felt, went considerably beyond the original terms of the resolution.

Congress did not oppose the President during this period and the anticipated confrontation of the legislature and the executive over the power to make war simply did not occur. Their solidarity on the matter of the Vietnam war raised serious questions about the status of the constitutional division of powers. Had the President not extended executive power at the expense of Congress? Had not Congress, without facing the issue directly, yielded to the executive a power which it did not have the right to relinquish? This issue will emerge from time to time in the pages which follow.[6]

TURNING TO THE JUDICIARY

Congress, then, would not oppose the executive. If the peace movement was going to set the system of checks and balances in motion against the war, it would have to do this by appealing to the judiciary. It is not that the courts themselves were totally uncommitted in the matter of the President's war-making power. They had been asked to rule on this in the past and had endorsed the executive's prerogative. But the recent experience in the civil rights movement had shown that the courts were capable of changing their own stand and with it the nation's policy. There would be risks in this for the judiciary. The civil rights issue had recently brought the Supreme Court into conflict with state and local law and power. The war issue could bring it into conflict with Congress or the President or both.

Any court challenge must have some basis in law. Just what law could be invoked against our involvement in the Vietnam war? In

1928, the United States, along with sixty-one other powers, signed the Kellogg-Briand Pact. It said:

> The High Contracting Parties solemnly declare in the names of their respective peoples that they condemn recourse to war for the solution of international controversies, and renounce it as an instrument of national policy in their relations with one another. [Article I (46 Stat.2343)]

In 1945 we signed the charter of the United Nations, agreeing then that:

> All members shall refrain in their international relations from the threat or use of force against the territorial integrity or political independence of any state, or in any manner inconsistent with the purpose of the United Nations. [Article II, Sec.4 (59 Stat.1031)]

We also accepted the Nuremberg principles by signing an agreement in London, August 8, 1945, providing a charter for the International Military Tribunal. Among the actions which it defined as war crimes were:

> (a) Crimes Against Peace: namely, planning, preparation, initiation or waging of a war of aggression, or a war in violation of international treaties, agreements or assurances, or participation in a common plan or conspiracy for the accomplishment of any of the foregoing; . . .
>
> (e) Crimes Against Humanity: namely, murder, extermination, enslavement, deportation, and other inhumane acts committed against any civilian population, before or during the war; or persecutions on political, racial or religious grounds in execution of or in connection with any crimes within the jurisdiction of the Tribunal, whether or not in violation of the domestic law of the country where perpetrated.
>
> Leaders, organizers, instigators and accomplices participating in the formulation or execution of a common plan or conspiracy to commit any of the foregoing crimes are responsible for all acts performed by any persons in execution of such plan. [Article VI (59 Stat.1544)]

We did not sign the Geneva Agreement of 1954, which provided for unification of North and South Vietnam by elections within six months (with the consequence that its war would have to be considered a civil war). We did, however, commit ourselves not to disturb its execution.

Because these agreements have so often been violated and because their conceptions are morally so elevated, it is tempting to consider them simply to be pious sentiments, at best inspirational in character. But the Constitution of the United States, Article VI, Clause 2 says:

> This Constitution, and the Law of the United States which shall be made in Pursuance thereof; and all Treaties made, or which shall be made, under the Authority of the United States, shall be the Supreme Law of the Land; and the Judges in every State shall be bound thereby, anything in the Constitution or Laws of any State to the contrary notwithstanding.

It is doubtless this which Arthur Goldberg, United Nations ambassador and former Supreme Court justice, had in mind when, in commenting on the United Nations Charter, he said, "we forget that the Charter is also a *legal* document, a treaty, and we are bound by it—we have treaty obligations."[7]

Aware of the Nuremberg principles, David H. Mitchell III (whose trial is the subject of our following chapter) said during this period: "I . . . specifically condemn the United States for crimes against humanity." To this judgment, shared by many other peace militants, he added an intention, which was also theirs: "If I am brought to trial I plan to use my trial as a forum to try the United States government before the world."[8]

The legal grounds for the peace movement's court challenges to the government were not limited to these particular treaties and charters. As we shall see in the cases which follow, the Hague and Geneva Conventions were also invoked. The peace movement also challenged a series of war-related laws and practices on grounds which were not connected with international agreements at all. They argued that the war was illegal on the constitutional ground that it lacked congressional declaration. They developed constitutional grounds for attacking government restrictions on dissent (First Amendment) and statutory grounds for attacking punitive reclassification by the Selective Service System. They also appealed to the history of the exercise of judicial power to defend the rights of the jury.

But what, precisely, could the peace militants hope for? One type of expectation was expressed in a remark by George Mische, a defendant in the trial of the Catonsville Nine: "If just one judge would rule on it, it would no longer be a serious thing. It would be over. . . ."[9] The judge presiding at the trial disagreed and responded: "Oh, I think you misunderstand the organization of the United States. One judge ruling would not end the war."[10] The latter is correct, of course, if one takes him literally. One judge ruling would not end the war, though the judiciary at its highest level *might* declare the war illegal. This could conceivably begin a train of events which would bring about its end, and this was probably what Mische meant.

If a result of this scope was only a distant hope, bringing the war issue to court could at least help to change the attitudes prevailing in the nation and especially among those in authority. Daniel Berrigan described this change in an interview with one of the authors:

> . . . what the minority in the peace movement are really pleading for as a minimal accomplishment is that the law of the land be respected by the authorities of the land, from the police department, to the courts, to the bureaucrats of the university, to the President. That is to say, pick up your own charter, your own Constitution, your own by-laws and respect them. Follow them, and the real problems of the land will begin to be dealt with, because all of those instruments of law and order to which all of these men in authority have sworn adhesion—all of them speak in decent and civilized language about limitation of violence first of all and secondly about the common good and about pursuit of peace.[11]

This raising of the level of consciousness—and conscience— could be accomplished even in trials where defendants were found guilty and the government was vindicated in strictly legal terms.

STRESS IN THE LEGAL SYSTEM

When the judiciary describes itself, it pictures an "instrument of law and order" of the sort which Berrigan praised. Each judge, as he assumes his office in the American court system, takes this oath:

> I, _____, do solemnly swear (or affirm) that I will administer justice without respect to persons, and do equal right to the poor and to the rich, and that I will faithfully and impar-

tially discharge and perform all the duties incumbent upon me as
_____, according to the best of my abilities and un-
derstanding, agreeably to the Constitution and laws of the United
States. So help me God.[12]

By these words with which it commits the judge to his responsibility, the legal system claims to be what the community expects it
to be (and what the peace militant challenges it to be), the place
where justice is done. The judge does not occupy this vital moral
position alone, but shares it with the jury. This is to say that he
shares it with the community which the jury represents. Our ideal
governing the availability of justice is essentially bound up with the
prospect of carrying one's case to the community in this way. The
impartiality which the oath prescribes—"without respect to persons
. . . equal right to the poor and to the rich"—is incumbent on both
judge and jury, and we expect to see it in all court proceedings. This
is the famous blindness of justice, its indifference to considerations
such as race, religion, politics, personal philosophy, and the like. It
is the judiciary's commitment to the propositions that only the
breaking of the law is to be punished and that, at the same time, no
one shall break the law with impunity.

All of this is, to use Berrigan's terms, decent and civilized. Legal
institutions which lived up to this description would be a worthy response to society's expectation of justice. Of course an institution
which lived up to such a description might welcome a Socrates or a
Jesus and even willingly accept the challenge which the peace militant issues when he insists that the government has broken the law.
It is at this point, the point where the legal system claims that no one
shall break the law with impunity, that the peace militant initiates
his critical stress. Cannot the government, and in particular the
President, break the law with impunity? This is the issue pressed by
Mitchell, who refused induction; by David Miller, who burned his
draft card; by David A. Samas, Dennis Mora, and James A. Johnson, soldiers who refused orders to go to Vietnam; by Dr. Benjamin
Spock and his associates, by the Berrigan brothers and their colleagues, and by the Oakland Seven, all of whom found ways to
attack the operation of the draft. We shall devote a chapter to each
of these cases.[13]

Asked how they pleaded, all those charged said *not guilty*. They contended that they were *not* lawbreakers. And the infraction with which they were charged—Mitchell's refusal to be inducted, the Berrigans' draft board raid? This, they said, was a *moral* and *legal* refusal to be an accomplice in a series of crimes then being committed by the government.

The crisis in judicial response lay in whether the legal system would or could face these issues. It was a dilemma in the courtroom, where the freedom or imprisonment of just men and women was at issue. And it was a dilemma for the institution as a whole, in which its integrity was the question. Perhaps it was pointless to maintain expectations of justice so high that they could not be met by a normal, decent institution.

Consider the courtroom. No judge wants to meet Socrates or Jesus professionally. Even the judge whose personal character is as exemplary as theirs and whose commitment to human values is as total and lucid as theirs would be disadvantaged in the encounter simply because he is a judge. Because of his role he is responsible for the established patterns for dispensing justice. These include stringent formal rules for the way in which cases shall be presented, and they are rarely flexible enough to adjust to the moral hero. The peace militant is the one on trial, for example, charged with refusing induction or with destroying draft records. Shall the judge allow his case to become a trial of the government for crimes against humanity? There is obvious wisdom in the rules which require that the trial of one person for a particular crime not in any sense become the trial of another party on another charge. But the crimes attributed by the peace militant to the government are the reasons he refused induction or burned draft records. He can scarcely present a meaningful defense for his behavior unless he can have these reasons carefully weighed. But to weigh his reasons is to be led to the question of the criminality of the government.

Prosecutors were quick to insist that breaking the law for the sake of the people of Vietnam is still breaking the law, and that high moral purpose is no defense. If the violation was intentional, the motive is irrelevant. The rules of evidence invite the judge to refuse to allow such a defense or, if they do allow it, to insist that it not be taken into account in deciding guilt or innocence. With this, the trial remains the trial of the accused and not of the government. But with this, the jury's independent judgment, its right to decide according to all the facts and its own lights, is thwarted by the rules of evidence. This distinctive community participation in the administering of justice is halted by technical legality. What kind of justice is it when the jury cannot take account of what everyone—jury members included —knows to be the real issues?

And what sort of law is there if the judiciary will not entertain a question despite the fact that it appears to raise a substantial issue of violation of the Constitution? This bears on the integrity of the institution as a whole. Consider, for example, those matters which arise out of treaties of the sort quoted a few pages ago. We noted there that the Constitution says that such agreements "shall be the Supreme Law of the Land, and the Judges in every State shall be bound thereby." With this in mind, the peace militant claimed that his behavior was not only moral but *legal*. This claim set judge against judge and at the same time drew upon the judiciary the charge that it was yielding indefensibly to the prerogatives of the President. Most judges faced with the question of the illegality of the war found that the issue was *non-justiciable,* that is, not susceptible to resolution by a court. They held the issue to be a "political question," the category indicating questions which, though they may be constitutional in character, are the province of the other two departments of government. Thus we find that Judges Miller, Burger, and Coffin of the United States Court of Appeals for the District of Columbia responded to a request in *Luftig* v. *McNamara* to rule on the legality of the war by saying:

> It is difficult to think of an area less suited for judicial action than that into which the Appellant would have us intrude. The fundamental division of authority and power established by the Constitution precludes judges from over-seeing the conduct of foreign policy or the use or disposition of military power; these matters are plainly the exclusive province of Congress and the Executive.[14]

Supreme Court Justice William O. Douglas, speaking on the same question, had remarked earlier: "The Chief Executive as Commander-in-Chief makes decisions in which no one else can participate. But what he does often gives rise to claims that the courts should adjudicate."[15] In the same work, he added: "The political question should no longer be used as a thicket behind which the judiciary retreats."[16] But Justice Douglas was a minority voice, and though the view which he expressed would more and more frequently appear in decisions toward the end of the period which concerns us, still at the time when it was delivered (1967) the decision in *Luftig* v. *McNamara* exemplified the prevailing view among judges on the justiciability of the war.

If the judges were divided on the validity of judicial intervention, legal experts were also divided on the consequences of the judiciary's refusal to involve itself. According to Professor Herbert Wechsler: "The only proper judgment that may lead to an abstention from decision is that the Constitution has committed the determination of the issue to another agency of government than the courts."[17]

In this light, a decision on the part of the Supreme Court that a question was political and a consequent refusal on the part of the Court to rule in the matter would be, as another commentator called it, "a decision in constitutional law that the question is to be decided by the executive or legislature and not by the courts."[18] If Wechsler is correct, the refusal of the judiciary to review the chief executive's acts in prosecuting the war would be a declaration by the Court that it had no right to review them. By taking such a position, the judiciary would have joined Congress in relinquishing power to restrain the executive in this area.

Professor Bickel of Yale disagrees with Wechsler's view of the implication of nondecision. He insists that the Supreme Court can call a question political and refuse to decide it without thereby deciding upon the way in which the Constitution allocates power. Without giving up its own rights of review, the Court could refuse to decide certain issues as an act of prudential discretion. Such an exercise of prudence might be justified for reasons which include: "the strangeness of the issue and its intractability to principled resolution; the sheer momentousness of it, which tends to unbalance judicial judgment" and "the inner vulnerability and self-doubt of an institution which is electorally irresponsible and has no earth to draw strength from."[19]

The Vietnam situation was not only highly complex, but was replete with military and political dimensions which the court might well feel it lacked the standards to evaluate. At the same time, there could be no question of its momentousness. The undisputed exercise of power by the President had placed the nation on a wartime basis and resulted in a draft for military service where American men—including many with the most serious doubts about the legitimacy of what they were doing—were required to risk their lives and to kill.

As the description of the period will make clear, self-doubt did characterize much of the judicial response to the peace movement. It should be no more difficult to understand a sense of vulnerability in an institution than it is to appreciate it in an individual. In the face of the very strenuous expectations of so many, the judiciary might well have said, "Why us?" and invited the peace militant to concentrate on the Congress and the President. But the peace militants had done this and electoral politics had already failed. Even had the direct political approach been more successful, one wonders if the expectations of justice in this matter did not demand recourse to a much more refined instrument. Did it not require the intervention of an institution much more accustomed to justifying itself? If it did, then the courts should have taken a risk of their own.

CHASING
THE GOVERNMENT

Chapter Two

The Trials of
David Henry Mitchell III

> You see the case, Mr. Mitchell, as far as the
> law is concerned, is a relatively simple case. . . .
> JUDGE WILLIAM TIMBERS
> I do not agree that the issue of my
> defense is clearcut and simple. . . .
> DAVID HENRY MITCHELL III

On May 20, 1965, a grand jury in New Haven, Connecticut, indicted David Henry Mitchell III, for wilful failure to report for induction into the armed forces, in violation of 50 U.S.C. App. 8462, of the Universal Military Training and Service Act. He was arrested ten days later, and on September 13 he came to trial before Judge William Timbers in the United States District Court of the District of Connecticut in New Haven. Mitchell pleaded innocent.

From the government's point of view, the question was simple: Did the defendant refuse induction into the armed forces, or did he not? What engaged the legal process in this instance, they felt, was a question of fact, susceptible of being determined yes or no. But Mitchell did not deny that he had refused. What he denied by pleading innocent was that his refusal was unlawful, and his denial rested on his contention that the induction order was unlawful because it would make him an accomplice in a crime, specifically the war of aggression that the United States was waging in Vietnam in violation of international law and of its treaty obligations. The wrong party

was on trial. If there were to be criminal charges, they should be preferred against those responsible for the induction order, the United
States government.

To defend his refusal as lawful, then, Mitchell would have to demonstrate that the government had broken the law. More than a year
before he faced the court, he had publicly said that he intended to do
just that. In an article directed toward draft resisters, he wrote: "If
I am brought to trial, I plan to use my trial as a forum in which to
try the United States government before the World."[1]

The government, however, was not about to go on trial. Prevent-
ing this was the other side of the coin of the prosecution strategy,
which aimed at maintaining the *simplicity* of the case. Government
attorneys would keep to the issue of did he or did he not refuse induction, would cut off any attempt to introduce a question of national policy, and would thereby prevent the defense from raising
the question of the government's behavior. For them there was no
question of the legitimacy of the induction order.

Mitchell had registered for the draft on January 30, 1961, apparently accepting at that time, along with so many others of his age, the
prospect of induction. In the months which followed, however, he
became convinced that American foreign policy was bent on the
domination of other nations and committed to aggression in order
to achieve this domination. Believing this, he joined in a series of
protests, including two on nuclear arms policy which resulted in his
arrest.[2]

His belief that American foreign policy was illegal led him to
decide not to cooperate with the draft, for which he had already
registered. Consequently, when his draft board (No. 17 in Norwalk,
Connecticut) attempted to classify him, the second step in its procedure, he refused to fill out the questionnaire. Instead, he sent a letter
which read in part:

> I will not play any part in the conscription system. I will not even
> play a part in seeking or serving alternative service for then I would
> be contributing to an immoral system and hardening all men's ac-
> ceptance of this system without dissent. . . . My dissociation and my
> non-cooperation is not complete if I cooperate with the crime being
> prepared by being silent, so I pledge that my resistance to militarism
> shall be heard. . . .[3]

For a variety of reasons, some of which are not clear, Draft Board No. 17 was to take three years before pressing for Mitchell's induction. On various occasions during this time he answered their correspondence by reasserting his position, at one point sending them a copy of an article which he had written. In it he remarked:

> In my own case, my draft refusal rests not on an abstract philosophy, but on the political situation as it exists. I non-cooperate with my government, not because I am a pacifist or occupy a position somehow uninvolved with the world, but on the contrary because I am very involved and specifically condemn the United States for crimes against peace and humanity. I refuse to cooperate with the Koreas, Cuban invasions or blockades, Vietnams, or with the nuclear arrogance with which we threaten to blow up the world. . . .[4]

THE TRIAL

The case came to trial on September 13, 1965. During the preceding week Mitchell's attorney, Conrad Lynn, moved to have the indictment dismissed, and in arguing for his motion introduced Mitchell's claims before the court. With respect to the war in Vietnam he said that the Universal Military Training and Service Act was being unconstitutionally applied because Congress had not declared war and because intervention in Vietnam was in contravention of various treaties and international conventions of which the United States was a signatory. In view of these conditions, his client was legally as well as morally obliged to dissociate himself from the war crimes of his government. This pretrial motion was denied by presiding Judge William Timbers, who regarded its grounds as irrelevant.[5]

The court was ready to proceed on the following day, September 8, but when it convened, it became known that Attorney Lynn was ill. Because of this, Judge Timbers continued the case until September 13. At this point, Mitchell announced that he was dismissing Lynn as his counsel because he disagreed with him over the way that the case should be presented. He asked for a longer continuance, saying that the five days just granted were not enough to allow him to obtain new counsel and for the latter to acquaint himself with the case. In arguing for this, Mitchell remarked:

> I do not agree that the issues of my defense are clearcut and simple. . . . I think they involve many things—Nuremberg trials, inter-

national law, conventions on war crimes and torture and genocide, et cetera. And I think it would take a lot of time for a lawyer to acquaint himself with all of these points in my case. . . .[6]

But the judge, who did not regard these issues as part of the case, did not agree about the need for time to prepare them. The request for a longer continuance was denied.

The defendant's attempts to engage a new lawyer failed. He said later that he had contacted some fifteen attorneys, a process made more difficult by the fact that the continuance included a weekend, but was unable to find anyone ready to accept his case on such short notice. The trial took place without his having counsel to present the defense that he wanted. The court appointed an attorney, but Mitchell refused to allow him to act as his counsel. With the defendant participating only minimally in his own defense and declaring that he neither approved nor disapproved of the proceedings since he had no choice in the matter, the trial took place. It was very much the simple case which the judge had envisioned: three days' testimony bearing almost exclusively on draft board procedure. Thereupon, a jury, instructed by the judge in the law bearing only on unlawful refusal, found Mitchell guilty.

THE JUDGE EXPLAINS

Mitchell was sentenced to from eighteen months to five years in prison and fined $5,000. A pair of recommendations accompanied the sentence: first, that the full five years be served unless the defendant, after serving eighteen months, was willing to be inducted; second, that the prison term be served outside of Connecticut.

During his remarks at sentencing, Judge Timbers said that the court had no comment to make on the defendant's philosophy. Yet he also said on this occasion that Mitchell's "so called cause . . . appears not to have cut any ice in this country or in this community . . ."[7] and he wondered aloud:

> What would be the fate of Mr. Mitchell and ones of his ilk if he were to attempt to conduct the sort of disaffiliation with recognized authorities of this country, if he were to attempt that behind the Iron Curtain or behind the Bamboo curtain?[8]

It might be unfair to Judge Timbers to see only ambiguity here, however awkwardly he may have juxtaposed his "no comment" with his comment. He is obviously attempting to meet the conflicting demands of the strictly legal questions and those of the context of the moral, political, and social concerns of the community which must surface in some form or other when a decision is explained. The task is particularly difficult when the decision relates to a public issue of national importance and when it has received intense local publicity. To attempt to place a verdict in its more general context and to take judicial notice of local agitation of the question is not necessarily to intrude on the legal issue, to ignore the difference between it, the "simple" case, and its context.

At the time of sentencing in this instance, the question of what was the legal issue not only was still open, but had also been aggravated. By refusing to participate in his own defense and by doing so on the grounds that he could not have the defense he wanted, Mitchell had succeeded in attaching issues which Judge Timbers held to be irrelevant—the questions of national policy—to an issue which even the most narrow legal scruples would have to admit was relevant: the right to a fair trial. The complaint that this right had been denied would be the ground for appeal.

But Mitchell had not only aggravated the question of what the issues were (and who was the criminal), he had said before the trial that he intended to do just that. To his remarks about trying the government before the world he had added: "I will fight my case through the courts as far up as necessary and utilize every other means available to stir up a storm."[9] In the same article in which this remark appeared, Mitchell recommended that this sort of thing become a general policy among draft resisters, one in which the government's efforts would be turned against it:

> The government helps increase the interest in the issues by prosecuting draft refusers. Our job is to utilize every threat, FBI visit, court fight, or jailing as a means of following through on our prosecution of militarism and the real criminal. When the government acts and creates publicity on the issue, we must utilize every means to make sure that they end up with burnt fingers and a kick in the behind.[10]

During the trial, there had been picketing and other demonstrations by those who supported the defendant, with pickets and demonstrators drawn not only from the students and faculty of nearby

Yale University, but also from outside New Haven. It is not surprising, then, that Judge Timbers' remarks had a somewhat beleaguered ring. Nor is it altogether surprising, given Mitchell's public statements about using his trial, that the judge considered the request for a longer continuance as an attempt to subvert the judicial process. He called it "degenerate subversion" in fact, when he told his side of the trial story in his Memorandum of Decision after Trial.

The memorandum is a rather rare, but not unprecedented, device which can be used by a judge to explain and justify a decision. Judge Timbers devoted seventy-one pages of his to the point around which the "fair trial" question revolved: did the refusal of a continuance longer than the one from September 8 to September 13 result in the defendant's being denied proper counsel and consequently a fair trial? The trial, Timbers asserted, was "scrupulously fair." In a detailed review of each step in the proceedings, he pointed to thirty-six instances of the "scrupulous care which was exercised to advise the defendant of his rights at every stage of the proceedings."[11] These ranged from the granting of frequent recesses to the dismissal of a juror who had briefly conversed with a witness during a recess. Timbers quoted from the transcript a lengthy exchange with a New Haven Civil Liberties Union lawyer who supported a posttrial motion for dismissal or for a new trial, an exchange which clearly conveys the judge's willingness to retry the case on condition that Mitchell defend himself or be defended within the "simple" framework that he, Timbers, had originally proposed.

What emerges from Judge Timbers' description of the case is his own conception of justice as fairness within sharply defined and mutually accepted patterns of laws and procedures. He was obviously convinced that his view was widely shared, at least among lawyers, for in speaking of the request for a longer continuance, which he had denied, he said: "It was perfectly clear to the court that no responsible counsel would submit to the conditions imposed by the defendant for acceptance of a retainer to defend him."[12] He condemned Mitchell for "his insistence upon defending the case upon the issues rejected on his motion to dismiss the indictment, thus effectively precluding voluntary representation by any lawyer worthy of his profession."[13]

Timbers also maintained that the shortness of the continuance made a fair trial more, rather than less, likely and in this way served the defendant. The behavior of Mitchell and his supporters—press conferences and releases, street corner speeches and picketing—had built up a situation which the judge called "explosive." Its effect, he felt, was to make it more and more difficult to get impartial jurors, meaning in this instance jurors not biased against Mitchell by the picketing and other demonstrations. The quick invocation of the rules protected the defendant, then, against his friends and against himself.

Finally, Timbers defended the limits that he had set upon issues and procedures by appealing to legal precedent (that is, that the draft was constitutionally applied and that the President is authorized to commit the nation militarily) and by appealing to the public interest: "after all, defendant had undertaken, in not the most restrained language, to inflame public opinion against a vital instrument of national policy—the draft law."[14]

Then he returned to the question of retrial and to Mitchell's challenge. The defendant does not have

> a right to a second day in court . . . when his avowed plan is "to use my trial as a forum in which to try the United States Government before the world . . . and utilize every other means available to stir up a storm . . . to make sure that (the Government) ends up with burnt fingers and a kick in the behind."[15]

THE APPEAL

The United States Court of Appeals for the Second Circuit thought differently about the "second day in court," however. Circuit Court Judges Lumbard, Kaufman, and Medina reversed Judge Timbers' decision and returned the case to the U.S. District Court for retrial. The reversal was accompanied by the recommendation that, in the interest of "sound judicial administration," the retrial hearing be assigned to another judge. The Court of Appeals held that the continuance granted was too brief to allow the defendant to obtain effective counsel and that Judge Timbers had abused his discretion by refusing additional time.

In arguing the government's case before the Court of Appeals, United States Attorney Jon Newman had, like Judge Timbers, maintained that the case was simple and that its simplicity was an important justification for limiting the continuance to only five days. As for Mitchell's complaint about this, he said:

> His only claim to prejudice arising out of the manner in which the court permitted him to exercise his right to counsel is that he was not able to present a defense *which as a matter of law was not available to him.*[16]

This defense was not available to him because the judge had excluded it (in quashing the pretrial motion). It was quite proper, the government maintained, for the judge to have taken upon himself the decision about whether the defense could be introduced rather than placing it in the hands of the jury, because what was at issue was a question of law rather than of fact. It is the duty to decide the former as distinguished from the duty to apply the law to the facts which separates the role of judge from that of jury. Finally, the decision was the proper one, according to the government, because Mitchell's defense was political and philosophical in character, and American courts had long since decided that a person can be compelled to serve in the nation's armed forces "without regard to his objections or his views in respect of the justice or morality of the particular war or of war in general."[17]

Mitchell's lawyer, Fyke Farmer, charged that the government's case was an "evasion of the question" and "a retreat from the gage of battle which the defendant threw down."[18] He argued that the government's claim that the defendant's objections were political and philosophical was a misapprehension, one which confused the defendant's motivation with the legal basis of the case and which directed attention away from the compelling affirmations of international law on which his defense was based.

To have kept the defense based on this—the arguments which drew attention to American war crimes—from the jury was to disregard the jury's function. The defendant was insisting that the draft board's order, because of its relation to war crimes, was not a valid exercise of government power. This drew the government behavior into the realm of fact, fact upon which the application of law depended. Elimination of such consideration by judicial ruling and by the accompanying instruction to the jury prevented the latter from considering whether Mitchell was being required to engage in criminal activity, something that no citizen can be asked to do. The defense was not properly excluded, then, and the denial of the time needed to prepare it was a violation of due process.

The Court of Appeals, as we noted, agreed that the continuance was too brief to prepare the defense properly. In its opinion, which was written by Judge Medina, it also showed signs of an interesting and (for the defense) promising sensitivity to the larger issues involved:

> In essence, what the trial judge failed to take into consideration is that this is not "a very simple case." It has decided First Amendment overtones. It is always difficult to obtain counsel to defend an unpopular cause, especially in a time of active hostilities. Moreover, a reasonable time was required for counsel to familiarize himself with the various intricacies of the Selective Service Law and to decide upon the proper strategy to be followed at the trial in order, if possible, to obtain an acquittal, or to make a record for purposes of appeal, or to obtain as light a sentence as the circumstances might warrant.[19]

The Court of Appeals was not accepting Mitchell's attempt to use international law as his defense. Its response was more narrowly based: whether the defense was valid or not, the case involving these issues was complex to a point where the time allotted for its preparation was too short. But the Court of Appeals did not rule out such a defense either, and this open door must have been encouraging to Mitchell as he faced the prospect of a retrial.

RETRIAL

The second hearing of the Mitchell case by the District Court began on March 15, 1966. Judge T. Emmet Clarie presided, while the government case continued in the hands of Assistant U.S. Attorney Jon O. Newman: Mitchell was represented by Mark Lane of New York.

Mitchell took the stand to testify for himself and, in response to questions asked by Lane, explained his position. He put special emphasis upon its legal character, which, he and Lane felt, the government perservered in misunderstanding. Mitchell was *not* challenging the right of Congress to raise armies. His objections were *not* philosophical or moral: he was *not* a pacifist and he would fight to defend the United States if it were attacked. But defense is one thing and aggression another, and present use of Selective Service for an aggressive war rather than for the constitutionally sanctioned common defense opened the obligation to cooperate with that system to legal challenge and not simply to moral objection. This legal challenge was precisely the point of this case.

Mitchell had already said all this to the draft board, to the judge in his first trial, to the Court of Appeals, and to whoever read his article or heard his speeches. But this was the first time that a jury was hearing it. It was reaching them over the predictable government challenge to its relevance. In overruling Prosecuting Attorney Newman's motion to strike, Judge Clarie said:

> The Court has been allowing it to stand on the record, to go to the question of intent. The Court will instruct the jury when the time comes to instruct the jury. It may be technically irrelevant, counselor, but broad latitude should be allowed, and the Court is so ruling.[20]

(Later, in his instructions to the jury, Judge Clarie did in fact rule it out as a legal defense, whatever it may have revealed about Mitchell's state of mind.)

Among other things, the defendant added:

> I was obliged and had a duty and responsibility, not just morally, but also legally, because of the Nuremberg judgment, which laid down principles of individual responsibility and guilt, which transcend those of a nation, to refuse to cooperate with the draft which was engaged in, as the major instrument for securing manpower for various criminal activities around the world; notably Vietnam, where we were stepping-up activity there in behalf of Diem at that time.[21]

Mitchell wanted to amplify his own characterization of the government position and of its activities by introducing a series of witnesses who, he felt, would add to the specifics of his contentions. Two had been sergeants who had been captured in Vietnam. Recently released, they had made widely-published statements charging that the United States had no right to be in Vietnam. Both men were in government custody. Judge Clarie refused to order their appearance on the grounds that their testimony would be immaterial to the issues of the case. For reasons of immateriality he also refused to issue subpoenas to two reporters who had been assigned to Vietnam as correspondents from the *New York Times* and the *New York Post,* to a former sergeant with the Special Forces in Vietnam, and also to the director of the Selective Service System. Immateriality was also given as the reason for the court's refusal to allow depositions to be taken abroad from one American and several Vietnamese who would testify to the bombing of civilian personnel by American bombers or to the extensive and regular use of poison chemicals and toxic gases by the American forces.

The government case was supported by documentary evidence of Mitchell's refusal to be inducted (draft board files, for example) and by a single witness from the draft board who elaborated on this. This was, in fact, the only evidence with which they felt that the jury should be concerned. In the summation of his case, Attorney Newman underscored this point, reminding the jury of its duty "to perform a very old and honorable function in the history of our jurisprudence, and that is to apply the law as the judge gives it to the facts that are in evidence."[22] As for the defense contention about the relevance of laws other than those designated as such by the judge, the jurors should remember that "If every person could decide for himself what the law is or should be, the result would be anarchy."[23]

When Mark Lane summarized the defense case, he also spoke of evidence, evidence which Mitchell had presented in his testimony about the war and which doubtless related to knowledge that the jury already had, thanks to the news media. Lane noted that:

> The government did not contest or offer any evidence to show that the Geneva Accords of 1954 had provisions contrary to those Mr. Mitchell told you about, which motivate Mr. Mitchell. The Government offered no evidence to show that American participation, armed participation in Vietnam, is not contrary to the U.N. Charter, the Kellogg-Briand Treaty, or to the principles of Nuremberg.[24]

By the time Lane had finished summing up, though he did not speak at great length, the jury had heard the Mitchell contentions a second time and would deliberate with the benefit of whatever reinforcement happened to result. The summation climaxed in the citing of Supreme Court Justice Jackson on the implications of Nuremberg:

> If certain acts in violation of treaties are crimes, they are crimes whether the U.S. does them or whether Germany does them, and we are not prepared to lay down a rule of criminal procedure against others which we would not be willing to have invoked against us.[25]

THE SIMPLE CASE: PATRIOTISM AND MORALITY

But this rule would not be invoked in the United States District Court of the District of Connecticut. In instructing the jury, Judge Clarie was quite emphatic:

> . . . as a matter of law, I charge you that none of the treaties referred to in the evidence in this case, namely the Treaty of London, referred to as the Nuremberg Trial; the Treaty of Paris, referred to as the Kellogg-Briand Pact; the United Nations Charter; the Geneva Agreement of 1954, or the Hague Convention, interfere in any manner in respect to this defendant's filling his duty under this order.[26]

Earlier, when instructions to the jury were being prepared and objections to them heard, the defense asked that the above charge, requested by the prosecution, not be given. They also asked that the jury be instructed that "uncontradicted testimony has to be accepted as binding, unless the jury does believe that the person is not telling the truth."[27]

Judge Clarie refused on both counts. The jury, having been instructed in a way that tended to restore the "simplicity" of the case, found Mitchell guilty. He was again sentenced to five years. Accompanying recommendations urged that the term should be served outside of Connecticut and New York and that no early release be contemplated until the defendant served a sentence equivalent to the term in the armed forces of a selective service recruit. The fine of $5,000, imposed in his first trial, was not reimposed.

There was a dramatic exchange between judge and the accused at the time of sentencing. Mitchell, strong-willed as ever, again condemned American policy at length and in the strongest terms. This time he gave the court in which he stood a place in his condemnation:

> This Court has wiped the slate of history and legality clean of all the principles by which we tried the Germans. This Court has sold

justice to power and morality to patriotism. The Court has proved itself guilty as the Germans were guilty, and has taken a step toward attempting to force that guilt on all individuals in the country by enforcing the crimes of its Government.[28]

After listening to this, Judge Clarie responded: "one would also believe that he had the firm conviction that there is nothing good about the United States of America."[29] He continued:

It is refreshing that one day of each month of the year there comes into the courtroom one hundred or more people from all the nations of the world. They come in here with tears in their eyes and stand up and swear and take the oath of allegiance to the United States, and swear their allegiance to bear arms, without any qualifications that they believe in this or believe in that or don't believe in this or that policy of the Government.[30]

Mitchell's attacks not only triggered this response on behalf of patriotism, it also drew a rejoinder in the name of morality:

It is difficult for the court to rationalize the defendant's reference to morality and virtue at this time to justify his position. . . .
According to the probation officer, the defendant is an agnostic: he doesn't believe in a Supreme Being. From April '62 to the summer of '64 he was in a common law relationship with a woman in New York. It is difficult to understand virtue and morality as being personal motivations at this time, in respect to his appearance before the bar of this court.[31]

Lane requested that these remarks be stricken from the record, but this was refused.

SECOND APPEAL

The District Court had not prevented the statement of what the U.S. Circuit Court of Appeals had acknowledged to be an unpopular case. It was, in fact, stated twice, once by the defendant and once by his attorney. But having been stated, it was limited in its usefulness to the defense by being allowed only to clarify Mitchell's intent; it was then eliminated, by the judge's instructions, from the jury's deliberation on guilt or innocence. Apparently the door which the appellate court had opened by its reversal and by its statement that the case had "First Amendment overtones" had been shut. Perhaps its being open was an illusion in the first place. The appellate court would have the opportunity to declare itself satisfied or not with the lower court's second handling of the case. The same three-judge panel which had reversed the first decision declared itself satisfied with this one.

Attorney Mark Lane reminded the Court of Appeals of its own previous view that the case was not a simple one. He argued that the District Court, by refusing to hear the evidence of those whom Mitchell wished to subpoena and by instructing the jury that the evidence of war crimes and statements of international law were not relevant, had "repeated the substance of the position taken at the first trial, that this was a very simple case."[32] He asked for a second reversal and yet another trial on the grounds that these exclusions and restrictions made the trial just concluded unfair.

The government, Jon Newman arguing again, continued to insist that Mitchell's defense was based on "personal philosophical or political views" and was, therefore, not a defense at all. It also added that this defense was "inappropriate for judicial examination" because of its "most sensitive nature."

This time the Court of Appeals decided that the District Court had acted properly, though in doing so it (the appellate court) left itself open to the complaint that it too was misconstruing that defense. Judge Medina, writing the opinion, said that the power of Congress "to raise and support armies" is distinct from the executive use of those armed forces and that an objection to the legality of the latter is not a justifiable reason for refusing service in the former. This line of argument seems to assume that Mitchell was challenging the congressional power, and the text of the decision makes it clear that the appellate court did assume this: "appellant asserts that the Selective Service, and not merely the war in Vietnam, is illegal . . . he seeks a declaration, in effect, that the Service must cease to function. . . ."[33] Mitchell immediately asked for a rehearing on the ground of this misunderstanding of his contention, but his petition was denied without comment.

THE SUPREME COURT

The normal way for a person to appeal a lower court decision in his case to the Supreme Court of the United States is to petition this body for a writ of certiorari. The Supreme Court declares itself willing or unwilling to review the decision of the lower court by granting or refusing to grant the writ. New York Attorney Robert L. Bobrick argued Mitchell's petition for a review of the decision by the United States Court of Appeals of the Second Circuit, which affirmed the verdict arrived at in Judge Clarie's courtroom. The "Brief for the United States in Opposition" was signed by, among others, Solicitor General Thurgood Marshall and Assistant Attorney General Fred M. Vinson, Jr.

Mitchell followed this ultimate stage in the legal process from prison. Despite the usual practice of continuing bail during appeal, and despite the stipulated consent of the government prosecution to continued bail, the Court of Appeals denied a stay of execution of sentence. So did Supreme Court Justice Harlan, before whom the question was then pressed. Mitchell surrendered to authorities on February 6, 1967 and was in Lewisburg Penitentiary when the Supreme Court's decision was announced. He would remain there: the Court refused his petition for a writ of certiorari.

Bobrick, Mitchell's attorney, obviously saw no reason to understate the importance of the case:

> In terms of the depths of the present tragedy and potential catastrophe facing the United States of America, this is the most important appeal to be filed in this Court since the Dred Scott decision.[34]

He called the opinion of the Court of Appeals a "bland, head-in-the-sand opinion" which denied the defendant due process of law:

> All that petitioner is asking is before he may be convicted of a crime of violating a draft board order, that its constitutional validity not be presumed and that there be a judicial resolution by the normal legal processes of trial and evidence of whether or not the order is the end product of a constitutional process or of an unconstitutional one.[35]

Bobrick repeated all of the basic assertions of Mitchell's position, including the more telling quotations from international law, and added remarks of such persons as Senator Fulbright and Reinhold Niebuhr. All of this was aimed at insisting that the question of the constitutionality of the use of force in Vietnam should be open to judicial review.

The government's brief was short and succinct. The contention that the United States is engaged in an illegal war, it said, is "inappropriate for resolution by the courts. The ability of the Chief Executive to conduct the foreign affairs of this country would be impaired if every such decision were subject to judicial examination."[36] What the appellants raise, in short, is a *political question,* and the courts should not decide it. Not only were the courts not the agency to decide these questions, but Mitchell was not the person to raise them; he lacked *legal standing,* "since his induction into the army would not necessarily result in his being sent to Vietnam."[37] And finally, none of the treaties cited by the defendant "suggests that individual soldiers are entitled to refuse to serve in wars with which they disagree."[38]

There is, quite evidently, a curious management of the issue in this last remark. The claim of the war's illegality is reduced, or at least transformed, to a matter of the personal preference of the defendant. The other two contentions had been made as part of the case when the government presented it to the Court of Appeals. The latter had rejected the contention about standing and had declined to discuss the appropriateness of judicial review of foreign policy.

Supreme Court Justice William O. Douglas said of the issues which the Mitchell case brought before the Court:

> These are extremely sensitive and delicate questions. But they should, I think, be answered. Even those who think that the Nuremberg judgments were unconstitutional by our guarantee relating to ex post facto laws would have to take a different view of the Treaty of London that purports to lay down a standard of conduct for all the signatories.
>
> I intimate no opinion on the merits. But I think the petition for certiorari should be granted. We have a recurring question in present-day Selective Service cases.[39]

But Justice William Douglas was alone in this opinion, dissenting from the position taken by the remainder of the Court. The writ of certiorari was denied and review refused. The majority did not explain the refusal. It is Supreme Court practice not to explain in these instances.

The legal process had been appealed to at all of its levels and stages, and the issue which Mitchell had attempted to force on the judiciary had been refused. He petitioned on his own behalf for re-consideration of the request, but this was denied without further comment on May 8. In March 1968, an attempt was made to persuade the Court of Appeals to reduce his sentence on the ground that Judge Clarie had a personal animus toward the defendant. William Kunstler argued this for Mitchell, underscoring Clarie's remarks at sentencing about the defendant's agnosticism and his sexual morality. While one of the Court of Appeals judges (Kaufman) was willing to characterize Judge Clarie's remarks as "unfortunate," there was no inclination among them to suggest a reduction in sentence. They called attention to the "tirade character" of Mitchell's own speech and also noted that the sentence by Clarie was lighter than that imposed by Judge Timbers (by $5,000) and that it was quite in line with sentences dealt to other defendants convicted of the same crime.[40]

His Nuremberg defense rejected, Mitchell would serve his term.

Chapter Three

David John Miller

The Universal Military Training and Service Act of 1951—the draft law—makes anyone "who forges, alters, or in any manner changes any such [draft] certificate or any notation duly and validly inscribed thereon" a felon subject upon conviction to a fine of not more than $10,000 or five years imprisonment or both.

By mid-1965, Congress seemed convinced that the fourteen-year-old statute should be modified to stay abreast of developments in the protest movement. A report by the House Committee on Armed Services declared that that body was

> fully aware of, and shares in, the deep concern expressed throughout the Nation over the increasing incidences in which individuals and large groups of individuals openly defy and encourage others to defy the authority of their Government by destroying or mutilating their draft cards.[1]

On the fifth of August, Representative L. Mendel Rivers, the chairman of this committee, introduced a bill to amend the draft law in the direction of congressional concern. Speaking in the House in support of the bill on August 10, 1965, Rivers said:

> The purpose of the bill is clear. It merely amends the draft law by adding the words "knowingly destroys and knowingly mutilates" draft cards. A person who is convicted would be subject to a fine up to $10,000 or imprisonment up to 5 years. It is a straightforward clear answer to those who would make a mockery of our efforts in

40

South Vietnam by engaging in the mass destruction of draft cards.

We do not want to make it illegal to mutilate or destroy a card per se, because sometimes this can happen by accident. But if it can be proved that a person knowingly destroyed or mutilated his draft card, then under the committee proposal, he can be sent to prison, where he belongs. This is the least we can do for our men in South Vietnam fighting to preserve freedom, while a vocal minority in this country thumb their noses at their own Government.[2]

Senator Strom Thurmond introduced an identical bill in the Senate on August 10, 1965, the day that the bill passed the House with 393 yea and 1 nay votes. His remarks echo Rivers':

Recent incidents of mass destruction of draft cards constitute open defiance of the warmaking powers of the Government and have demonstrated an urgent need for this legislation. . . .

The President has acknowledged that our country is engaged in a war. Attempts to interfere with the Universal Military Training Act or service in the Armed Forces constitute treason in time of war. Such conduct as public burnings of draft cards and public pleas for persons to refuse to register for their draft should not and must not be tolerated by a society whose sons, brothers and husbands are giving their lives in defense of freedom and countrymen against Communist aggression.[3]

By August 30, 1965 the amendment had become law. It had received congressional approval and President Johnson's signature only twenty-five days after being proposed. Amended, Section 12 (b) (3) of the Universal Military Training and Service Act now embraced anyone

who forges, alters, knowingly destroys, knowingly mutilates or in any manner changes any such certificate or any notation duly and validly inscribed thereon—guilty of a felony subject upon conviction to a fine of not more than $10,000 or five years imprisonment or both.

On October 15, 1965, David J. Miller burned his notice of classification at a public rally held in front of the induction center at 39 Whitehall Street in New York City. Four days later he became the first person indicted for the knowing destruction and mutilation of a draft card in violation of the draft law as recently amended.

Miller had originally registered with his draft board on November

30, 1960, while a student at LeMoyne College in Syracuse, New York. He had received a student deferment. By the end of his junior year he had become profoundly disturbed over conscription and the war and during his senior year he became a pacifist. He described himself as "an absolute pacifist":

> I would not kill anyone under any circumstances. I would resist evil and injustice non-violently, and while engaging in non-violent resistance, I would use no means that I thought might harm my opponent, physically or mentally.

> I came to this position via a personal religious development during college and via the civil rights movement that I took part in while in college. The ideology and non-violent tactics of the civil rights movement appealed to me. I joined Syracuse Core, participated in a number of demonstrations and was arrested in two demonstrations.[4]

This describes the type of moral commitment that we see in the classic figures of civil disobedience—Gandhi and Dorothy Day, for example. In theory it might promise a style of resistance more pure and more passive than the tactical stand of a David Mitchell and of other resisters who were not pacifists.

When Miller graduated from LeMoyne he returned his classification card and gave up his student deferment. Then he adopted what can be called a position of relative noncooperation with his draft board (Local Board 58 in Syracuse). He would not allow himself to be processed for military service. He refused to apply for conscientious objector status, but he answered all correspondence from the board conscientiously, spelling out to them the reasons for his position. In the summer of 1965, he moved to New York City and joined the staff of the Catholic Worker,[5] informing the board of his new address. When they asked him to appear for a hearing, Miller wrote them saying (in part):

> Sorry, but no deal. I have chosen to regard your authority over me as unjust and not binding. I'm going to remain here in New York. You may take the course of action that you think best.[6]

Because he did not attend the hearing, he was declared delinquent. When the board ordered him to report for induction—on September 3—he sent them yet another letter telling them that he had not changed his mind.

Gentlemen,

    I have in my possession the order to report for induction on September 3rd. Be advised that I do not intend to appear. I have not changed my mind about conscription. I would not comply to it in any country of the world. To say as some people do that an individual like me who proposes to refuse recognition of such laws as the draft would be shot in some totalitarian countries concluding then that I should comply here because the treatment is better in the United States is no argument at all. Rather, it is just the opposite, it is much more an incentive to do the right thing and not take part in such an aberration of conscience. I shall remain here at the Catholic Worker where I can be reached at anytime.[7]

On September 3, 1965, his induction order was cancelled by the board "in order to protect his appeal rights." He was reclassified 1-A, and a new notice of classification was mailed setting forth the new classification. Miller signed it and thereafter carried it until he burned it.

The Whitehall Speakout was the first event in three days of protest activities scheduled for New York City from October 15 to 18. It was followed the next day by a parade down Fifth Avenue in which, according to its organizers, thirty thousand persons participated. The speakout was sponsored by an ad hoc group and scheduled for the afternoon of October 15 in front of the induction center at 39 Whitehall Street in New York City. Those attending would hear representatives from the War Resister's League, Du Bois Club, Student Non-Violent Coordinating Committee, Committee on Non-Violent Action, Movimiento Pro Independence, and the Catholic Worker, all speaking in opposition to government policy in Vietnam and to the draft.

The meeting lasted from 4:30 to 6:30 p.m. According to estimates, the size of the audience varied from one hundred to three hundred. Thirty-five to fifty police officers were reported to have been present and at least fifteen representatives from the news media. Close to a hundred hecklers were also present, separated from the protest audience by police barricades. At one point or another during the meeting, given the usual crowd fluctuation at affairs of this sort, there may have been as many hecklers as protesters.

Miller was introduced in the middle of the program. Taking the microphone, he said that he had decided not to give the speech which he had prepared. Instead he "would let the action of burning my draft card speak for itself." He told the audience that he was a Catholic pacifist. He said that he was opposed to all wars and that he was particularly opposed to the war in Vietnam and to the conscription of young men for it. He added: "I hope this will be a significant political act" and then ignited the card.[8] It burned to the cheers and clapping of the protest audience and the excited booing from the barricaded crowd of hecklers. According to witnesses at his trial, this reaction was the emotional climax of the meeting, which then wound on to its conclusion with neither violence nor disorder.

Miller was arrested on October 17, 1965 in Hooksett, New Hampshire. He was on his way to Saint Anselm's College as a member of the Catholic Worker team which had been invited there to discuss pacifism with the student body.

THE TRIAL

The case was tried on February 9 and 10, 1966, before Judge Harold R. Tyler, Jr. of the United States District Court of the Southern District of New York. Miller had waived a jury trial. He was represented by two American Civil Liberties Union lawyers, Marvin Karpatkin and Osmond Fraenkel.

At first, Miller intended to represent himself and "only to bring up moral issues in my defense."[9] As the trial approached, however, he came to feel that the Constitution offered a basis in law for his moral position. It was even possible, he thought, that the case might be won, or at least that some of the judges might be influenced. Consequently, he accepted the services of the American Civil Liberties Union lawyers for his defense, agreeing with them, however, that only constitutional issues be raised.

During the trial the prosecutor, Assistant District Attorney Peter E. Fleming, moved into the issue of the morality-law relationship and the following exchange took place:

> FLEMING: Do you consider what you did on October 15 an act of conscience, Mr. Miller?
> MILLER: I already answered that. In part, yes.
> FLEMING: Did you consider it an obedience to a higher law?
> MILLER: Well, I considered it a constitutionally protected act.[10]

Fleming then persisted, until twice overruled by Judge Tyler, with questions aimed at establishing that the defendant's case was a pure personal-conscience-versus-the-law defense. But Miller's personal conscience had found legal expression, and it is the law—the Constitution—that he, Karpatkin, and Fraenkel would oppose to the law —the draft law. Specifically, they would oppose the First Amendment guarantees of free speech and Fifth Amendment guarantees of due process to the draft law as recently amended, insisting that by the insertion of the words "knowingly destroys, knowingly mutilates," Congress had turned that statute into a device for the suppression of an important type of protest.

Conflicts of law with law, of course, are the province of the judges —either in an original trial or at some stage of appeal. But they only arise when someone is charged with breaking a law. Establishing that the law has been broken is the job of the prosecution, and in this Fleming anticipated little difficulty:

> The indictment in this case could not be simpler. It contains only one count. It names only one defendant. It involves uncomplex conduct. This is not, for example, a stock-fraud case. . . .[11]

He was right: Miller admitted that he burned his draft card. Testifying in his own behalf he said: "I burned my draft card as a symbolic protest in opposition to conscription, to the Selective Service System, to the war in Vietnam, and to the draft card burning law itself."[12]

Yet Fleming did have to deliver on his simple case, and he took elaborate care to do this. To prove that Miller destroyed a draft card that had been properly issued, he presented documents as evidence to trace the exchange of correspondence between Miller and Local Board 58, the processing of his case, and finally the issuance of his 1-A notice of classification. A draft board official testified to explain this evidence. Fleming also had testimony from the FBI agent who had seen Miller burn his card and from the two agents who had arrested him. Procedurally, the work of the police, like that of the draft board, seemed impeccable.

Karpatkin and Fraenkel placed Miller himself on the stand along with two others who had taken part in the speakout. They also had testimony from a member of the speakout audience and from two character witnesses. Their questioning aimed at two things: to show that the October 15 scene at Whitehall was a carefully circumscribed speech situation, and that the burning of the card was itself a reasonable speech act. Both of these objectives served the defense's First Amendment position.

Pursuing the first of these, they led the witnesses through an account of the preparation for the gathering. The organizing committee had arranged for the necessary permits, sound truck equipment, police patrol, and street barricades—all the requirements for an authorized public demonstration. The leaflet announcing the speakout was placed in evidence, and it said at one point:

> We have secured all the necessary licenses for the Speakout. This means that there will be no *civil disobedience*. Our job now, as originally announced, is to communicate our views about the draft and the war in Vietnam to Selective Service employees, young men facing the draft and the many spectators in the street—and to do this as effectively as we can.[13]

There would be "no civil disobedience"; Miller had respected this, the defense maintained, and had not broken a law. "Our job . . . is to communicate our views"; the speakout was an exercise in *communication,* and Miller had simply worked at communicating, attempting to affect public opinion in this eminently authorized way. There had been no violence, no disorder, no "clear and present danger." Miller did not urge anyone else to burn his card, and no one else did in fact burn a card at the meeting.

When he cross-examined these witnesses, Prosecutor Fleming sought to establish through their testimony on the same events not only that Miller had burned his card but also that there was no sound reason why he should have done so. There were no restrictions placed on his right to speak out: no one tried to stop anyone from speaking on that day. All the Constitutional free speech guarantees were operating for the protestors: the site that they requested was made available, accessibility to their designated audience of "Selective Service employees, young men facing the draft and spectators in the street" was made possible. There was police protection from a hostile audience, loud speaker equipment, and press coverage. There was no need for Miller to violate a criminal statute in order to communicate.

But Karpatkin, in developing his second theme, maintained that all Miller did was speak out. From the point of view of the Constitution, the defense insisted, the burning of a draft card was no different from any other act of speech and:

> . . . this symbol in the middle of his speech was no different than if he had sung a song in the middle of a speech, or recited a poem in the middle of a speech, or did some juggling or acrobatic acts in the middle of a speech.[14]

> . . . the eloquence of his speech which contained this gesture and which indicates that he, in fact, succeeded in that which the Constitution allowed him to try to succeed in doing, namely to get people to listen to him . . .[15]

Judging from its effects, the defense continued, the burning acted as eloquent speech might; not only did it provide the emotional climax of a meeting devoted to speeches, but it made for what Karpatkin called a "before and after situation." Before the demonstration, Miller was relatively unknown. Since that time, Miller received numerous requests to speak to various organizations throughout the country. Neither Judge Tyler nor the government considered the latter line of defense relevant to the case.[16]

To appreciate the thrust of defense argument and prosecution rebuttal, it is important to know just what the Constitution does regard as speech. The defense had begun to develop this theme in its pretrial motions for dismissal. They noted that according to one or another First Amendment decision by the Supreme Court, certain kinds of conduct, known as "symbolic speech," were held to be protected. For example, the flying of a red flag in protest of a community action was to be protected as speech;[17] so was the refusal to salute the American flag;[18] picketing is also a form of protected speech from the point of view of the First Amendment.[19] Given this apparent latitude in the understanding of speech—its inclusion of expressive behavior or symbolic speech—the defense could consider itself in a position to raise a serious First Amendment challenge.[20]

They had also raised their Fifth Amendment challenge as a pretrial motion to dismiss: the August '65 amendment to the draft law served no valid legislative purpose and consequently violated Miller's rights to due process. The argument here was that the legislative

history of the amendment revealed it to be aimed at the suppression
of political dissent, an intention which they found in the remarks
of Senator Thurmond and Representative Rivers. Describing this
legislative history further, they noted that there had been no request
for such legislation by the Selective Service System, or by any agency
concerned with national defense or military manpower. The views of
such agencies were not even solicited, nor were their comments invited. No legislative hearings were held, and there was no floor debate on the matter in either chamber. They added that there was no
legitimate relationship between the war-making powers necessary
for national defense and the implications of draft card burning, since
such burning in no way affected the military and economic capabili-
ties of the United States. Within the Selective Service System there
were many protective and alternative resources, such as duplicate
files on all registrants. The hurried enactment of the amendment, the
imposition of a five-year sentence and/or $10,000 fine, served as a
"hypocritical cloak of propriety" for an oppressive piece of legislation which was contrived to suppress political dissent.

These two themes, First and Fifth Amendment arguments, would
be advanced at each level of the case up to the Supreme Court. They
would, of course, be refined and refocused at various points along
the way. Two other arguments, also introduced to support motions
to dismiss, were rather quickly abandoned. One of these stated that
no crime had been committed because what had been burned was a
notice of classification, not a certificate of registration, and another
that the indictment violated prohibitions against cruel and unusual
punishment.

Judge Tyler responded to the defense pretrial motions in a written
opinion, the first of two such opinions that he would offer in connection with the trial. (The second was delivered after the verdict.) He
held the claim of cruel and unusual punishment to be premature:
prior to conviction there was no punishment, cruel or otherwise. He
also said that the language of the draft law simply did not leave it
open to the sort of attack that the defense was making in its other
three motions. The notice of classification, for one thing, was certainly included among the selective service documents not to be
burned. Discussing legislative history in connection with the Fifth
Amendment argument, he held that what motivated Congress in

enacting the draft amendment was irrelevant. Even if one assumed
that it possessed motives totally unrelated to proper legislative purpose, the courts could only look to the statutory language and ask if
Congress had the power to do what it had done. In the present case,
the law could be considered a reasonable exercise of the congressional
power to raise armies.

Judge Tyler gave the First Amendment motion to dismiss more
attention than the others, but he also rejected it. He said that the
cases in the Supreme Court decisions which the defense had cited in
exemplifying the latitude of the First Amendment all involved the
overturning of statutes whose very language proscribed some form of
symbolic speech. This was simply not the case with the amended
draft law. However, he agreed with the defense that the statute might
affect the freedoms of speech and assembly under certain circumstances. Whether or not the present case involved such circumstances
could only be decided by the trial.

The Judge seemed to have his own reservations about the significance of the recent amendment to the draft law. He observed at one
point during the trial that:

> it seems to me that if a man's classification card is destroyed or lost,
> or whatever, the government still had the adequate paper work at
> least to underpin a notice to report for induction.[21]

This appeared to sustain the defense argument that there was no
valid reason for the enactment of the disputed amendment to the
statute. So did his later remark that the statute in question was not
"the most earthshakingly necessary law." Still this did not prompt
him to side with the defense on the issue:

> But even assuming that you (the defense) and I have that opinion,
> I am not sure that it amounts to much. . . . I can see why Congress
> could have thought that it would have a valid purpose.[22]

Actually, the only defense argument which Judge Tyler found
relevant was one which Miller's attorneys had not presented—at
least not directly. In Tyler's own words:

> It seems to me that what the defendant really means to urge here is
> that you balance what this statute on its face quite evidently pur-
> ports to achieve in the total scheme of things in this country as

against the First Amendment rights of Mr. David John Miller, or anybody otherwise similarly situated, that under all the facts and circumstances that we now know it is more reasonable to say that the First Amendment cloaking should get the upper hand; isn't that really what you are saying?[23]

Defense Attorney Fraenkel said that the defense felt that the proper standard for judging a speech's entitlement to First Amendment protection was the "clear and present danger" test. According to this norm, speech is constitutionally protected unless it can be established that it is likely to result in immediate and serious violence. There had, of course, been no violence at the Whitehall speakout. However, taking up the balancing test which Judge Tyler had explained, Fraenkel said that in cases like the present one the First Amendment "should get the upper hand in any situation where there can be any remote doubt about it."[24] The Judge sharply disagreed with such a conception of First Amendment protection:

> It rarely has been suggested that the constitutional freedom for speech and press extends its immunity to speech or writing used as an integral part of conduct in violation of a valid criminal statute.[25]

The defense attempt to ground their constitutional argument on the concrete facts of this case failed where Judge Tyler was concerned, and his position at the conclusion of the trial remained what it had been during pretrial hearings. He put it this way:

> Isn't the simple answer to this case dependent upon how he would answer this question? Wouldn't you say that David John Miller could have made the protest without burning his card that afternoon?[26]

He then addressed Miller:

> I find you guilty under this statute, David Miller, even though it is perfectly true that I also find, by the way, as a practical matter, that you were undoubtedly sincere in your purposes, that you rather freely expressed in answers to questions posed by your own lawyers and by government counsel.[27]

THE SENTENCE

In his second opinion, Judge Tyler took up certain developments which had occurred during the trial. One of these was the emergence of the balancing test. During the trial he had suggested that the defense was promoting a balancing test between Miller's rights as an individual and the claims of the law in question. Now he declared such a test unfeasible. One of the reasons why it was unfeasible was that it would require a substitution of his court judgment for Congress' attempt to maintain an effective means for drafting citizens for military service. A second reason was the familiar worry that the exemption of Miller would result in widespread draft evasion:

> . . . to strike the balance in favor of Miller would be to virtually li-
> cense him and others so inclined to ignore their responsibilities to
> the national defense requirements of this nation.[28]

Then, addressing himself to what he called the "ingenious defense contention" that the First Amendment fully protects the most dramatic speech available, he said that he could find no authoritative precedent for such protection, especially where other adequate if less dramatic means were at hand. "To bespeak the obvious," he said, "he [Miller] could have spoken against all of the things he desired without burning his notice of classification."[29] This point seemed every bit as obvious to Prosecutor Fleming, who restated it emphatically at the time of the sentencing.

Both judge and prosecuting attorney were correct, of course, about Miller's having bypassed the more ordinary forms of protest on October 15. But during the preceding months Miller and many like him had become convinced that the ordinary forms of protest achieved nothing against the growing war and conscription. Miller's commitment to extraordinary protest was well established. It had brought him two arrests and one jail sentence as a civil rights activist. It had led him to refuse conscientious objector status and openly and dramatically to refuse induction. On September 3, the day he was to report for induction, he was picketing outside the selective service office. At one point he left the picket line to enter the office. He told the clerk what he was doing outside and that he would not report for induction. Then he returned to his picketing. Finally on October 15, he burned his draft card. This uncompromising, risk-taking posture was not likely to be satisfied by writing to his Congressman, as the prosecuting attorney had suggested, or even by delivering the speech that he had prepared for the speakout. The risk that he assumed on

Whitehall Street corresponded to the enormity of what he saw himself protesting.

At the time of sentencing (March 15, 1966) Karpatkin and Fraenkel attempted in another way to have the symbolism of Miller's act acknowledged. They asked for a suspended sentence with an appropriate symbolic sentence attached: one hour in the custody of a United States Marshal. The government attorney, however, pressed the argument that Miller's crime deserved treatment no different from that accorded other crimes enumerated in the statute, such as refusal to report for induction, false use of a selective service certificate, etc.

For his part, Judge Tyler expressed deep interest in David John Miller "as a person" and took notice of his sincerity and good works with the Catholic Worker community. He felt, however, that somewhere along the line the defendant "had gotten a bit of bad advice":

> . . . what I am troubled with is that I think we have a problem here that nobody has pointed out with clarity to Mr. Miller. It is perfectly all right to dissent. It is perfectly all right to express your views. But it isn't all right to thumb your nose at everybody else and say, "I will only do it on the basis which I selfishly maintain is the only way. I won't go along with the government of laws, even where that government of laws provides a system for airing out the merits of my position."[30]

Miller did not get his symbolic sentence. He did get a suspended sentence however. It was for three years. Two years of probation were assessed, with the conditions that were symbolic in a way that Miller could not appreciate: that he carry a draft card on his person at all times and obey all orders and directions from his draft board. This probation would terminate upon Miller's induction into the military service.

THE APPEAL

In introducing the opinion which he wrote for the appellate court, Judge Wilfred Feinberg recognized that Miller's case "raised perplexing issues of whether symbolic conduct is speech protected by the First Amendment."[31] Karpatkin and Fraenkel had indeed massed most of their argument behind the First Amendment considerations, with the due process (Fifth Amendment) ground presented in a rather secondary position. Speaking also for Judges Lumbard and Kaufman, Judge Feinberg said that "the ultimate question before the court is the power of Congress to enact the legislation."[32] If David Mitchell's case had drawn the courts toward a confrontation with the President over his use of the power to make treaties and conduct foreign affairs, the Miller case was raising the prospect of a confrontation between the judiciary and Congress over the latter's use of its lawmaking power.

The defense brief contended that the amendment to the draft law was "an unconstitutional abridgement of freedom of expression guaranteed by the First Amendment, both on its face and as applied to the facts of this case."[33] The objection to the statute on its face was the attack on its legislative history, which the brief restated. Judge Feinberg rejected it as inconclusive. Even though some of the remarks by congressmen indicated a desire to suppress political dissent, he said, "the more authoritative" committee reports show a concern that the destruction of draft cards "represents a potential threat to the exercise of the power to raise and support armies."[34] Confirming a government argument, he added that even prior to the August 1965 amendment the destruction of a draft card by a registrant would have opened him to indictment for wilful nonpossession. Thus by the amendment under consideration Congress only strengthened and clarified what was already an existent obligation.

When they turned to the facts of their case, the defense argued a very broad conception of First Amendment latitude:

> It is the appellant's contention that a constitutionally proper definition of the scope of the First Amendment is one which is broad enough to include all modes of symbolic speech, or communication of ideas by conduct.[35]

Here they invoked the words of Justice Frankfurter, who said, in a 1941 opinion, "Back of the guarantee of free speech lay faith in the power of an appeal to reason by all the peaceful means for giving access to the mind."[36] In burning his draft card, Miller had chosen a dramatic and unquestionably effective way of gaining access to the minds of his audience. Here the brief for Miller added that there was a constitutional right to make one's speech as effective as possible, subject to the proper constitutional standard.

The government said that Miller's First Amendment argument "boggles the mind." While it was true that pure speech was constitutionally protected, the attempt to protect symbolic speech in Miller's sense would extend First Amendment protection to any human act performed in a dramatic context, even a crime. This was clearly untenable. But the defense was not claiming that the First Amendment protected what was uttered in the context of a crime. To pretend that they did was to ignore the provision "subject to the proper constitutional standard," which was an integral part of their argument. The "proper constitutional standard" as far as Miller's lawyers were concerned was the clear and present danger test, which, in its classic expression by Justice Holmes, states:

> The question in every case is whether the words used are used in such circumstances and are of such a nature as to create a clear and present danger that they will bring about the substantive evils that Congress has a right to prevent.[37]

According to such a standard, Miller's carefully circumscribed act was acceptable.

But Judge Feinberg insisted that the speech issue was even more complex than the defense maintained, and he pointed to a series of cases in which a combination of speech and symbolic conduct had been held not to be protected. In these instances, it would be legal to restrict speech in order to regulate conduct. He regarded the case before him to be of this type and said that the appropriate constitutional standard for judicial decision here was that of balancing the two conflicting interests.

The defense felt, however, that it could justify Miller's actions even with the standard of the balancing test. Expanding the theme which emerged during the trial, they held that American society loses more in free speech than it gains in selective service administration by applying the statute to Miller. To punish a citizen who destroys his own certificate as a form of public protest is to strike at conduct too remote from the waging and preparation of war. Indeed, a government witness (Gladys Leverette, coordinator of Local Boards 57, 58, and 59 in Syracuse, New York) had testified at the trial that the board had all of the documents necessary to process Miller for induction.[38] Consequently, the defense argued that Miller's conduct had a high degree of rationality, with no degree of danger to the administration of the Selective Service System. They were willing to acknowledge, not knowing what lay ahead in the development of modes of protest, that destruction of records in various city, state, and national headquarters might endanger national security.

However, Judge Feinberg discounted the remoteness and uniqueness of Miller's act in favor of what he foresaw as its aggregate consequences: "the seriousness of an individual's acts must often be assessed not only in isolation but under the assumption that they may be multiplied manifold."[39] In this light, he felt, conduct like Miller's, when subjected to the balancing test, had to be restricted in the interest of public order. Such regulation results in an indirect and minimal abridgement of "speech" in favor of public order, which demands the greater protection under the particular circumstances presented. The statute, as the opinion noted earlier, did not prevent political dissent. Judge Feinberg added to his conclusion by reminding Miller that he and those who agree with him were free to criticize national policy as vigorously as they desired by written and spoken word, and that they did this on October 15, 1965. "But they are simply not free to destroy Selective Service Certificates."[40]

Reflecting very briefly on the Fifth Amendment argument, the Court of Appeals opinion said of the judiciary: "Our function is to determine only the power of Congress in enacting the statute, not its wisdom."[41] In the light of the court's preceding discussion of legislative history and congressional prerogative, it decided that Congress did have the power.

The Court of Appeals held the draft law as amended to be constitutional and, on October 13, 1966, it affirmed Miller's conviction.

THE SUPREME COURT

In carrying Miller's case to its final appeal, Karpatkin and Fraenkel repeated their First and Fifth Amendment arguments. Their experience with the Circuit Court of Appeals prompted them to add two further issues to their grounds for requesting high court review. One was an affirmation of the legitimacy of the Court's examination of expressed legislative purpose to determine the constitutionality of a statute. This they separated out as a distinct ground. In the second they argued that the Court of Appeals had erred by saying that the Supreme Court no longer applied the clear and present danger test in questions of the constitutionality of statutes affecting First Amendment rights, but applied only the balancing test in such cases.

In advancing the question of legislative history as a separate issue, Miller's defense underscored what it considered to be uncertainty on the part of the Court of Appeals over whether legislative history could be introduced in the way in which the defense wished to use it. They supported this contention by pointing to language in the decision which said in one place that the appeal to legislative "motive" is rarely if ever done by a court, but denied in another place that such an appeal would never be permissible.

In support of its contention that the Circuit Court of Appeals misunderstood the high court's attitude on the use of the clear and present danger test in First Amendment issues, the petitioner's brief pointed to language in the latter's decision according to which it was felt that Judge Feinberg maintained that such decisions "seemed to require" the use of the balancing test.[42] It added that while the clear and present danger test was most appropriate, the balancing test properly applied would also vindicate Miller.[43]

The government brief began with the Fifth Amendment issue first, listing the valid purposes which the amended statute served by prohibiting destruction of selective service certificates:

> They facilitate communications between the holder and his local board by keeping him aware of his Selective Service number, his board's address, and his current status. They enable him to prove his draft status and remind him of his legal obligation to notify his local board of changes in his personal circumstances which might alter his current classification or require changes in official records. The Notice of Classification could also aid in reconstructing a local board's files if they were ruined by some catastrophe. It also contains sufficient information to enable a local board which is not the one where the holder is registered to assign him to duty in the event of an extreme national emergency.[44]

They added, in connection with the same defense argument, that the long established reasons which justify the requirement that the card be carried in the first place sustain legislation prohibiting its destruction.

Turning then to the tangled matter of the intentions of Congress, the key to the petitioner's argument based on legislative history, the government pointed to the House and Senate committee reports and said that these, rather than the remarks of particular individuals, were the indicators of legislative purpose. They carefully avoided reference to Senator Thurmond and Representative Rivers by name as they distinguished "certain statements on the floor of Congress . . . (which) . . . seem to support . . . the petitioner's . . . claim" from those reports which reveal no intention of suppressing speech. The role of the senator and the representative as sponsors of the legislation did not make their explanations of it declarations of legislative purpose as the defense claimed.

Finally, addressing the questions of symbolic speech and the attendant issues, the government brief insisted upon the mixed speech-conduct character of Miller's act. It is in the area of such mixed behavior and here alone that it has become the Court's practice to apply the balancing test rather than the test of clear and present danger. Hence there is no merit in Miller's claim that the Court of Appeals misunderstood high court practice in this connection. The government brief concluded by reasserting the appropriateness of the balancing test in connection with this statute because of the mixed speech-conduct character of the act in question: "The statute is violated even if the document is destroyed in privacy, with no intention of expressing protest or making any kind of communication whatever."[45]

The Supreme Court denied the petition for writ of certiorari. Mr. Justice Douglas, however, was of the opinion that it should be granted.

The Miller case did not end here. As we shall see shortly, the defendant's most dramatic encounter with the judiciary was still to come. But now the peace movement was reaching toward a climax, with resistance to the war and to conscription spreading and intensifying. It would force the courts to respond to a variety of positions and tactics, but it was not yet finished with the burning of draft cards and neither therefore were the courts.

On the morning of March 31, 1966, David P. O'Brien, along with three others, burned his registration certificate on the steps of the South Boston Courthouse. Arrested there, he was charged with destroying his draft card and came to trial on June 1 of that year before Judge Sweeney of the United States District Court in Boston. O'Brien, a pacifist like Miller, elected to defend himself. He was found guilty and sentenced.

His appeal was argued by Marvin Karpatkin, who, along with Melvin L. Wulf, legal director of the A.C.L.U., and Howard S. Whiteside of Boston, would later prepare the case for the Supreme Court. Certain specifics aside, they made the same First and Fifth Amendment arguments for O'Brien as had been made for Miller. In fact, with the exception of a single phrase, the very wording of the questions presented for review is identical in the briefs for the two cases.

But why did the Supreme Court, which had denied certiorari to David Miller, decide to review the O'Brien case? Because there was a conflict in the lower courts over the law itself, something which had not happened in Miller's case. While the District Court in O'Brien's case had accepted the card-burning amendment as legal, the Court of Appeals, First Circuit, reversed its decision. In an opinion which he wrote to explain the decision of Judges McEntee, Coffin, and himself, Judge Aldrich asserted that the draft law as amended ran afoul of both the First and the Fifth Amendment. As regards the latter: because the conduct in question—draft card burning—was already punishable under the nonpossession regulation, the draft amendment served no valid purpose. And because the draft amendment was directed at public rather than private destruction of cards, it singled out one group—protestors—for special punishment. This was contrary to the First Amendment.

The Court of Appeals, though it reversed the decision on constitutional grounds, still considered O'Brien guilty of nonpossession and remanded him to the District Court for resentencing. At this point, then, both O'Brien and the government had an important stake in Supreme Court review. The latter wanted it because they held that the Court of Appeals had been wrong in declaring the statute unconstitutional; the former because they felt that the Court of Appeals had sustained a sentence for a crime for which O'Brien was neither tried nor convicted.

Still another group, it should be noted, felt that it had a stake in the high court's *not* rendering a decision in the O'Brien case. This was the Boston Five—Benjamin Spock, William Sloane Coffin, Michael Ferber, Mitchell Goodman, and Marcus Raskin—under indictment as of January 8, 1968 for having conspired to counsel nonpossession on the part of selective service registrants. In a brief as friend of the court they argued that a series of important legal issues would not be squarely presented in the O'Brien case, issues which had risen in their own.[46] We shall consider the case of the Boston Five separately and see that the overt acts alleged to be criminal were also different from those in the O'Brien or Miller cases.

However, the Supreme Court did review the O'Brien case and did decide. Chief Justice Earl Warren delivered the opinion for the Court on May 27, 1968. It quickly shrugged off the argument that the amendment was illegal on its face.

> A law prohibiting the destruction of Selective Service certificates no more abridges Free Speech on its face than a motor vehicle law prohibiting the destruction of driver's licenses. . . .[47]

The law's application to O'Brien was quite another matter, however. The Warren opinion saw the case as a mixed speech-nonspeech situation. When it balanced O'Brien's right to "speak" symbolically as he had against the government's right to regulate conduct in the national interest, the Supreme Court held that the government was entitled to restrict the nonspeech elements in the interest of the nation's security:

> . . . both the governmental interest and the operation of the 1965 Amendment are limited to the noncommunicative aspects of O'Brien's conduct. . . . For this noncommunicative impact of his conduct, and for nothing else, he was convicted.[48]

The First Amendment argument was rejected.

As for the Fifth Amendment argument, the opinion noted that the defense had referred to what only a small handful of congressmen —actually there were only three—had said in making the defense claims about illicit congressional purpose. But the entire body was involved in its passage.

> What motivates one legislator to make a speech about a statute is not necessarily what motivates scores of others to enact it, and the stakes are sufficiently high for us to eschew guesswork. We de-

cline to void essentially on the ground that it is unwise legislation
which Congress had the undoubted power to enact and which could
be reinstated in its exact form if the same or another legislator made
a "wiser" speech about it.[49]

The 1965 amendment, then, was held to be constitutional both as
enacted and as applied. With this the Court vacated the judgment of
the Court of Appeals and reinstated the judgment and sentence originally arrived at in the Boston District Court.[50]

VIOLATION OF PROBATION

Unlike David H. Mitchell III, David J. Miller was free on bond
while he exhausted all of his rights to appeal. Within fifteen days
after the writ of certiorari was denied, the conditions of his probation
were to go into effect. On April 6, 1967, he appeared before Judge
Tyler to answer a petition filed by his probation department, which
alleged that he was in violation of the conditions of his probation for
not having obtained and carried a draft card. His lawyer, Marvin
Karpatkin, told Judge Tyler that Miller himself came forward and
revealed this information to the probation department.

When Judge Tyler asked if Miller was ready to plead to the charge
that he did not obtain and carry a draft card, Karpatkin protested
that Miller simply could not utter the word "guilty." Judge Tyler
didn't demand the word itself but insisted that Miller speak and indicate to the court that he was aware of the implication of his decision. Miller admitted the allegation and added that he did not intend
to fulfill the conditions of probation.

The government attorney, Peter Fleming, Jr., renewed his attack
on Miller's altruism. The defendant's rhetoric during the case suggested to him that "personal vanity best explained David Miller's
conduct." After the Court of Appeals' unanimous confirmation of
his conviction, Miller's violation of parole could only be characterized as the "unrestricted exercise of personal whim."[51]

Attorney Karpatkin countered with a description of the demands
of Miller's conscience, pointing to its development as a result of long
search and deep meditation into the position of absolute pacifism.
He appealed then for a judicial response based on equity rather than

law, one which would acknowledge the distinctive quality of Miller's moral character. Miller added his own appeal to Judge Tyler along similar lines:

> I would like to see you take the opportunity not to put me in prison because, as a matter of fact, I think that I am just in this case and in other areas, and that I am innocent and in my own way maintain innocence; I am doing what is right. And I would not want to put it on your conscience that you would be sentencing an innocent man to jail. I hope that you would take this opportunity, and it is a personal one and I suppose the only way you could do it is to beg out, or one of the ways, anyway.[52]

Faced with the prospect of sentencing Miller for the second time, Judge Tyler restated his belief in Miller's sincerity and his appreciation for Miller's dedication to social service. He admitted, however, that he could no longer understand Miller's determination. He had had, after all, every legal and practical opportunity to test the law and to express his views without official interference while his case was pending. He could continue to do this if he would only "live with our system as it is and to go with your conscience." He spent some time attempting to convince Miller that he had other moral responsibilities in addition to those springing from his pacifist conscience. These responsibilities were themselves of a profound human and enduring kind—to his wife and child, for example.[53] He encouraged Miller to apply for a conscientious objector classification as one of the means of living up to these requirements. Should he refuse this offer to reconsider the conditions of probation, Judge Tyler would impose a sentence equivalent to that of a draft evasion case.[54] This he felt would be consonant with his responsibility as judge to the public as well as to the hundreds and thousands of men in the service who were perhaps as severely opposed to war as Miller was in the philosophical and moral sense.

Present in court at this time was Father Daniel Berrigan, whose peace movement activities would subsequently involve him in a series of spectacular confrontations with American law enforcement and the judicial system. Berrigan, a Jesuit priest, was a former professor of Miller's at LeMoyne and had officiated at his wedding. Having requested and received permission to speak, he voiced his concern for the encouragement of alternatives to public and social violence, for the encouragement of:

> the feeling among free men that the war is not inevitable and that free men always have at their recourse alternatives to what they are doing, and that a democracy allows in full knowledge and generosity the free activity of responsible men to discover alternatives to public and social violence.
>
> It is for this reason I would plead, quite pragmatic, it is important that good men not be removed from the public scene in wartime but that their example shine out for all thoughtful men, soldiers, civilians, clerics, judges, all of us, in order that all of us may realize that war is outmoded and that man in order to survive must seek out other works to do.[55]

But Judge Tyler opted for duty to the nation:

> . . . there comes a time really, not withstanding one's own conscience and strongly held views, when as a young man in a country like ours he really ought to go, and that somehow even though the war may be wrong and even though we may all agree that war as a resolution of policy is wrong. . . nevertheless that young man ought to go.[56]

This was not a divine but a "temporal solution," as it must be in our legal system, Judge Tyler said, and added: "I must conclude under all circumstances that there must be rendered unto Caesar what Caesar must have in these circumstances."

Miller then spoke: "Caesar does not have me, Judge."

> JUDGE TYLER: He may not have you but you may have to render unto him what the law requires.
> MILLER: I will never.[57]

Miller served his sentence at Allenwood Prison.

Chapter Four

The Fort Hood Three

The case of the Fort Hood Three unfolded in both the military and civilian court systems. While the civilian court is permanently established by federal, state, or local government to try all law violations within its jurisdiction, the military court is convened by the commanding officer of the accused serviceman on the occasion of a violation of military regulations. The very term *court* in its military application—court-martial—is applied to what the civilian system calls the jury: the group that renders the verdict. In addition, the military system has its own system of review and does not grant bail. But these and other differences are not of much importance for the discussion of the issues which concern us. Indeed, we shall see the judicial process in each system struggling in very similar ways with the same difficult questions, and we shall be reminded that the two spring from the same matrix of legal experience.

On June 7, 1966, David A. Samas, James A. Johnson, and Dennis Mora were ordered to duty in Vietnam. They were Army privates stationed at the time at Fort Hood, Texas, and they were directed to report to the U.S. Army Overseas Replacement Center in Oakland, California on July 13 for actual shipment. On June 13, they left Fort Hood on the month-long leave that the Army customarily accords its soldiers prior to overseas assignment.

On June 30, during this leave, the three held a press conference in New York to announce:

> We have made our decision. We will not be a part of this unjust, immoral, and illegal war. We want no part of a war of extermination. We oppose the criminal waste of American lives and resources. We refuse to go to Vietnam! ! !

Of themselves they said:

> We represent a cross section of the Army and of America. James Johnson is a Negro, David Samas is of Lithuanian and Italian parents, Dennis Mora is a Puerto Rican. We speak as American soldiers.[1]

They also announced at the press conference that they had begun action in the United States District Court for the District of Columbia seeking an injunction to restrain Robert S. McNamara, as Secretary of Defense, and Stanley Resor, as Secretary of the Army, from shipping them to Vietnam. In addition to the injunction, they were asking this court for a declaratory judgment that they not be made to commit illegal acts in an armed conflict which was in violation of the Constitution, laws, and treaties of the United States.[2]

On July 7, the Army answered the challenge issued at the press conference by changing the military orders of the three soldiers: their leave was terminated and they were directed to report immediately to Fort Dix in New Jersey. Before these new orders reached them, however, they were arrested in New York City and taken under guard to Fort Dix, about thirty miles away. There they were confined under "administrative restrictions"—a sort of house arrest. They were told at that time that they were being held for investigation of charges that they had violated Article 134 of the military code, which forbids uttering disloyal statements with intent to cause disaffection and disloyalty among the civilian population and members of the military forces.

This confinement lasted until July 14, when they were again ordered to report for shipment to Vietnam. When they refused to obey an order aimed at effecting this deployment, they were charged with insubordination and held for courts-martial.

Before their military trials began, they lost the first round in their attempt to move the government by action in civilian courts. On July 11, Judge Edward M. Curran, sitting in the District Court for the District of Columbia, rejected their claim that his or any other civilian court had jurisdiction in such a case. His opinion said in part:

> The propriety of transferring a member of the Armed Forces from one part of the world to another is not only political but a military question over which the courts have no jurisdiction. . . .
>
> In addition, it is not the function of the judiciary to entertain such litigation which challenges the validity, the wisdom, or the propriety of the Commander-in-Chief of our Armed Forces abroad.[3]

The language of the opinion leaves no doubt that the court's refusal of jurisdiction is one side of a coin, the other side of which is the court's affirmation of the prerogatives of the President, particularly his war-making power.

Judge Curran's decision would be appealed, of course, and the case for court jurisdiction reasserted. The appeal was before the United States Court of Appeals for the District of Columbia when the military trials of the trio began.

THE TRIAL

The Fort Hood Three were tried separately between September 6 and 9, 1966 before three courts convened for that purpose at Fort Dix by the commanding general of the First U.S. Army. Each court was a ten-member panel composed exclusively of officers, all three defendants having waived their rights to enlisted representation. The Army prosecution team for each trial consisted of Lt. Col. Richard L. Rice and Captain Donald H. Partington, trial counsel and assistant trial counsel respectively, according to military designation. The Army assigned Major Edward A. Lassiter to the three as defense counsel and Lieutenant Jason M. Cotton as assistant defense counsel. The defense was led, however, by a civilian lawyer, Stanley Faulkner from New York. Faulkner served as individual counsel to each of the three.

Col. Robert F. Maguire presided over each trial as law officer. As he opened the proceedings at Dennis Mora's trial, Col. Maguire spoke to the court members of their responsibility and of his own. They would have to decide guilt or innocence, and, if the defendants were guilty, they would also decide the sentence. In connection with the first obligation he said:

> When you come to vote upon the guilt or innocence of the accused your responsibility is basically that of fact finders. . . . Since you are fact finders, you do have the right to question the witnesses who testify before you.[4]

As for his own role—

> As the law officer of this court, I have generally speaking the duties and responsibilities of a trial judge. It is my duty to insure that these proceedings are conducted in full accordance with the law and in the discharge of this duty I rule with finality on all issues of law that may arise during the trial. The members of the court are required to accept my ruling as final. . . . They must look to me as the sole source of law.[5]

This difference between matters of fact and matters of law is the basis for distinguishing the roles of jury and judge in the civilian court system too, as we have already noticed. We shall find it a matter of debate in several of the trials which follow this one in these pages. It will also—at least briefly—become an issue in the present instance.

Dennis Mora was the first to be tried, and we shall concentrate our attention on his case. Virtually every argument introduced by both prosecution and defense at any of the trials arose here. Evidence remained basically the same in each trial, and the court rulings made in Mora's case were maintained throughout the subsequent hearings.

The opening statements of prosecution and defense laid out the lines to be developed by each side—just as they are expected to. Col. Rice said that the prosecution would show that

> the accused's superior officer Captain Damaso DeVera, gave the accused a direct order to board the sedan provided to take him to Maguire Air Force Base and the accused wilfully disobeyed the same.[6]

Attorney Faulkner opened for the defense by saying that Captain DeVera's order was unlawful, and that this justified Mora's disobeying it. They would show that the order was unlawful for a pair of reasons which would be developed in two lines of argument. According to the first,

> the Department of the Army proceeded to invoke the order to go to
> Vietnam, knowing that it would not be obeyed, only for the purpose
> of imposing the greatest penalty that could have been imposed. . . .[7]

In its second line of argument, the defense would hold the command to be unlawful because it issued from an unlawful source. In order to show this, Faulkner said: "we will attempt to prove to you that the conduct of the war in Vietnam is illegal. We will . . ."[8] But now he was interrupted by Col. Maguire. The law officer promptly recessed the court and brought both defense and prosecution attorneys to an out-of-court meeting. Addressing Faulkner, he began:

> Defense counsel, I recessed the court to call this hearing because
> listening to your opening statement it occurred to me that you must
> have misunderstood me yesterday. . . .[9]

Yesterday—the morning of the previous day, September 6—had been spent in hearing pretrial motions by the defense. Just as it would have been in civilian court, the pretrial hearing was the occasion for the defense to put its case as an argument for dismissal or for some other interventions by the judge which would either end the proceedings or alter them seriously before they even reached the jury. Where motions of this sort fail to elicit judicial intervention, they nonetheless give prosecution, defense, and judge an initial "reading" of each other which can be useful in the trial proper. Faulkner and his colleagues had in fact sought disqualification of the law officer, dismissal of the charges, change of venue, and continuance during this pretrial session.

The first thing the defense had done was to attempt to introduce the issue of the illegality of the war. The content of the argument was familiar enough: American military presence in Vietnam violated the War Powers Clause in the Constitution and our treaty obligations. However, the strategy for presenting it was curious: it took the form of a challenge to Col. Maguire to disqualify himself as law officer:

> The question I intend to ask is whether you have any preconceived
> convictions regarding the legality of the Vietnam war: If you have

will you please express them for the record for the purpose of determining whether challenge for cause is present?[10]

Attorney Faulkner apparently adopted this approach because he
felt that a motion to dismiss based simply on the claim that the war
was illegal had no chance. He probably didn't expect his question to
prompt a series of first-person ruminations by the law officer about
his own impartiality. If he had expected this, he would have been
disappointed. Sidestepping whatever personal thrust the challenge
contained, Col. Maguire raised the distinction between law and fact:

> I am certain that you realize Mr. Faulkner that if your question
> is based on a question of fact, it is to be submitted to the court. If it
> is a matter of law it is not proper.[11]

"Your question," as subsequent exchange makes clear, is the question of the illegality of the Vietnam war rather than that of possible
bias on the part of the law officer. Faulkner argued that from the
point of view of international law, the legality of the American military presence in Vietnam was a matter of fact that had to be decided
in court. The prosecution contended, and the law officer agreed, that
the court-martial was an exercise of domestic rather than international law. In this perspective, the former argued, "the legality of the
war in Vietnam is a construction of the laws and treaties of the
United States . . ."[12] and Col. Maguire subsequently announced:

> Gentlemen, I rule the legality of the presence of our troops is a
> pure matter of law—and, therefore, that the question put to me by
> the defense counsel with a view to possible challenge legally is im-
> proper and I so rule.[13]

With this handling of the motion, any question of personal bias was
resolved by reference to the law officer's role as judge. If he is wrong
about ruling, an appeals body can reverse him—but what will be at
issue will be legal judgment, not impartiality.

Having ruled that the question of the American military presence
was a matter of law, Col. Maguire, in the face of another request by
Faulkner, ruled that, from one important angle at least, that presence
itself was legal. Faulkner had requested that the defense be allowed

to obtain testimony and depositions from six witnesses: Secretary of State Rusk, Under-Secretary of State Ball, Secretary of Defense McNamara, General Westmoreland, Vice President of South Vietnam Ky, and North Vietnam Premier Phan Van Dong.[14]

Faulkner said that he wanted to introduce these people not as experts familiar with certain problems but as *participants* in the events in connection with which his client stood accused. The issue was Mora's responsibility as regards this war, and some of these men (Rush, Ball, and McNamara) were the makers or administrators of our treaty commitments and the makers of the war. The other witnesses were needed to testify out of personal experience on the situation where crimes against peace and humanity were the issue.

The prosecution insisted that an order to a soldier to move from one point to another simply could not be considered a violation of international law. Col. Maguire took up this theme, seeing the issue as a simple one: "it boils down to this, whether on July 14, 1966 the President of the United States had authority to order members of the Armed forces to go to Vietnam." Noting lack of precedent on both sides in the matter, he denied the defense motion, ruling: "for the purpose of this trial that as a matter of law the President of the United States has the power and had the power on 14 July, 1966. . . ."[15]

In view of the fact that he had laid this ruling and the previous one on the defense, it is not surprising that Col. Maguire reacted sharply to Faulkner's declaration before the court that he intended to defend by reference to the illegality of the war. At the out-of-court meeting with the attorneys, Col. Maguire emphatically restated his rulings against the introduction of the question of the illegality of the war and in support of the President's power to move troops. Faulkner argued that the rulings on the preliminary motions to disqualify did not prevent the raising of the same issues when the question became that of the refusal to obey military orders deemed illegal. Maguire saw no merit in this and said:

> I now forbid you in any manner, shape or form to present to the court that our troops are illegally in Vietnam. I have made my ruling as a matter of law for the purpose of the legality of the order involved in this case that they are legally there.[16]

Faulkner intimated (and Maguire denied) that this was in effect a ruling that the order to Mora was legal and that therefore his defense was being prejudiced. He renewed the challenge to Maguire:

> I would now like to enter into the record a direct challenge to you, Mr. Law Officer, to continue to sit on this case. I think you have expressed an opinion which a judicial officer should not have expressed. You have ruled already on the legality of the command which I think should have been reserved until the accused's case was fully into the record. I think you have predetermined at this point that the defense is not a good defense and I respectfully ask that you remove yourself from this case.[17]

The law officer said: "Your request is denied."[18]

Though it is mentioned again later—with Col. Maguire's permission—at the time of sentencing, the issue of the illegality of the war was now eliminated as a defense in the question of guilt or innocence.

Now if Faulkner and his collaborators were going to prove the order illegal, it would have to be because it had been given to entrap Mora. The Manual for Courts-Martial gave them this to work with:

> Disobedience of an order . . . *which is given for the sole purpose of increasing the penalty for an offense which it is expected that the accused may commit, is not punishable under this article.*[19]

In a brief submitted to the Commanding General U.S. First Army, who would review the trial results, the defense team said:

> There was every reason for the Department of Army to know that accused would refuse the command to go to Vietnam on 14 July 1966. The Department of Army knew on 30 June 1966 that accused had publicly announced the commencement of the said injunction action and the press conference. It is obvious that the latter two events so enraged the Department of Army that the change of orders came about. With all this foreknowledge the total confinement of accused was planned from 7 July to 14 July 1966. The plan was to entrap accused into a position where he would be given the order which it certainly could have been expected he "may" disobey. In these circumstances accused cannot be guilty of violating Article 90, U.C.M.J.[20]

This defense claim had sufficient support in testimony and documentation to justify taking it quite seriously. It was a matter of record that the press conference had elicited public comment from the Pentagon's general counsel, Frank Bartimo, and the chief information officer at Fort Dix, Major Allen Galfund. On the basis of various communications logs and duty records it was determined that on the evening of July 6 a meeting had been held among Pentagon officials in the office of one General Sedluck (Room 2E 737) at which plans were made to deal with the trio. At 11:30 P.M. of that evening a phone call was made to Fort Hood—and at 5:05 A.M. on the following day Fort Hood wired the Pentagon advising them that the orders for Mora and his associates had been amended to send them immediately to Fort Dix.

They were arrested before they had received these orders—which prompted the complaint of illegal confinement. On the 12th and 13th of July, meetings were held at Fort Dix and attended by the commanding general of that installation, his deputy, the public information officer, and a number of others. The decision which was apparently taken in this meeting was contained in a message from the Fort Dix commander, Maj. Gen. Hightower, to the Army Chief of Staff in Washington. Its opening paragraph read:

> With respect to Johnson, Mora and Samas there is sufficient evidence to warrant the preferring of charges alleging a violation of Article 134, uttering disloyal statements with intent to cause disaffection and disloyalty among the civilian population and members of the military forces. My decision is that in the best interest of the service, preferring of charges be deferred to afford Enlisted Men opportunity to comply with orders to proceed for duty to RVN.[21]

The opportunity to comply was to be established by separating the three on July 13, and then on the 14th ordering each individually to transportation to Vietnam. "Should orders be disobeyed," the message continued, "appropriate action will be taken." On the 13th, the Department of the Army responded approving the plan.

This situation was first made the ground for a series of motions at the pretrial hearing. With Major Lassiter arguing, the defense asked for dismissal because the order was given during a period of illegal confinement and then because the elaborate planning by the Army made the charges the result of an illicit scheme. The first motion was denied because even if confinement was illegal, its relation to the charge in question was not direct enough to justify dismissal. Col.

Maguire ruled against the second as a motion to dismiss, because these various discussions and communications always included the possibility that the order might be obeyed—in which case it would have been the occasion for avoiding prosecution rather than prompting it. He also denied a motion for a change of venue to a court with no knowledge of the interest which the communication with the Pentagon indicated on the part of the Department of the Army.

Finally, the defense asked for a continuance until after the appeals in civilian court had been decided. The prosecution argued against this motion by insisting that the court-martial was a tribunal of competent jurisdiction in the matter, and that, consequently, there was no valid ground for the requested continuance. This motion too was denied, with the law officer adding to the prosecution's reasons for the decision. The presentation of the case to the court then began.

The prosecution, whose case was presented on the afternoon of September 6, pursued the sharp line which its opening statement anticipated. They introduced into evidence the original order to report for shipment, the amended order directing Mora to report to Fort Dix, and the special order directing them to take transportation from Fort Dix and Maguire Air Force Base for shipment to Vietnam. They presented just one witness, Captain Damaso DeVera, who made the charge of insubordination.

Prosecution questions to DeVera elicited the facts that he was Mora's commanding officer during the latter's period at Fort Dix and that he had informed Mora on July 13 that the orders for his assignment to Vietnam were still in effect and that he should be prepared for shipment. According to DeVera's further testimony, the orders for actual shipment (giving place, date, and means of transportation) were handed to him—DeVera—on the morning of July 14. He passed them on to Mora, reading them to him and explaining certain of their contents. He then ordered Mora into a car which would take him to Maguire Air Force Base for a flight toward Vietnam. Mora refused this order to get into the car each time DeVera gave it. After a third refusal DeVera made out a confinement order on the charge of insubordination and Mora was sent to the stockade.

Faulkner's cross-examination was directed at revealing DeVera's action to be part of a plan to entrap Mora. He hammered away at several points: prior conversations about Mora between DeVera and his (DeVera's) commanding officer; the fact that there had been publicity about the case; the fact that DeVera had gone to meet Mora on July 14 with blank confinement orders in his pocket. He succeeded in showing some inconsistencies between what DeVera said in direct examination and what DeVera said in previous questioning about the incident. However, DeVera's position at this time is summed up in the following exchange:

> Q. Did you have any foreknowledge that Pvt. Mora would not go to Vietnam?
> A. No sir.[22]

This meant, as his other testimony explicitly affirmed, that despite widespread national and local reporting he had heard only vaguely of a plan by certain soldiers to refuse to go to Vietnam. It meant further, according to the same testimony, that he had not associated the report he heard with Mora despite his presence at the meeting on the 12th of July, despite his exchange with Mora on the 13th, and despite conversations with his superiors about the matter. It meant too that his discussion with his superiors did not touch on what he was to do in case of a refusal and that the carrying of the confinement orders as well as the decision to charge the accused with insubordination (rather than some lesser infraction) was strictly his own.

The defense introduced two witnesses: Lt. Col. Craig T. Wesley, Commanding Officer, United States Army Personnel Center at Fort Dix, and Private Mora himself.

Col. Wesley's testimony bore primarily on the meetings of July 12 and 13. Questioned by Major Lassiter, he said that he had attended each. DeVera was present for part of the second. Asked about the purpose of these meetings of Fort Dix authorities, which in the minds of the defense represented part of an illicit plan, Wesley said that their aim was "to accomplish the continued movement of the accused to their destination."[23] He added that those at the meeting expected that the movement orders would meet with compliance.

Pvt. Mora then took the stand in his own behalf. Under direct questioning by Faulkner, Mora first reviewed his personal history prior to the trial. He was a Puerto Rican from the Bronx, graduated in history from C.C.N.Y., was drafted in December 1965, was trained as a switchboard operator in the Signal Corps, and on June 6, 1966, was ordered to Vietnam. He recounted his arrest—"around the corner from my house"—and his confinement at Fort Dix. This seven-day confinement preceding the direct order to go was apparently very severe ("We were restricted to the immediate area of our bunks") and without formal charges: "Col. Wesley told us we were being investigated under Article 134 of the U.C.M.J. which amounted to making statements detrimental to the morale of the armed forces."[24]

When questioning turned to the reasons for his refusal to be moved into the war zone, Mora cited extensive reading which had convinced him that the war was wrong, and spoke of moral commitment hardened in the ghetto:

> I believe to act contrary to what you know is right is to die a little . . . whenever the cop on the corner would tell us we had to keep our place, keep within our boundaries at that time I told them, no. The fact that you reaffirm what you believe you cannot backtrack. If a man is without a moral code he is like the sea without water. That is the only way I know how to act.[25]

On cross-examination by the trial counsel, Mora clearly conceded that he had knowingly disobeyed the order given by Captain DeVera.

When the prosecution summarized, it called attention to the fact that Mora had admitted under oath every act with which he was charged. Under the circumstances there could be no doubt—reasonable or even conceivable—of his guilt. The defense summary stayed with the issue of the illegality of the order, underscoring the evidence which seemed to point to its having been given only for the purpose of entrapping and punishing Mora.

When he instructed the jury, Col. Maguire reminded them that if such was the purpose of the order then it was indeed illegal and Mora was innocent. For the rest, he cautioned them that only the order to get into the car was at issue here, not the orders to go to Vietnam. He added that the motives which prompted Mora to disobey were irrelevant.

The court deliberated for twenty-seven minutes before arriving at the finding of guilty.

The maximum sentence authorized for the violation of Article 90

U.C.M.J. is five years imprisonment, dishonorable discharge, forfeiture of all pay and allowances, and reduction to the lowest enlisted grade. Prior to court deliberation over the sentence, Faulkner addressed them again about his client. He introduced Mora's service record, which was a history of "excellent" ratings and quick promotion. Mora was, in short, a good soldier. For the rest, he underscored the defendant's conscientiousness despite its high cost and that the rehabilitation aim of imprisonment was scarcely relevant in the case of this sort of moral character.

Army trial counsel argued the need for obedience to orders if there is to be the efficiency and discipline necessary to the Army. Conceding the excellence of the defendant's previous record, he insisted that on July 14 Mora had lost his right to be called a good soldier. His conduct was, in fact, dishonorable. The government asked for dishonorable discharge, forfeiture of all pay and allowances, and "an appreciable period of confinement to adequately punish Dennis Mora and to deter others."[26]

Col. Maguire exhorted the members of the court:

> . . . you sit in judgment upon this man not to wreak vengeance on him but for the purpose of taking that action which you believe will serve the best interest of society in general and the military society in particular as well as the needs of Private Mora as an individual.[27]

The court recessed at 3:50 P.M. to allow deliberation on the sentence. At 4:05 P.M. it opened to allow the president of the court, Col. Walter R. Bruyere, to inform Mora that he had been sentenced: "To be dishonorably discharged from the service, to forfeit all pay and allowances, and to be confined at hard labor for three years."[28]

The court which tried James Johnson and the one which tried David Samas also found them guilty, but sentenced them to five years in prison. There is no right to bail in the military system of justice, and convicted servicemen are normally required to begin serving their sentences immediately upon conviction. The Fort Hood Three went to prison while their appeals were made. There were brief stays in the Fort Dix and the Fort Meade stockades. Then they went to the U.S. Disciplinary Barracks at Fort Leavenworth, Kansas, to serve their sentences.

THE APPEAL

The first appellate action in the military court system in this case was taken with the Commanding General of the First United States Army, who had convened the court and who had authority to review the results and to reduce the sentence. Faulkner, Lassiter, and Cotton submitted a brief, and the case was summarized in detail by Army Staff Judge Advocate James K. Gaynor. Gaynor's role was to appraise the trial and advise the general on a course of action.

He advised that the sentence be approved. The general agreed. This was early November, 1966.

Now the scene shifted to the federal court system and to the appeal by the three from the ruling made by Judge Curran of the District Court for the District of Columbia on the previous July 11. The legal question which completely dominated the appeal was that of the justiciability of the case, or to put the matter another way, that of the willingness of the court to intervene. Interestingly enough, the same point was at issue in another case which was before the United States Court of Appeals for the District of Columbia, a case which was also being argued by Stanley Faulkner. This was the appeal by one Robert Luftig, also a soldier, who had requested and been denied an injunction and a declaratory judgment against Secretary of Defense McNamara and Secretary of the Army Resor prohibiting Luftig's being sent to Vietnam. Since the cases differed only on a point of fact—Luftig had not actually received orders to Vietnam while Mora, Johnson, and Samas had—Faulkner and government attorneys agreed that the decision in the Luftig case would apply to the case of the Fort Hood Three.

Faulkner was able to draw upon some noteworthy opinion and some precedent to make his case for the justiciability of the question. A remark from a speech by Justice Douglas presents the theme of one series of citations: "But the political question should no longer be used as thicket behind which the judiciary retreats."[29]

Thus in one case, *Nixon* v. *Herndon,* Justice Holmes wrote:

> The objection that the subject matter of the suit is political is little more than a play upon words. Of course the petition concerns political action but it alleges and seeks to recover for private damage. That private damage may be caused by such political action and may

be recovered for in a suit at law hardly has been doubted for over two hundred years, since *Ashby* v. *White,* 2 Ld. Raymn. 938, 3 id. 320, and has been recognized by this Court.[30]

In another case, *Baker* v. *Carr,* the Court wrote: "Yet it is an error to suppose that every case or controversy which touches foreign relations lies beyond judicial cognizance."[31]

There was precedent, Faulkner maintained, for injunctive relief against a government official when his acts were constitutionally void.

> Not only no such power is given, but it is absolutely prohibited both to the executive and the legislative, to deprive anyone of life, liberty or property without due process. . . .[32]

Faulkner reminded the court that President Truman's attempt to seize Youngstown Sheet and Tube under the wartime powers at the time of the Korean conflict was stopped by injunction; then he turned back to Justice Douglas:

> Yet even though power is given exclusively to one department to do a certain act, when the power is exercized justiciable rights may arise. Private rights commonly derive from treaties. The Chief Executive, as Commander-in-Chief, makes decisions in which no one else can participate. But what he does often gives rise to claims that courts should adjudicate.[33]

The Court of Appeals reaction was itself rather striking. It affirmed the lower court's decision on Luftig, and therefore on the three, abruptly and quotably:

> The District Court was, of course, eminently correct on both its primary and alternative grounds for dismissal; these propositions are so clear that no discussion or citation of authority is needed. The only purpose to be accomplished by saying this much on the subject is to make it clear to others comparably situated and similarly inclined that resort to the courts is futile, in addition to being wasteful of judicial time, for which there are urgent legitimate demands.
>
> It is difficult to think of an area less suited for judicial action than that into which Appellant would have us intrude. The fundamental division of authority and power established by the Constitution precludes judges from overseeing the conduct of foreign policy or the use of military power; these matters are plainly the exclusive province of Congress and the Executive.[34]

This decision was rendered on February 6, 1967 and would be appealed to the Supreme Court. Meanwhile, the verdict of the court-martial was reviewed, according to military practice, by the Army Board of Review.[35] The brief submitted by Faulkner and by Captain Paul V. Melodia of the Judge Advocate General's Office, who also acted for the defense, attributed nine errors to the original courts-martial. The first two were that the courts-martial had dealt improperly with the question of the legality of the war, which violated international law on war crimes, crimes against humanity (error I), and which also violated the laws of land warfare (error II). The soldier who went to war would be liable under both of those laws. A third error lay in the refusal to call the witnesses which the defense requested. Two other errors related to the refusal of a continuance pending civilian court action and the prior involvement of the convening authority in the case. There was also a pair of complaints about insufficiency of evidence and then a lengthy argument about the restraint of free speech, something barely touched upon in the courts-martial and the federal Court of Appeals. They did not renew the complaint about violation of the war powers provision of the Constitution, however.

The Army's case was presented by Captain Salvatore A. Romano and Major John F. Webb. They met the opposition's contention point by point, dwelling at particular length on the questions of the war's illegality and of freedom of speech. On the first of these they reviewed a series of precedents for the separation of powers and then turned to the "Nuremberg defense." Here they seemed to have done their homework carefully. They argued, primarily on the basis of Nuremberg documents, first that only individuals could be guilty of war crimes and crimes against humanity—an argument which seems to undermine the charge that a nation could be guilty. On the same documentary basis, they further argued that one could not hold everyone who fights guilty of waging aggressive war (where that might be a question), because such a charge could apply only to high-ranking officials. Neither could participation alone in a war where atrocities are committed make them guilty of atrocities:

> . . . appellant cannot raise the Nuremberg defense simply because some atrocities may be committed in Vietnam. Appellant has not

been ordered to commit atrocities and consequently his refusal to obey the order cannot be rationalized on some vague assertion of a purported Nuremberg defense. . . .

If appellant was ever faced with the possibility (of being ordered to commit an atrocity), he could not only rightfully disobey such an order, but would be required to do so for no other reason than that obedience would violate the regulation and policy of the Department of the Army.[36]

Their handling of the restraint of free speech issue consisted of a short argument to the effect that there was no causal relation between the appellants' exercise of free speech at the press conference and the order which they were convicted of disobeying and then a long documentation of the need to limit the right of free speech in the armed forces. The short argument seemed to maintain that the entire sequence of events could be accounted for without considering the speech issue, which therefore lost its causal character:

To the extent that appellant was already under orders for Vietnam the subsequent updating of the orders was part and parcel of the initial decision to deploy appellant to the theatre of operation. Appellant was convicted for wilfully disobeying a direct order which implemented his order to go to Vietnam. Therefore there is absolutely no causal connection between his alleged exercise of free speech and the order to board the sedan.[37]

This is a curiously abstract and rather unimpressive argument following, as it does, the admission that the appellant had been confined as a result of the press conference. The argument for the need to restrain the speech of military men is quite complete, however, and carefully developed. After reviewing a long series of favorable court decisions and comments by supporting authorities, they turned to the restraints in the present case:

Faced with an open and publicized defiance by appellant not to go to Vietnam as required by order, some steps had to be taken to mitigate the demoralizing impact such activity had upon good order and discipline. Appellant's leave was cancelled and he was placed in administrative confinement. Certainly, in view of the threat posed to good order and discipline, such steps were not unreasonable.[38]

The Board of Review evidently felt that this was the case. The board affirmed the guilty verdict for all three but reduced the prison terms of Samas and Johnson to three years each making them the same as that of Mora.

Judge Advocate Edward Fenig added four pages of discussion to the opinion signed by Judges Joseph J. Crimins and Joseph H. Chalk in which he concurred. Characterizing the appeals of the three soldiers, he said that "they would substitute for themselves as accused a more transcendent matter: American policy in Vietnam."[39] This, of course, correctly identified the legal tactics of these—and most other—war resisters, though Judge Fenig did not generalize in this way.

The tactics did not succeed with him, though. He joined in the defense of the legality of the war by affirming the President's power. He also briefly argued for the limitation of the free speech of servicemen and for the irrelevance of treaty commitments to the trial. He concluded with classic observations about individual conscience and the law:

> In matters of conscience the law does not give carte blanche for individual stirrings and sincerity of purpose is often of dubious legal merit. So are political opinions. In a recent Supreme Court decision involving a deliberate violation of a state court injunction it was held ". . . that in the fair administration of justice no man can be judge in his own case, however exalted his station, however righteous his motives and irrespective of his race, color, politics or religion . . ." *Walker* v. *City of Birmingham,* 35 L.W. 4584 (13 June 67).[40]

The decision by the United States Court of Military Appeals was given in a very brief opinion on September 27, 1967. After reviewing both the history of the case and the briefs submitted for both sides—identical in substance with those submitted to the Board of Review—this body affirmed the sentences. Supporting this decision the court briefly affirmed the legality of the presence in Vietnam, the nonjusticiability of the issue of presidential power, and the dubious legal merit of the accused's notions of legality.

THE SUPREME COURT

When Faulkner (with the collaboration of attorney Selma Samols) petitioned the Supreme Court to review the dismissal of the federal court case, he said that it should be—and should have been—distinguished from the Luftig case because of the difference in factual situation. One would imagine that Faulkner's having agreed on the level of U.S. Court of Appeals to let the Fort Hood Three be subject to the Luftig decision did not help things here. The government, in a memorandum signed by Solicitor General Thurgood Marshall, declined to repeat the arguments which it made in the Luftig case. They said that the appellants' "belated effort to distinguish their case" did not touch the basic grounds for dismissal, namely that it was an unconsented suit against the government and that the legality of the American involvement in Vietnam is a nonjusticiable political question.

The appellants' brief was devoted in great part to the arguments for the justiciability of the issue, arguments which Faulkner and Samols attempted to buttress by pointing to recent historical developments: "With the increase of Federal power both nationally and internationally more and more situations come within the orbit of the loose definition of a 'political' question."[41] The petition for a writ of certiorari was denied.

The number of those who wanted the Court to rule, however, increased by one: Justice Potter Stewart joined Justice William O. Douglas in dissent. The position of Justice Douglas was not surprising because he had already dissented from the Court's refusal in the Mitchell and the Miller cases. Justice Stewart, on the other hand, is considered a traditionalist, or in the words of the *New York Times* editorial occasioned by the decision, "a stickler for constitutional tradition and precedent."[42] His dissent had considerable impact: the *Times* editorial suggested that an important turning point had been reached:

> Case No. 401
>
> No one really expected that Case No. 401 on the appellate docket for the 1967 term of the United States Supreme Court would legally halt Army draftees from going to Vietnam. . . .
>
> Yet the purpose of the case has been served: to the legislative debate about the war's legality has now been added judicial questioning. Although the appeal to hear arguments of three soldiers was denied, the dissenting opinions of Justices Potter Stewart and William O. Douglas are significant. Their effect is to raise anew

constitutional questions that require steady examination—and, under another set of circumstances, future justiciable findings.[43]

Stewart and Douglas wrote separate opinions. The latter explored
the history of the issue, both recent and distant, while Stewart raised
a series of questions for which judicial logic, applied to these circumstances, seemed to require an answer. Whether by accident or by
design, history and logic reinforce each other noticeably. Here are
the questions that Justice Stewart asked:

> I. Is the present United States military activity in Vietnam a "war"
> within the meaning of Article I, Section 8, Clause 11 of the Con-
> stitution?
> II. If so, may the Executive constitutionally order the petitioners
> to participate in that military activity, when no war has been
> declared by the Congress?
> III. Of what relevance to Question II are the present treaty obliga-
> tions of the United States?
> IV. Of what relevance to Question II is the joint Congressional
> ("Tonkin Bay") Resolution of August 10, 1964?
> (a) Do present United States military operations fall within the
> terms of the Joint Resolution?
> (b) If the joint Resolution purports to give the Chief Execu-
> tive authority to commit United States forces to armed conflict
> limited in scope only by his own absolute discretion is the Reso-
> lution a constitutionally impermissible delegation of all or part
> of Congress' power to declare war?[44]

Article I, Section 8, Clause 11 of the Constitution is the War
Powers Clause: "The Congress shall have power . . . to declare war."
Justice Stewart pressed, among others, the point that if the Vietnam
conflict is *war* in this sense, then need it not have been declared by
Congress in order to justify the assignment of the soldiers? Is it
permissible even for an acquiescent Congress to delegate such
power?

Justice Douglas began his dissent by noting the administration's
position—articulated before the Senate Committee on Foreign Relations by Nicholas D. Katzenbach—that the Vietnam activity is not
a war in the sense of Article I, Section 8, Clause 11: "A declaration
of war would not, I think, correctly reflect the very limited objectives
of the United States with respect to Vietnam."[45] Douglas then went

back to 1863 to point out that this issue has been subject to debate from the time of the Prize cases of that year to the present.

> During all subsequent periods in our history—through the Spanish American War, the Boxer Rebellion, two World Wars, Korea and now Vietnam, the two points of view urged in the Prize cases have continued to be voiced.[46]

But if the Vietnam action is not a war in the sense of the War Powers Clause, does this then leave the President—even a President supported by a Tonkin Gulf Resolution—a military blank check? In Douglas' words:

> Does the President's authority to repel invasions and quiet insurrections, his powers in foreign relations and his duty to execute faithfully the laws of the United States, including its treaties, justify what has been threatened of petitioners?[47]

Douglas thought that the Court should answer, as did Stewart. To use the latter's concluding words—echoed by the *Times*—

> These are large and deeply troubling questions. Whether the Court would ultimately reach them depends, of course, upon the resolution of serious preliminary issues of justiciability. We cannot make these problems go away simply by refusing to hear the case of three obscure Army privates. I intimate not even tentative views upon any of these matters, but I think the Court should squarely face them by granting certiorari and setting this case for oral argument.[48]

Encouraged by the reaction, Faulkner and Samols quickly asked the Court for a rehearing, one which would take into account, among other things, recent congressional interpretations of the Gulf of Tonkin Resolution. Along with the restatement of a number of previous arguments (bearing on the relevance of treaties and of the laws of land warfare, for example), he cited a list of authorities, which began with von Clausewitz, according to whose definitions the Vietnam action was indeed war.

But the legal system had apparently moved as far as it could on the impulse supplied by Mora, Samas, and Johnson. The petition for a rehearing was denied without comment. If these problems were to be raised again, they would have to be posed in another case.

The likely effect of Justice Douglas' uncovering of the legal history upon the prospects of the next resisters was unclear. On one hand he made it clear that their case is not the groundless and traditionless exercise in individual conscience that many lower court jurists seem to have felt that it was. It had a place in the history of the legal establishment. But its very perennial (or near-perennial) character indicates that a decisive resolution had not been achieved and would be difficult to promote.

Writing in the *New York Times* at the time of the decision, Fred P. Graham said that the Supreme Court had at least twice declared wartime acts of the American military to be unconstitutional. These were in the cases of Lincoln's suspension of habeas corpus during the Civil War, and the imposition of martial law in Hawaii during World War II, "but both (decisions) came after the wars were over and public feelings had cooled."[49] An attempt to overrule certain war-making powers during the Civil War led to a move by Congress to withdraw jurisdiction in this area from the Court.

The resisters would keep coming, maintaining their demands upon the legal system and testing both the speed and the direction of its reflexes. It would come as a surprise to no one, of course, that the rhythm of change in institutions does not necessarily synchronize tightly with the rhythm of the life and sacrifices of the individual. Whether it was made to do so in succeeding cases we shall see.

Mora, Samas, and Johnson did their time in Leavenworth.

CONSPIRACIES TO
SAVE LIVES

Chapter Five

The Conspiracy of
Dr. Spock et al.

The 1967 peace offensive reached its peak in the week of October 16 thru October 21—Stop The Draft Week—with a nationwide series of demonstrations. Protests occurred in New York, Philadelphia, Portland, Seattle, Madison, Boston, Chicago, Washington, D.C., and the Bay Area of California, with protesters demanding immediate withdrawal of United States forces from Vietnam, the end of the draft for Vietnam, and a reallocation of American resources to fight poverty at home. The activities of Stop The Draft Week were planned and carried out by many organizations, both national and local. Coordination among them was uneven, extending from instances of cooperative planning to the bare awareness of each other's existence.

At the same time, there was a dramatic escalation in the level of risk-taking on the part of peace militants. On one hand, an increasing number of people who had previously avoided direct confrontation with police were now ready to risk that confrontation to express their opposition to the war. Some of these were persons of national reputation. There was a second group, which was used to confrontations, but according to the style and tactics traditional to the peace movement—with prior consultation with police, planned arrests, and no attempt at resistance or escape. Many of these were now ready to assume a more militant style. The incidence of borderline law violation increased sharply; the October protests not only included traditional acts of civil disobedience but extended beyond into direct and violent confrontation. Government agencies responded with stricter enforcement policies.

In a memorandum to all local draft boards, dated October 24, 1967, Selective Service Director Lt. General Lewis B. Hershey recommended that any selective service registrant who mutilated or surrendered his draft card as an act of protest be declared delinquent and reclassified for prompt induction. He followed this two days later with a letter that recommended the same treatment for draft registrants who participated in any illegal demonstrations against the draft or public policies. The Justice Department itself soon disowned the Hershey policy, and draft registrants, for their part, promptly challenged one after another of its provisions. As their cases reached the Supreme Court, the challenges were upheld and during the ensuing two years punitive reclassification was dismantled piece by piece.[1] "We deal with conduct of a local Board that is basically lawless," said Justice William O. Douglas, who wrote the majority opinion in the Oestereich case.[2] To hold that the boards had the power to resolve draft exemptions by means of delinquency proceedings, he continued, would be to make of them "free wheeling agencies meting out their brand of justice in a vindictive manner."[3] He then added:

> once a person registers and qualifies for a statutory exemption, we find no legislative authority to deprive him of that exemption because of conduct or activities unrelated to the merits of granting or continuing the exemption.[4]

All of this took a certain amount of time, during which the prospect of punitive reclassification did hang over the peace militant. But the response from the side of the government to the 1967 offensive of the peace movement did not come from the Selective Service System alone. A special unit was organized in the Criminal Division of the Justice Department during December 1967 to speed up the investigation and prosecution of violations of the Selective Service Act and related statutes. There were also grand jury investigations in several localities directed at acts previously tolerated as civil disobedience or general advocacy.

Two notable indictments for Stop The Draft Week activities emerged from these investigations: conspiracy charges were preferred against the groups which came to be known as the Boston Five and the Oakland Seven. The Boston Five were prosecuted for a series of acts which culminated in a demonstration at the Justice Department on October 20, 1967. The defendants in this trial included Dr. Benjamin Spock and Rev. William Sloane Coffin. They and others who took part in Pentagon and California Bay Area demonstrations exemplify the trend among prominent persons to become more visibly active. Thus Joan Baez, Rev. Robert McAfee Brown, Kay Boyle, Noam Chomsky, Rev. Daniel Berrigan, Robert Lowell, and Norman Mailer participated in demonstrations at this time with all but Brown and Lowell being arrested. The Oakland Seven, who had challenged the legitimacy of the police and had planned to defend themselves against police violence, exemplified the move beyond traditional civil disobedience practice. They were indicted for their role in the California Bay Area Stop The Draft Week protest.

Conspiracy was the charge in both cases, and it merits some attention even prior to the account of the trials. Conspiracy is an agreement between two or more persons to achieve an unlawful object, or to achieve a lawful object by unlawful means. Legally, it is a quite intricate matter, difficult to prosecute and difficult to defend. It is the *agreement* among two or more persons that is its essence rather than what is agreed upon, and indeed, criminal conspiracy can have taken place even if the criminal act planned is never carried out. Some people claim that prosecution for conspiracy aims to punish intent alone, something which legal precedent and practice would not allow. But proponents of conspiracy prosecution note that intent is the purpose of an individual, so that to establish an agreement among individuals is to establish an act that goes beyond intent. They point to the increased potential for social harm which is achieved by cooperation among persons; mutual encouragement, division of labor and the like make possible a far more imposing threat than would the intention of an individual.

Every party to a conspiracy is liable for the acts of any other member in furtherance of the unlawful purposes, a fact which gives a certain indeterminate character to one's participation. In addition, the act is usually clandestine, and to come to grips with this, the courts are much more likely to accept circumstantial evidence than they would be in other types of crime. The informer is likely to play an important role as well. Circumstantial evidence, informers, and prosecution skill must convince a jury that the act aimed at by each alleged conspirator was known by him to be unlawful and that he knew himself to be cooperating with others for its accomplishment.

THE BOSTON FIVE

On January 5, 1968 the Boston Five were indicted by a federal grand jury of the District of Massachusetts for conspiracy to violate the draft law. According to the indictment, their illegal activity included the sponsoring and support of "a nation-wide program of resistance to the functions and operations of the Selective Service System."[5] This suggests a conspiratorial effort of considerable scope.

It is true that the acts that they were accused of conspiring to commit were part of Stop The Draft Week, and that this was an event of no mean magnitude. But Stop The Draft Week grew out of the efforts of a great many individuals and groups. Why, the defense would wonder, were William Sloane Coffin, Michael Ferber, Mitchell Goodman, Marcus Raskin, and Benjamin Spock selected for federal prosecution? "Well, I don't know that I can say exactly the reason why these five . . ."[6] the prosecuting attorney would respond during the trial. It was during his closing argument to the jury that he dealt with the question, and in handling it he underscored the pragmatic dimension of prosecution: the government traditionally has a discretionary power in deciding whom to prosecute,[7] and the exercise of this discretion is linked to the nature of prosecution as a deterrent to crime.[8] The latter consideration would, presumably, favor the indictment of persons like the defendants, whose national reputations gave them high visibility.

In any event, "there has always been somebody, always, who says: Why me? Everybody else was doing it or everybody else agreed. . . ."[9] However many others may also have been guilty, the matter at hand was the guilt or innocence of these five of the crime with which they were charged.

The indictment was on a single count, alleging one conspiracy. But the one conspiracy had four alleged aims, said to have been furthered by a series of acts, some of which were participated in by some, but not all, of the defendants. Thus the single count was articulated into several considerations. Taking the four aims first, the government claimed that the defendants conspired that they would "counsel, aid and abet diverse Selective Service registrants"[10] (1) to refuse to serve in the nation's armed forces; (2) to refuse to carry selective service notices of classification; and (3) to refuse to carry selective service registration certificates. In addition to this action aimed at draft registrants, the five were accused of conspiring that they would *themselves* "hinder and interfere, by any means, with the administration of the Military Selective Service Act of 1967. . . ."[11]

The conspiracy was said to have gone on from August 1, 1967 to the date of the indictment—January 5, 1968—and the things said to have been done to advance it were woven into four events, the discussion of which would dominate the trial. These events were the circulation for signatures of the statement "The Call to Resist Illegitimate Authority," a press conference, the accepting of draft cards from draft registrants, and the turning in of these cards to a government agency. The defense did not deny that any of these events occurred.

From the point of view of the Boston Five a single current of purpose animated their behavior in all these activities. This was to allow persons whose age made them relatively secure in their opposition to the war to ally themselves with men of draft age who were extremely vulnerable in their resistance. An estimated one thousand young men were already in jail for refusing induction, and, as we have seen, the trials of David Henry Mitchell III, David J. Miller, and the Fort Hood Three had already resulted in convictions.

"The Call to Resist Illegitimate Authority" condemned the war as illegal and immoral and insisted that "every free man has a legal right and a moral duty to exert every effort to end this war, to avoid collusion with it, and to encourage others to do the same."[12] To sign would be to support draft resistance and to oppose war policies which, it asserted, were destructive of the country. Eventually "The Call" would bear 23,000 signatures. Its profession of concern for the national good undoubtedly contributed to the willingness of some to sign despite the warning contained in the covering letter to the effect that signing might violate the law.[13]

Promoting "The Call" was one of the purposes of the press conference to which the indictment referred. The conference was held at the Hilton Hotel in New York on October 2. Coffin, Spock, Goodman, and Raskin—but not Ferber—were there. So were such anti-war intellectuals as Robert Lowell, Dwight McDonald, Paul Goodman, Ashley Montague, and Noam Chomsky. All spoke, most to denounce the war and to encourage participation in Stop The Draft Week. A few—Mitchell Goodman was one—simply made announcements about activities which were to take place on the week of October 16. These included the demonstrations in New York, Oakland, California, Washington, D.C., and elsewhere.

A central feature of most of these Stop The Draft Week demonstrations was to be the turning in of draft cards by draft registrants. This turn-in at many points around the country had been planned for October 16 by Resistance, an organization of draft age men formed to resist induction.[14] Some of those at the press conference said that they would participate in these turn-ins by accepting cards. They would later—on October 20—attempt to present the cards to the Attorney General at the Justice Department.

On October 16, Coffin and Ferber helped preside over a demonstration in Boston, which became the third major event alluded to in the indictment. Though it was a draft card turn-in of the sort planned generally for Stop The Draft Week, it had not been announced at the New York press conference, apparently because plans for it were not completed (and may not have been begun on October 2). This demonstration began as a rally on Boston Common and then moved to the Arlington Street Church, where it became a religious ceremony. Coffin and Ferber, along with others, delivered sermons. Fifty draft cards were burned, though Coffin and others discouraged this. Ferber turned in his card, which was among the approximately two-hundred-fifty received there that day. These, along with others turned in around the country, would be taken to Washington on October 20.

The October 20 Justice Department demonstration was primarily Coffin's idea. He had suggested it when asked by Mitchell Goodman about ways for the over-draft-age to support the resistance by prospective draftees. It seemed to offer an appropriate climax for the nationwide draft card turn-in as well as the prospect for provoking a court test of the legality of the war and of the draft. This would be the only one of the four events specified in the indictment at which all five of the defendants were present.

Unfortunately, from their point of view, Attorney General Ramsey Clark did not appear at the Justice Department on the 20th. The encounter which did occur was anything but the legal and moral confrontation which the Coffin-Goodman scenario had sought. Two Assistant Attorneys General—John R. McDonough and John Van de Kamp—met the protestors, served them coffee, and heard them out. They refused to accept the draft cards, however, McDonough commenting that he might himself be violating the law by doing so. The cards were simply left on the table, to be taken by an FBI agent who was present, Oustide, after the meeting, Coffin castigated the government for refusing to take up their challenge:

> But I think it's an incredible thing, when you stop to think of it, that one of the highest officers of the law in the United States was really derelict in his duty to accept evidence of an *alleged crime,* and simply to refuse to accept the cards which we put on the table.[15]

During the first week of the new year, the government dealt some cards of its own.

THE TRIAL

The case would be heard before a jury in the United States District Court in Boston. Assistant United States Attorney John Wall was assigned the prosecution, along with Joseph J. Cella of the Justice Department. Wall did almost all of the courtroom work.

For the accused, there was less a single defense than five independent defenses. Reacting to the charges in a way quite suited to his denial that he had conspired with the others, each of the five retained his own lawyer and each lawyer prepared and carried out his work with very little consultation with the others.

Acting for Coffin in this rather unusual drama was James D. St. Clair; for Ferber, William Homans; for Mitchell Goodman, Edward

Barshak; for Marcus Raskin, Calvin Bartlett; and for Benjamin Spock, Leonard Boudin.[16] Each would present his own opening and closing to the jury; each would cross-examine not only prosecution witnesses but other defense witnesses and the other defendants.

Judge Francis Ford presided. A veteran of the federal bench—eighty-five years of age—he was disposed toward a strict construction of the issues. At the very opening of the hearing devoted to pretrial motions, he ruled out all discussion of the legality of the war and of the draft: they were irrelevant to the case. He held the contentions of the Nuremberg defense to be non-justiciable and denied defense motions based on these—a motion to take depositions abroad, for example. He also denied a motion to dismiss the indictment for vagueness and insufficiency of evidence and another for a bill of particulars naming all co-conspirators.

Judge Ford's handling of jury selection showed him to be committed to a brisk managing of procedural matters. On the first day of the trial proper, defense attorneys noticed that out of eighty-eight prospective jurors, only five were women. They protested the unrepresentative character of the group. The judge allowed some questioning of the court clerks about the way in which Bostonians were chosen for jury duty, but rejected defense objections to the panel's makeup. He also rejected all the questions which they had submitted to be asked of prospective jurors. As a result, twelve white male jurors and three white male alternates were selected in rather short order, subject only to peremptory challenge by each side. They would be sequestered for the remainder of the trial.

It was clear from Mr. Wall's opening statement to the jury that the government's case rested in large part on the public statements of the defendants. He quoted these at length during his extended speech, and quite accurately. Accuracy in this area would be no problem for the government: "The Call" was in print in thousands of copies, and as for the press conference, the draft card turn-in (at Arlington Street Church in Boston), and the Justice Department drama, these were all on film thanks to commercial television.

The government's case placed all five at the Justice Department on October 20. All save Ferber had been at the press conference and all save Ferber had signed "The Call." Ferber and Coffin had been at the Arlington Street Church ceremony. As for the planning of these events, Coffin and Goodman were shown to have had a planning role in the Justice Department visit and Raskin to have helped compose "The Call." Prosecution witnesses included Assistant Attorney General McDonough, who described the Justice Department encounter, and several FBI agents, one of whom was present at the October 2 press conference and another who had interviewed Spock in early December.

Now this December interview, though it was within the time period which the indictment covered, was later than any of the events which were specified as advancing the conspiracy. The last of these events, at the Justice Department, was on October 20, 1967. Government film and testimony extended to several such incidents, including a speech by Spock to Women's Strike for Peace in Philadelphia in late November, his appearance along with Goodman at a demonstration in New York on December 5, and a television interview of Coffin on December 14. Finally, the prosecution reached beyond the time of the indictment (August 1, 1967 to January 5, 1968) to introduce a speech which Ferber had given on April 3, 1968. Through all of this, the government emphasized the defendants' frequent and emphatic associating of themselves with the resisters' defiance of the law and challenging—at times even taunting—the government to arrest them.

When the prosecution finished and ritual defense motions for dismissal had been denied, the attorneys for the accused made their opening statements—all five of them. With Boudin leading the way, they had asked that each be allowed to open immediately prior to presenting the rest of his case. But Judge Ford ruled that they must open one after another so that all opening statements would be completed before anyone presented his case. The order, like that of the presentation of evidence, would be determined by the initials of the defendant: Coffin, Ferber, Goodman, Raskin, Spock. Each attorney began by introducing his client.

Coffin, currently chaplain at Yale, had been in the Army during World War II, and from 1950 to 1953 had been in the Office of Strategic Services. He had been a freedom rider in the South during the early sixties, had organized and advised for the Peace Corps, had lectured in India, and from 1965 onward had devoted himself to anti-war activities.

Ferber, at twenty-three, was the youngest defendant. A Swarthmore graduate and Harvard graduate student, he had been classified IA delinquent in the draft. He was Unitarian Universalist in background, and while not a pacifist he did come closer than any of the others to being that.

Goodman, a Harvard graduate with field artillery service in World War II, was a teacher and writer with a novel and articles in prestigious periodicals to his credit. Since 1965 he had been devoted to the anti-war movement, primarily as a writer and organizer.

Raskin, thirty-four years old, was 4F in the draft. A University of Chicago graduate and law school graduate, he was formerly legal counsel for a group of Congressmen and from 1961 to 1965 a member of a White House staff committee researching disarmament. He was coauthor with Bernard Fall of *Vietnam Reader,* and, since 1965, a codirector of the Institute for Policy Studies, an independent research and education organization.

Spock, a pediatrician, sixty-five years old, was the author of seven books. He had been a Lieutenant Commander in the Navy in World War II. He moved toward the peace movement through nuclear disarmament activity, which he began in 1962. He had campaigned for Johnson in 1964 and, subsequently disillusioned, had devoted most of his time since 1965 to anti-war activities.

With the prospect of testing the legality of the war and of the draft eliminated by judicial decision, the five were left with the rather demeaning task of staying out of jail. The jury heard them state their convictions about these broader issues, but under the justification that they were making clear their state of mind. Judicial instruction ruled out its being anything else. Their chief work was to refute the government's case: they did not conspire . . . , they did not hinder . . . , they did not counsel, aid, abet. . . .

They did not conspire. . . . Mr. St. Clair would tell the jury at one point: "if there is a conspiracy in this case—and I suggest to you that there isn't—it has to be a conspiracy of strangers."[17] Each of the five was led by his attorney through a description of his relation as a stranger to the other four. Prior to the period mentioned in the indictment, prior to August 1, 1967, that is, Coffin had exchanged a dozen or so words with Spock on the stage of a Madison Square Garden SANE rally in 1965 and Raskin had shaken the pediatrican's hand, though he didn't recall when and Spock didn't recall at all. There had been no other contacts among the five during this time.

Within the period specified by the indictment, Goodman had spoken with Coffin in planning the Justice Department rally. He had also phoned Raskin for help in making arrangements. (Raskin turned him down.) There had been no conversation among the four at the press conference and only the most miminal exchanges between Coffin and Ferber at the Arlington Street Church and between Coffin and Raskin at the Justice Department. Ferber met Raskin and Coffin only at the arraignment.

They did not conspire, then. Theirs was the behavior of persons with similar views arrived at individually and participating as individuals in public demonstrations elicited from the responsible by a momentous crisis in the nation's history. It was parallel action by like-minded men. But as the prosecution argued, conspiracy does not demand that they know the others directly, nor that the work be secret. It requires only that they knowingly cooperate with others in planning to break the law. Quite clearly most did know of the others' position on the war and on the draft and of their presence and intentions in the various activities mentioned in the prosecution case.

They did not hinder. . . . The prosecution's case for conspiracy to hinder the operation of the Selective Service System rested on the defendants' roles in accepting draft cards (Coffin and Ferber) and on the participation by Spock and Goodman in a December sit-in in front of the Whitehall Street induction center in New York. Defense argued that the surrender (and accepting) of draft cards tended to speed up induction, rather than hinder it. As for the Whitehall sit-in, it was purely symbolic, with arrest arranged beforehand with the police in the style of a radical pacifist demonstration. No one imagined that it would actually shut down the facility.

They did not knowingly and willingly counsel, aid, and abet the committing of any infraction. Here the five would have to combat the first impressions left by their own words. "The Call" listed a series of forms of resistance including refusal to obey orders and going

AWOL by servicemen and refusal to be inducted and leaving the country on the part of the draft aged. It said:

> We believe that each of these forms of resistance against illegitimate authority is courageous and justified. . . . We will continue to lend our support to those who undertake resistance to this war.[18]

Coffin, at the Arlington Street Church ceremony, had said: "Well, I am afraid that the government is afraid of a moral confrontation of those who today and this week are determined to counsel, aid, and abet those of you who are in the resistance."[19] Goodman, at the Justice Department and elsewhere had used the "counsel, aid, and abet" language in describing his intentions. Ferber, at the Arlington Street Church, urged his listeners to "help anyone and everyone to find ways of avoiding the draft."[20]

Spock used similar language in the post-indictment interview with FBI agents, where he also observed that he was risking arrest. In another incident, in Philadelphia on November 29, he had said, "Let us not stop for a minute. I am in favor of civil disobedience right up to the hilt."[21]

Coffin had conceded "aiding and abetting" in a postindictment television program, and Ferber, in a speech just a few weeks prior to the trial, spoke of induction refusals, the exodus of hundreds to Canada, riots, desertions, and mutinies, and then remarked: "If that is what they want to face, then we are ready, stronger than ever, to give it to them."[22]

When the prosecution confronted them with these words, defendants responded in several ways. Goodman and Coffin disavowed a lawyer's understanding of the terms "counsel, aid, and abet," and the former testified that he used them for their dramatic impact. He was not declaring criminal intent, but "using language as I saw it commensurate with the desperate situation that our country was in."[23]

Coffin, Ferber, and Spock insisted that their efforts were directed only toward the converted. They did not aim to convince or to induce anyone to resist. They wished only to support those who had already reached their own decisions to do so. Thus Coffin testified to asking those surrendering cards to him in Boston, "Are you sure you know what you are doing?"[24] and of returning one to a law student with the admonition "You're out of your mind."[25]

Ferber said that those surrendering cards at the Arlington Street Church ceremony were strongly cautioned against emotionalism and warned of the possible consequences of their decisions. Then, Ferber continued, "I also said: The draft cards will remain in Boston for the next four days and that anyone who wished to obtain his back should do so with no trouble."[26] Spock, in expounding his own insistence that he did not attempt to persuade, said "I explained that it was against my professional principles to try to persuade anybody to do anything that he is not ready to do himself."[27]

As for the challenge to the government to arrest them, could this be other than the acknowledgment of a crime, knowingly and willingly committed? "Alleged crime,"[28] Coffin responded, and then proceeded to explain what he understood civil disobedience to be:

> My understanding . . . of civil disobedience . . . is the deliberate testing of a statute or regulation whose constitutionality is in question; and that by violating the law you are apparently civilly disobedient, but it may turn out that you were totally legal.[29]

It was an "alleged crime" then, for Coffin, who had, as a freedom rider, once been vindicated by a Supreme Court decision declaring a law which he had broken to be unconstitutional. His description of the motive forces behind his civil disobedience leaned heavily on the sanctity of the conscience of the individual, and Wall challenged him strongly on this: What of the rights of the sincere segregationist to civil disobedience in the interest of resisting integration? Spock was pressed on the question, by both Boudin and Wall, and opted for law. Thus when Wall asked, "did you base your claim of right to oppose the war upon your conscience, or upon your view of law?" Spock answered:

> I always based it on the rule of law. I never felt I had to differentiate between law and conscience or fall back on conscience, because I always believed that a citizen must work against a war that he believes to be against international law. This is the Nuremberg principle which I believe is part of the United States law.[30]

The defense lawyers closed their cases by reiterating the "conspiracy of strangers" theme and by underscoring the upright character of their clients, their convictions about the war and the draft, as well as the nature of free speech and dissent in American society.

A surprisingly large amount of Mr. Wall's closing statement was devoted to the nature of conspiracy law, ground which would soon be covered by Judge Ford in his instructions to the jury. But its dramatic climax lay in his attack on the moral stance of the defendants—particularly on the issue of the sovereignty of conscience. "I submit to you, some of these or most of these defendants seem awfully self-righteous about what's legal and what's moral and what's immoral."[31] After returning briefly to the conscientious segregationists, Wall drew out the implications of their view of conscience:

> The result, members of the jury: Anarchy. Every man a law to himself. . . . Is this country to be tied to a string that is tied to Mr. Coffin's conscience? Is it going to be tied to a string, even to the conscience of a man as sincere and dedicated and as great as Dr. Spock? It can't be.[32]

There is a far better conscience to be tied to. It is to be found in Congress—"our conscience as expressed through those people who are voted in. . . ."[33] This conscience has several times decided that, conscientious objectors aside, "no body has got a right not to go in the service."[34] Concluding, Wall asked for "an appropriate verdict," and added, "The Government of the United States asks you to do justice under the law."[35]

INSTRUCTIONS TO THE JURY

> "Conspire" is a word of Latin origin and means "breathing together."
> It means a common undertaking, a common plan.[36]

To supply the law which the jury would apply to the facts in order to decide whether or not the five had "breathed together," Judge Ford gave a series of instructions which were standard in conspiracy cases: that it could have taken place without any formally expressed agreement; that circumstantial evidence was sufficient to justify a verdict; that it was not necessary that the conspiracy should have succeeded, nor that each conspirator clearly understood its scope. It was necessary to show that each knowingly and willingly participated, and once this was established, each co-conspirator became liable for the acts of every other. Of course, mere association with a member of a conspiracy is not evidence of one's own membership, and a person may be identified as a member of a conspiracy only by his own statements and conduct.

The defense had been distressed over Judge Ford's ruling out of the questions of the legality of the war and of the draft, a ruling which he repeated in his instructions. They were further upset by his rejection of *all* of their requested instructions. His final direction to the jury raised unanimous defense protest. He said:

> In addition to your general oral verdict, in the event that, and only in the event that, your single verdict is guilty on the conspiracy charged, you will make and return special written and unanimous answers to ten questions. All requested special answers to questions relate to all the offenses charged as the objections of the single alleged conspiracy.[37]

The first three questions asked if the five conspired—yes or no—to (1) counsel, (2) aid, and (3) abet registrants to avoid the draft. The next six related in the same way to the matter of registrants carrying registration certificates (4, 5, and 6) and notices of classification (7, 8, 9). The tenth asked if all conspired to hinder the draft. The defense complained that to ask these questions was to lump all the defendants together in a way calculated to promote the impression that they conspired. Their protest was rejected.

VERDICT AND SENTENCING

Four of the Boston Five—Coffin, Ferber, Goodman, and Spock—were found guilty of having conspired with each other and with other unnamed persons to violate the Military Selective Service Act of 1967. Raskin was acquitted.

At the sentencing, on July 10, 1968, Judge Ford lectured his listeners severely: "Rebellion against the law, is in the nature of treason."[38] He continued:

> High and low, the intellectual as well as all others, must be deterred from violation of the law. . . . Where law and order stops, obviously anarchy begins. . . . It is reasonably inferrable that the defendants here played some material part in inciting certain draft evaders to flout the law. It would be preposterous to sentence young men to jail for violation of the Selective Service Act and allow those who, as the jury found, conspired to incite Selective Service regis-

trants to take action to violate the law . . . to escape under the guise of free speech.[39]

All of the convicted defendants were sentenced to two years imprisonment; Ferber was fined $1,000 and the other three were fined $5,000.

THE APPEAL

The United States Court of Appeals for the First Circuit reversed the convictions. The majority opinion, written by Judge Bailey Aldrich and concurred in by Judge McEntee, acquitted Spock and Ferber and ordered a new trial for Coffin and Goodman. According to a dissenting opinion by Judge Frank Coffin, all defendants should have been acquitted. The contrast between these two opinions offers an interesting case of varied judicial response.

Before the Appellate court, the defense had reiterated its argument that the behavior of the defendants was not conspiracy in the conventional legal sense. It not only lacked the usual criminal qualities, but was public, based on an honest belief, and aimed at sensitizing the government and fellow citizens to a position supported by a reputable body of opinion on a most important issue.

There was also a series of charges against the way in which the trial had been conducted. Evidence, it was claimed, had been improperly admitted from non-defendants, and insufficiently limited to the one person to whom it properly related. The charge on conspiracy had been in error (had not made it clear that a single one of the defendants could have been guilty), the jury had been improperly selected, and the request for special findings was improper.

The Court of Appeals did not take up most of these questions, preferring to resolve the case on First Amendment considerations, from which the contrasting opinions emerged, and on the issue of the special findings, where there was unanimity.

In his dissent, Judge Coffin said First Amendment considerations —particularly the public character of the activity—ruled out the application of the conspiracy doctrine. He quoted Supreme Court Justice Harlan to the effect that "conspiracy is by its very nature secret"[40] and insisted that in instances where ideas and issues are

brought into the public marketplace, the situations recommend the
protection of the First Amendment.

> There is no legal precedent for applying the conspiracy theory to
> such an effort. This is, to my knowledge, the first attempt to use
> conspiracy as a prosecutorial device in such circumstances. . . . I
> would not—for the first time—grant this weapon to the government
> in this kind of a case without the alternative assurance that hazards
> to individual rights would not be increased, or that the interest in the
> nation's well-being and security cannot be as well served in less
> repressive ways.[41]

It is not the public character of the defendants' activities alone
that moved Judge Coffin. He did not maintain that publicity is sufficient to "pasteurize" conspiracy in every case. In this case, the public
character in combination with other weaknesses in the broad conspiracy charge, as well as the availability to the government of other
less repressive ways of protecting the community, prompted him to
rule out conspiracy.

Judge Coffin's perspective on the matter was distinctive, and as
he began his dissent he noted that while the court (the majority) had
asked whether or not anything *barred* prosecution for conspiracy, he
asked if any reason or authority *compelled* such prosecution in this
case. There was not, in his opinion. Beyond the public character of
the activities, the group itself was ill-defined and involved in many
alliances. Finally he felt that the use of "The Call" to inculpate defendants both by the district court and by the majority opinion was
untenable.

The question of "The Call" merits more attention. It was bifarious
in nature; that is, it supported acts some of which were legal and
others illegal.[42] As a result, it raised a question of specific intent, the
question of whether the defendants in supporting "The Call" as a
whole specifically embraced its illegal dimension. This question had
been posed before, and the answer by the Supreme Court decisions
was clearly *no*.[43] The majority opinion in this case maintained, however, that the defendants could be connected with "The Call" in an
inculpatory way by something they said or did, either before or after,
which specified their intent to support the illegal dimension. In fact,
Judges Aldrich and McEntee held that Coffin and Goodman might

have inculpated themselves by subsequent statements (the former at the Arlington Street Church and the latter at the Justice Department), and these judges made them subject to another trial rather than acquitting them. Judge Coffin's sharp and direct rejoinder:

> I cannot believe that this delayed fuse approach to determining the conspiratorial culpability of signing a document like "The Call" would have anything other than a pronounced chilling effect—indeed that of a sub-zero blast—on all kinds of efforts to sway public opinion. For example, such diverse groups as Clergy Concerned, a consumer's boycott of California grapes, a parents' group for so-called "freedom of choice" plans within a southern school district might find themselves facing a conspiracy indictment. Even if the court's safeguards were rigorously applied the ranks of individuals enlisted in a controversial public cause would visibly shrink if they knew that the jury could find them to be members of a conspiracy on the basis of either their subsequent statements or legal acts.[44]

He objected to "The Call's" being accorded any legal significance at all.

Judge Coffin agreed with the majority that the nation had the right to raise an army and to protect that right by legal action. But that legal action should not be at the expense of First Amendment rights:

> I conclude that prosecution for substantive offenses or for a narrow, discrete conspiracy would fully serve the government's interest— perhaps even more than the court's sweeping conspiracy theory— without delivering such a serious blow to First Amendment Freedoms.[45]

Judges Aldrich and McEntee were certainly not insensitive to First Amendment concerns. They were, however, less impressed with the claim of immediate threat to free speech and at the same time more impressed with the dangers of mass defiance of the selective service process. They did not accept the defense contention that conspiracy was necessarily secret, agreeing with the prosecution that the lack of secrecy is not decisive, particularly in a case where one of the aims of the defendants was publicity. They did maintain, however, that the government had not proved the defendants' specific intent to adhere to the illegal purposes of "The Call." The government had argued this on the basis of statements by third parties. But only the defendants' own statements or acts could legitimately be used to establish specific intent, though these could have been (to the distress of Judge Coffin) subsequent to the undertaking in question. Spock and Ferber had not said anything that might have allowed a properly instructed jury to find them guilty. Coffin and Goodman had. Hence the latter should be tried again despite Judge Coffin's "delayed fuse" protest. (They were not, in fact, tried again.)

On the central issue of the appeal, and the chief reason for the reversals, Judge Coffin concurred with the majority, and the opinion written by Judge Aldrich speaks unanimously for the three-member court. This was the issue of the instructions given to the jury by Judge Ford and, more specifically, the special questions with which those instructions concluded. The defense had not been consulted about the special questions,[46] though consultation with both parties about instructions is normal. They had protested the questions when they were posed and argued against them vigorously before the Appellate court. The defense position was, as we noted, that the questions linked the defendants together in a way irreconcilable with the necessary determination of *individual* guilt or innocence. The government replied that the questions had been posed in a way that clearly distinguished them from the general verdict: they were labelled special *questions* and not special *verdicts,* and were introduced with the instruction that they were to be answered if and only if a guilty verdict was reached. They also cited precedent for the use of special questions in criminal cases.

But, the Court of Appeals maintained, the labelling and the association with a guilty verdict alone was certainly insufficient to prevent the questions from being a prejudicial influence on the jury. "There is no easier way to reach, and perhaps force, a verdict of guilty than to approach it step by step."[47] And as for the question of precedent, the court maintained that the few instances where special questions were admissible in criminal cases were clearly distinguishable from the case at issue and constituted no precedent for it; such questions were admitted only where they obviously benefitted the defendant and where the latter did not object.

The issue of the special questions was taken with the greatest seriousness by the Appellate panel, which associated it with the very meaning of the jury and of its role. Among several citations, the unanimous opinion offers the following to this point:

> To ask the jury special questions might be said to infringe on its power to deliberate free from legal fetters; on its power to arrive at a general verdict without having to support it by reasons or by a report of its deliberations; and on its power to follow or not to follow the instructions of the court. Moreover, any abridgement or modification of this institution would partly restrict its historic function, that of tempering rules of law by common sense brought to bear upon the facts of a specific case.[48]

More than any of the cases treated so far, that of the Boston Five turned on the role of the jury and on its relation to the judge. In the cases which follow, this issue will continue to be central as the peace movement induces stress at yet another point in the legal system.

Chapter Six

The Oakland Seven Conspiracy

One of the Stop The Draft Week goals of the California Bay Area organizations was to close down the induction center in Oakland, the second largest center in the country. At times six to ten thousand people participated in this week-long demonstration, in which the events of Tuesday, October 17, 1967 have been described by a local newspaper as one of the "bloodiest outbreaks of violence in anti-Vietnam protesting."[1]

A number of organizations planned activities for Stop The Draft Week in the Bay Area. The Civil Action Day Committee and the War Resister's League projected a non-violent sit-in blocking entrances to the induction center on Monday, October 16. Typically the membership of these groups were clergymen, professors, housewives, and students who were, by this time in the evolution of protest, not considered to be militant activists. They had met with the police, communicated to them their plans to commit civil disobedience, and negotiated, so to speak, their own arrest.

Two other groups—Resistance, and the Campus Stop The Draft Week Committee—were composed of militants who had become disillusioned with this passive approach of civil disobedience. David Harris, one of the organizers of Resistance, felt that the focus on getting arrested was obscuring the real goals of such actions. Resistance, as we have already noted, planned a nationwide draft card turn-in for October 16. In the Bay Area, these cards would be pre-

107

sented at the Federal Court Building in San Francisco. Resistance would not aim directly at the induction center.

The Oakland Seven were members of the Campus Stop The Draft Week Committee, organized at the University of California, Berkeley. Like the first two groups they aimed directly at shutting down the induction center, but like Resistance they rejected the traditional passive style of civil disobedience. According to one of the leaflets:

> We hope that one of the accomplishments of Stop The Draft Week will be the development of a new kind of demonstration. Instead of a fixed plan of action, we have attempted to describe a set of alternatives which will provide the flexibility necessary to achieve our goal—closing down the Induction Center—with a minimum number of arrests and police violence.[2]

Turning to specific tactics, they further clarified their intended departure:

> Our attitude toward the inductees is: we are on their side, we are friendly, but we will stop them from getting in.
>
> If the police disperse us here or at any point we will regroup at the staging areas and come back.
>
> SELF DEFENSE. There will be no aggressive violence against the cops but people have a right to defend themselves from attack.
>
> ARRESTS. It may be possible to free individuals from the grasp of the cops and absorb them into the crowd. People may sit around the paddy wagons.
>
> BAIL. Bail will be raised while people are in jail. Each person should make arrangements for his own bail if possible.[3]

It was to the planning of such action that the Alameda County Grand Jury responded with the conspiracy indictment.

The grand jury had been called to investigate the events of Stop The Draft Week. County District Attorney Francis Coakley had spoken to them about the concern of municipal and state authorities that anti-war demonstrations might precipitate a riot destructive of human life and property like that in Watts. The latter explosion, in August 1965, was still fresh in California memory. Anti-war activities emanating from the University of California's Berkeley campus had given evidence of an increasing militancy since 1964. In a letter to the general counsel of the university in 1966, Coakley noted that a report from the United States Senate Internal Security Committee indicated that the control of the anti-Vietnam war movement was in the hands of Communists and extreme elements. He cited past instances of illegal activities planned on and off campus which had passed without sanction, but said that hereafter university personnel who allowed the use of facilities for planning, recruitment, and solicitation of funds for known illegal purposes could be charged with vicarious criminal liability under the law of conspiracy.[4]

On January 28, 1969 the grand jury charged Frank Bardacke, Terrence Cannon, Reese Erlich, Steven Hamilton, Robert Mandel, Jeff Segal, and Michael Smith with felony for conspiring to violate California Penal Code Sections 602j (trespass), 148 (resisting), and 370–372 (nuisance).[5]

The indictment specified ten acts which it alleged to have been performed in furtherance of the conspiracy. Reese Erlich arranged for and directed meetings prior to the week of October 16. Jeff Segal distributed leaflets and maps which described the organization and conduct of the demonstration. Mike Smith was charged with using and attempting to teach others the use of a wooden stick as a club. A bail fund at Wells Fargo Bank was initiated and maintained by Robert Mandel and Mike Smith. Terrence Cannon, Steven Hamilton, and Frank Bardacke met with others at areas close to the Oakland Induction Center to direct and plan for the demonstration. Terry Cannon was further charged with the display and distribution of wooden clubs.[6] Transportation for demonstrators was arranged and paid for by Robert Mandel, who also, it was further alleged, transported loudspeaking equipment to the area of the University of California campus. Finally Mike Smith, with the aid of loudspeaking equipment, directed persons on October 17, 1967, to move from the campus to the city of Oakland in the vicinity of the induction center.

It would be a full year before the case reached the courtroom. During that period, attorneys for the seven attacked the indictment from a variety of directions. For example, in May 1968, they asked the Superior Court of Alameda County to set it aside because it was without "reasonable and probable cause"—the activities condemned being protected by the First Amendment. Their request led to the elimination of the part of the indictment related to public nuisance, which the court held to be inapplicable. The parts relating to trespass and resisting stood, however. An attempt in July to have the Court of Appeals of the First Appellate District prohibit prosecution—also on First Amendment grounds—was rejected. In November a motion to quash the indictment on the grounds that the grand jury had been unconstitutionally established was also denied.

THE TRIAL

The trial began in mid-January of 1969, in the Superior Court of Alameda County, with Judge George Phillips presiding. Assistant District Attorney Lowell Jensen argued the case for the prosecution, while three lawyers, Charles Garry, Malcolm Burnstein, and Richard Hodge, worked for the defense. Burnstein and Hodge represented Jeff Segal and Terry Cannon respectively, while Garry (who had defended Black Panthers Huey Newton and Bobby Seale) represented the other five. Garry took a preeminent role in the defense.

The jury of eight men and four women would have to decide whether the defendants conspired to violate the law by resisting and trespass and/or by aiding and abetting others in these violations. The issue, according to the prosecution, was not the legality of the Vietnam war, the constitutionality of the draft, or the conduct of the police, but a conflict with rights protected by the Penal Code of the State of California. These rights include the federal government's right to run a business (the induction center) in Oakland and the right of a citizen to drive on its streets.

The defense denied any agreement to violate the laws of trespass and resisting. Many of the overt acts charged in the indictment (meetings, speeches, transportation) were the exercise of rights guaranteed by the First Amendment. Others (setting up bail bond, instruction on self-defense) were preparations for a confrontation in view of a propensity for violence on the part of the Oakland police. The defense also complained that these seven defendants were being held responsible and liable for everything which occurred during Stop The Draft Week.

The prosecution attempted to focus on events of Tuesday, October 17, 1967. On Monday, people had left the streets open although certain groups sat in the doorway of the induction center, and some 120 were peaceably arrested. On Tuesday morning, however, the streets were choked by a mass of people who were prepared to stay unless forced out. If the police made an attempt to keep the streets clear and the building available to admit inductees, there would be a confrontation.

There were two views of what occurred when the police did move down the block to clear the streets forcibly. Defense witnesses maintained that the police broke and went into the crowd on a rampage. They said that there was no place to which the crowd of six to ten thousand could go when the police wedge moved on them. These witnesses did not observe demonstrators attacking or taunting the police, but reported split heads, vomiting, and people being clubbed, crying and pleading for relief. On the other hand, no prosecution witness observed illegal use of force by police. They attributed the violence to the demonstrators, who, they said, taunted the police hysterically, threw bottles and stones, set fire to automobiles, set off stink bombs inside the induction center, and blocked entrances and streets. One police officer testified that he saw some police clubs raised in the air but he did not see them land.[7] The prosecution claimed that the description offered by defense witnesses was a product of the hysteria of the participants, particularly since the defense could prove no serious permanent injuries.

The Oakland Seven did not themselves testify, but their defense brought forty-seven witnesses to the stand. These represented a cross section of the community and were drawn from a wide variety of social and occupational groups. They reflected the increasing participation of formerly inactive opponents to the war. Mr. Garry had two reasons for introducing so many witnesses. The first was to leave no doubt that there had been police brutality and misconduct on Tuesday. Virtually every witness testified that they either personally experienced or observed some form of unprovoked use of force by the police. The second purpose was to demonstrate through these witnesses, most of whom did not know the seven defendants, that attendance at the widely publicized demonstration was a matter of individual decision and not something connived at by the defendants. Unless the testimony of individual decision for participation was accepted, the defense argued, one could only attribute the attendance of six thousand persons to some form of mesmerism on the part of the seven.

The prosecution responded that the participation of many persons on the basis of individual decision in no way disproved the existence of a common design. There was, on the contrary, considerable evidence to support the contention that such a design—such a conspiracy—existed. Police undercover agents testified to statements made by various members of the seven at meetings prior to the demonstration. The following remark by Terry Cannon was typical of what they offered:

> We have rejected non-violent actions concerning October 16 through 21. Our goal is to muck up the whole thing. The rally will be at DeFermery Park in Oakland—look it up on your trusty maps —and the next day we will attempt to keep that mother closed down.[8]

The defense reminded the jury that the agents had testified from notes taken at the meetings in question. It was inevitable, Attorney Garry maintained, that these were incomplete and that the remarks quoted were taken out of context. Under cross-examination one of the police witnesses admitted that note-taking had been selective and sporadic. Cross-examination further revealed that one police undercover agent used an alias, posed as a student, volunteered firecrackers to taunt the police, offered to turn in his draft card, participated in policy-making of the groups and attempted to recruit SDS members when he volunteered to speak at their meeting. Reflecting on these activities, counsel for the defense noted to the jury:

> . . . if the First Amendment means what it says, that you have freedom of expression and freedom of the persons to hear the person who is expressing himself, then it is a nullity when the man with the bugger will sit in there and take sporadic notes so that he can find some areas of being able to malign or to misquote you.[9]

The prosecution also introduced copies of material that Jeff Segal had read to those in attendance at various meetings prior to the demonstration and the tape of a radio broadcast of a rally which took place on the eve of October 17. The tape included a speech by Segal, whose activities were the object of special attention on the part of the prosecutor.[10] In the speech, Segal had reiterated the demonstration's purpose of stopping the operation of the induction center, adding that if it became necessary to stop the movement of buses filled with inductees, this would be done. He warned against seeking or provoking violence from the police, but also reminded his listeners of their right to defend themselves against police violence. He also reviewed the arrangements that had been established during the preceding weeks: organization into groups among monitors who had been instructed, communication among monitored groups by walkie-talkie, instructions for absorption of a police wedge, dispersal and reassembly where this was necessary, and behavior in the event of arrest. Literature that had been circulated and discussed at previous meetings had gone into these matters in considerable detail.

In the eyes of the prosecution, detailed organization of this sort could only have been the product of a group working in agreement. It could, in short, only mean conspiracy once it was demonstrated that its object was criminal. In the latter connection State Attorney Jensen said:

> . . . when you have an organization which is calculated deliberately and set out for a specific purpose regardless of what may be the truthfulness or the lofty emotion that goes with the purpose in its major sense, if it is set up in such a fashion where it is not simply in competition for the idea and the truth, but it is set up in a fashion to violate specifically the laws of this community to see to it that the business cannot be run by trespass, to see to it that the police cannot make arrests and they cannot keep the streets clear to vehicular traffic, then that is an unlawful demonstration.[11]

According to the defense, Segal's speech did not indicate that he had entered into an agreement with any person for any specific purpose. He told what he wanted to happen and what he would advise but not what he or anyone else had agreed to cause to happen. In addition, for the prosecution to establish that the defendants conspired as charged it would have to prove beyond a reasonable doubt that they agreed specifically to trespass and to resist. They admitted that they wanted to close down the induction center, that they expected it would happen and that it did—on the day before. But, the defense continued, there is no evidence that they caused it to happen on the 17th, nor did any witness who testified that he participated indicate that he trespassed at the request of any defendant. There is no evidence in the speeches which explicitly indicates a desire to confront or resist the police. If there was a conspiracy, it was on the part of government agencies to curtail free speech and opposition to their illegal policies. The defense also argued that the legal staff of the Alameda County District Attorney's Office had decided to make an example of these seven young men in order to discourage this form of demonstration.

As we have noted, the attorneys for the seven maintained that the overt acts specified in the indictment were either rights exercised under the First Amendment or legitimate preparations for defense against police violence. As they concluded, they reiterated their defense on the basis of honest belief. Conviction for conspiracy demands that the defendants be shown to have wanted and intended to violate specific laws. What was learned of the defendants' state of mind from speeches and testimony was that they believed the war to be illegal and that anyone who failed to take the steps to oppose the war after all other plans of political action had failed might himself be held to violate the Nuremberg principles. Thus, the defendants believed that even the police, in the context of the demonstration, were illegitimate. Whether or not one agrees with these beliefs, they argued, it must be recognized that they were honestly held, and therefore the intent requisite for criminal conspiracy was not present.

The prosecution responded that high purpose cannot relieve an individual of the responsibility of obeying the law. Observing analogous behavior on the part of Robin Hood, the prosecutor noted that however noble his aims, he remained a thief if he intended to steal. Criminality cannot be removed from conduct by purpose. The argument formulated in summary by the prosecution to describe the defense maintained:

> . . . the government is operating in an illegal fashion, and I am going to prevent that by my conduct, and my moral superiority puts me in a position where I may suspend the operation of law in terms of its application to me . . . the conduct on Tuesday, October 17th, where masses of people came down and said, "You can't operate that building" is outrageous, where they come down and say, "You can't operate those streets" is an outrage. . . . In our framework of law, everyone within that is within, neither below or above the law. When we have a situation where persons come and say, "My activities may include the violation of the rights of others . . . may include the violation of the law of this State, because I am morally

superior," I say, "Neither are you morally superior nor may you do that, because a framework of law exists or it doesn't. . . ."[12]

INSTRUCTIONS TO THE JURY

It was both the practice in the California state courts and the disposition of Judge Phillips to allow extensive questioning of prospective jurors (voir dire). The defense, of course, made the most of this, but both the prosecution and the judge also pursued the examination intently. Jury selection had taken almost four weeks, in fact, but having spent this time, the parties to the trial could feel that whatever could have been done at this stage of trial preparation had in fact been done. The complexities of conspiracy law and of the events of October 1967, as well as the connection of these events with the local and national mood faced with civil disorder and an unpopular war, would place heavy demands on those who had to reach a verdict. Still, as Judge Phillips pointed out, these demands were not unmanageable, and he made clear to the jury chosen in so exhausting a process that it had the confidence of the court:

> I think it is a fiction to say that we can get twelve jurors that are completely and absolutely devoid of any emotion, passion, or are completely and absolutely impartial. The important thing is that you be intellectually honest, on guard against your passions and emotions at all times. As long as you stay honest and intellectually put your passions and your emotions aside, you will arrive at the truth and a just verdict. And you should have faith in that.[13]

They were to decide whether the defendants had knowingly and willingly conspired to violate California laws against trespass and resisting. This and nothing else.

The judge's instructions laid out a series of guidelines for the decision process. The conspiracy charged in the indictment could have taken place without any formally expressed agreement among defendants. Agreement could have taken the form of tacit, mutual understanding. Direct evidence was particularly rare in a crime which was by very nature clandestine. Hence for the prosecution to prove it existed, circumstantial evidence would have to suffice: they need not prove an actual meeting among all defendants, for example. Even association among defendants prior to and after the alleged conspiracy could be taken into account in determining whether the conspiracy took place. If one adds to all this, as Judge Phillips did in the instructions, that each member of a conspiracy is liable for the acts and declarations of all the rest, that the overt acts performed in accomplishing a conspiracy need not be crimes, and that only one such act in addition to proof of criminal agreement was necessary to support conviction—then one can see why the prosecutor might be confident of this case.

However, the jury was also instructed that the defendants were not liable for what was done by persons not part of the alleged conspiracy even where what they did promoted conspiracy. This was important because the alleged planning and acts occurred in a context where there was planning by many groups and a week-long series of acts in Oakland and all across the nation. Evidence of association with one or more members, even though it could be of association prior to and after the alleged conspiracy, was not itself sufficient. The association had to be knowledgeable and wilfully directed toward accomplishing the conspiracy's goal.

In connection with the defendants' frequently asserted right of self-defense, the judge instructed that the police had no duty within the meaning of Penal Code Section 148 (resisting) to make an unlawful arrest or to use excessive force in the performance of any duty. Consequently, no one resisting unlawful arrest or the excessive use of force by the police could be guilty of violating this law. Definitions of assault and battery as related to self-defense were made very explicit with instructions which cited contrasting examples of police and persons participating in lawful and unlawful acts.

Two other instructions were crucial to the defense. One permitted the jury to take into account the beliefs of the defendants about the legality of the Vietnam war and of the Selective Service Act. The second instruction was to the effect that a person is not guilty of a crime if he acts under an honest, reasonable belief that what he is doing is legal. The importance of this lay in the relation which these defendants maintained between their behavior and the First Amendment. Many of the acts charged by the prosecution were not denied by the defense but were held to be protected by the Constitution, and the instructions made it clear that such acts as public speeches and press conferences on important public issues are protected by

First Amendment guarantees of freedom of speech, assembly, petition, conscience, press, and association. These could not be punished
unless it could be proved that they were calculated to incite someone
to act in a way which the government had the right to prevent.[14]

The defendants were acquitted by the jury. Of all the cases selected for study, this is the only one brought to trial in which all of
the defendants were acquitted.

TWO JUDICIAL RESPONSES: A COMPARISON

The Oakland Seven and the Boston Five trials were not identical,
of course. The former resulted from a county grand jury investigation and charged conspiracy to break state laws against trespass and
resisting. The Boston Five were indicted by a federal grand jury for
conspiring to break federal laws pertaining to the operation of the
Selective Service System. The latter were tried in Federal Court in
Boston, the former in Alameda County Superior Court.

Yet there are similarities between them of the greatest importance,
similarities which make possible a valuable comparison of types of
judicial response. Each indictment charged conspiracy and each
stemmed from activities in connection with Stop The Draft Week,
an event which was nation-wide in scope and intended by its proponents as an open, public, mass challenge to national policy on the
war and the draft. The challenge encountered the national mood of
frustration as well as the reflexes of the American legal system. And
it went deep—touching on American pride in the nation's traditional
willingness to admit the expression of every shade of opinion. The
defense in both cases argued that the behavior of the defendants was
protected by the Constitution, particularly by the First Amendment,
or by some other form of law. But judicial response varied, perhaps
revealing indecision in the legal institution or perhaps revealing an
experimental flexibility on its part according to which it would test
out and, if need be, revamp its reflexes in view of issues of such
importance.

At the very beginning of each trial the difference in judicial style
was evident. In Oakland there was a prolonged investigation of the
predispositions of jurors by the attorneys for both sides and by Judge
Phillips. There was only a perfunctory *voir dire* process in Boston.

In the latter case, the defense did not have the use of the grand jury court transcript to assist it in preparing its case for its clients. Only rarely does the federal court system make such transcripts available. The Oakland defense lawyers did have this benefit, which California law provides as a matter of right in any criminal case. Judge Phillips did not read the indictment himself, the clerk being assigned this task. Judge Ford not only read the indictment but in his instructions constantly repeated and elaborated the elements of the crime charged in the indictment.

If we move further and consider the way in which each judge viewed the jury's duty and also the way in which each instructed the jury on certain defense arguments which were offered in both trials, we shall see the contrasting patterns of judicial response even more clearly. The role of the jury offers a good point of departure.

Boston Five Trial Instructions to the Jury[15]

> A jury has a two-fold obligation: to assist in enforcing the laws of the United States and to protect those unjustly accused of crime. The government obviously wants no innocent man convicted, but on the other hand insists . . . that tryers of facts, which you are, allow no guilty man to escape. It is important, in a government such as ours, that the laws be enforced, not only for the maintenance of government alone but also for the protection of each one of us in our security and safety. . . . (pp.4–5)

> You must apply the law that I lay down. If I fall into error in laying down the principles of law, my error or errors can be reviewed by a higher court. If you apply your own law and make an error, it cannot be reviewed and corrected. (p.3)

Oakland Seven Trial Instructions to the Jury[16]

> . . . The function of the jury is to determine the issues of fact that are presented by the allegations in the indictment filed in this court and the defendants' plea of not guilty. . . . (p.2)

> . . . You are the exclusive judges of the facts and of the effect and value of the evidence but you must determine the facts from the evidence received here in court. . . . (p.5)

> I think it is a fiction to say that we can get twelve jurors that are completely and absolutely devoid of any emotion, passion, or are completely impartial. The important thing is that you be intellectu-

ally honest, on guard against your passions and emotions at all times. As long as you stay honest and intellectually put your passions and your emotions aside, you will arrive at the truth and a just verdict. And you should have faith in that. . . . (p.34)

Judge Ford's remarks indicate that the Boston Five jury is to walk a narrow and sharply defined path, one whose restricted latitude and definition he impresses on them by underscoring both the expectations of the government and his own role as the one who "lays down the law." By contrast, the Oakland Seven jury in Alameda County Superior Court hung loose. Judge Phillips emphasized their competence to deal with complex and emotional issues, rather than their obligations to the government and to him. No doubt personality differences play a role in this contrast, but merely as vehicles of contrasting possibilities which are part of the legal system itself.

The pattern of this contrast is reinforced if we consider the way in which each judge dealt in his instructions with the case made by the defense. Consider the contention of both defenses that statements and actions are legal if they are based on the honest belief that the Vietnam war is illegal and that the draft is unconstitutional.

Boston Five Trial

Before we proceed further, members of the jury, let me remind you what we are trying here. False trails and issues must be avoided. We are not trying the morality, legality or constitutionality of the Military Selective Service Act of 1967, and we are not trying the wisdom, morality, legality or constitutionality of the war in Vietnam or the right of a person to protest the war in Vietnam on these grounds. These questions—the morality, legality and unconstitutionality of the war in Vietnam—are irrelevant, are not issues in this case. . . . (p.16)

. . . sincere belief on their part that the Vietnam conflict, and the conscription of young men to serve in it was illegal, immoral or unconstitutional or a belief that they were protected by a constitutional right of free speech would be no defense or excuse whatsoever to an intentional and wilful violation. . . . (p.46)

Oakland Seven Trial

Evidence, if any of the honest belief and/or good faith belief or the defendants or any of them in the legality or illegality of the Viet-

nam War and of the Selective Service Act and all the ramifications
of those two matters may be weighed by the jury as part of the relevant evidence in arriving at a decision whether the defendants had
the specific intent to commit the crime of conspiracy as charged.
(pp.21–22)

An act committed or an omission made under an ignorant mistake of facts which disproves any criminal intent is not a crime.
Thus a person is not guilty of a crime if he commits an act or omits
to act under an honest and reasonable belief in the existence of certain facts and circumstances which if true would make such an act
or omission unlawful. (p.22)

In the instructions on motive and intent, which also relate to the
question of honest belief, the contrast continues to appear.

Boston Five Trial

Motive no matter how laudable or praiseworthy that motive may
be, cannot negative a specific intent to commit a crime. Good or innocent personal motive alone is never a defense where the act committed is an intentional violation of law—a crime. . . . (p.43)

Where a person has a specific intent to bring about a result which
the law seeks to prevent—what induces him to act, his motive, is
immaterial. Personal advancement, financial gain, political reasons,
religious beliefs, moral convictions, or some adherence to a higher
law are well-recognized motives for human conduct. These motives
may prompt one person to voluntary acts of good and another to
voluntary acts of crime. A person may not decide himself whether a
law is good or bad, and if he believes it to be bad be free to violate
it. If he does knowingly violate the law he must be held responsible.
(p.44)

Oakland Seven Trial

Motive is not an element of the crime charged and need not be
shown. However, you may consider the motive or lack of motive
as a circumstance in this case. Presence of motive may tend to establish guilt. Absence of motive may tend to establish innocence.
You may therefore give its presence or absence as the case may be,
the weight to which you find it to be entitled. (p.10)

Notice that in the Boston Five trial, Judge Ford himself settles the
question of intent, removing the praiseworthy motive from consid-

eration as a mitigating factor, while in the Oakland Seven trial it is left to the jury to accord motive its appropriate weight.

Something very similar occurs in connection with the question of incitement. The defense in both cases had argued that the behavior of the defendants was protected by the First Amendment, whose protection extends even to the advocacy of a crime if this advocacy is not accompanied by direct incitement.

Boston Five Trial

> I charge you that the defendants . . . have a right protected by the First Amendment of the Constitution of the United States to freedom of speech, and press and assembly . . . to criticize our form of government . . . even though the speaking or writing of such criticism may undermine confidence in our government. (p.34)

> Section 12 does not penalize utterance or publication of abstract doctrine concerning matters of public policy, or conspiracy to do so, having no attribute or quality of incitement of Selective Service registrants to concrete action to violate the law.
>
> Members of the jury, I charge you that what is denounced as offenses against the United States and condemned as unlawful action by Section 12 of the Military Selective Service Act . . . is the counseling, which means advising a person to pursue a particular course of action; or aiding, which means assisting, helping, supporting another in the commission of a crime; or abetting, which means encouraging, inducing, inciting another to commit a crime, or a plan or conspiracy to do so by speech or conduct. . . . (pp.35–36)

> . . . If you are satisfied that the defendants . . . are guilty of a violation of the provisions of . . . Section 12 as I have interpreted it to you, *I find as a matter of law that there is a clear and imminent danger—sufficient danger—of a substantive evil that Congress has a right to prevent,* to justify the application of Section 12 of the Military Selective Service Act of 1967 under the First Amendment of the Constitution of the United States.
>
> This, members of the jury, is a matter of law. It is no concern of yours in arriving at your verdict. (pp.50–51, emphasis added)

Oakland Seven Trial

> Public speeches, press conferences and public meetings on the subject of important public issues are protected by the First Amendment to the Constitution, which guarantees freedom of speech, assembly, petition, conscience, press and association.

> You may not find the defendants guilty if the evidence is limited
> to such activities and statements. (p.26)

> You are instructed that the United States Constitution protects
> even advocacy of crime in the absence of direct incitement.
> There is evidence of the writings, public statements and public
> speeches of some of the defendants. No matter what you find the
> content and purpose of any of those utterances to have been, none
> of them may be punished under the Constitution and none of them
> can support a finding of guilt on the part of any defendant unless
> *you find* beyond a reasonable doubt that it was expressed in lan-
> guage which, under the circumstances in which it was used, was rea-
> sonably and ordinarily calculated to incite persons to act in such a
> way as to bring about an immediate danger of acts which the gov-
> ernment has a right to prohibit. (pp.26–27, emphasis added)

There is additional evidence of the pattern of contrast in Judge
Ford's issuance of special instructions. By demanding collective responses by the jury to ten specific questions, Judge Ford further nar-
rowed the area of jury responsibility. Judge Phillips issued no such
instructions. Furthermore, because of these special questions an apparent conflict begins to emerge within Judge Ford's instructions
themselves. This is the conflict between the conception that guilt under our system is purely individual and personal, even in conspiracy
cases—something which Judge Ford had made the subject of an
early instruction—and the collective character of the involvement
referred to in the special findings. Here for example is Question
No. 1.

> Does the jury find beyond a reasonable doubt that the defendants
> unlawfully, knowingly and wilfully conspired to counsel Selective
> Service registrants to knowingly and wilfully refuse and evade serv-
> ice in the armed forces of the United States in violation of Section
> 12 of the Military Selective Service Act of 1967?

In his relations with the jury, Judge Phillips provides an example
of what can appropriately be called judicial disassociation. But-
tressed by an extensive *voir dire* in jury selection and by personal
confidence in the jury, he gave them latitude and then stood clear of
them. The verdict could go either way. As for Judge Ford, his demands upon the jury placed him in the position of advocate of the
government's position. His work in the Boston Five trial constituted
an instance of what is called judicial advocacy.

Post-trial interviews give us an idea of how some jurors from both trials responded to these different postures. "Of course you wonder if you made the right decision," one juror from the Boston Five trial reflected, "but the way the judge charged us, there was no choice."[17] Another juror from the same trial offered the following observation: "I knew they were guilty when we were charged by the judge. I did not know *prior* to that time—I was in full agreement with the defendants until we were charged by the judge. That was the kiss of death."[18] By contrast when asked what results would have followed if Judge Phillips had not given the instructions on the First Amendment and honest belief as proper defenses (instructions requested by the Boston Five defense but refused by Judge Ford), an Oakland Seven juror responded emphatically: "They would have been guilty. That's it."[19]

Chapter Seven

The Catonsville Nine

The prevailing view concerning the jury is that it is to be the judge of facts. This is what distinguishes its role from that of the judge, to whom belong all questions of law. The cases which we have discussed have already given us several opportunities to see this. In most of them a certain amount of stress developed over the jury's role. Should jurors be allowed to hear testimony about the motives of the defendants? Should they hear testimony about the legality of the Vietnam war? If they do hear such testimony, can they take it into account in deciding guilt or innocence?

One way of understanding these tensions is to see them as disagreements over just what is to be considered a fact. How broad or how narrow is that category to be? Some matters are held not to be facts as far as a particular jury is concerned because their connection with the case to be decided is not sufficiently direct. They are considered irrelevant. Other considerations may not be facts as far as the jury is concerned because they are matters of law and are to be settled by judicial ruling.

It is the judge who settles the issue of what is or is not a fact in the trial under way before him. This occurs despite his being—at least where what is in dispute is whether an issue is fact or law—a party to the conflict. If he makes a mistake, he reminds the jury, he can be reversed by a higher court. In the case of the Fort Hood Three, to

124

recall just one challenging instance, the judge decided that a key issue—the legality of the American presence in Vietnam—was not a
matter of fact but a matter of law. He thereby claimed it for his own
jurisdiction. Having claimed it, he ruled on it: that presence is legal.
The military courts which reviewed his decision agreed that his juris-
dictional claim was proper and that his ruling on the question to
which he had laid claim was no less proper.

In the case to which we turn now—that of the Catonsville Nine—
an effort was made to redress this apparent imbalance favoring judge
over jury. We shall see an attempt to stake a claim on behalf of the
jury in the area of the law. We shall also see the most dramatic courtroom encounter between civil disobedient and the law up to that
time. It would not, admittedly, equal the trial of the Chicago Seven
for extravagant and sustained pyrotechnics,[1] but neither did it have
the dimension of rage and bitterness among participants—defendants, attorneys, and judge—that emerged in and often dominated
the latter. Judge and defendants respected each other enough for the
dramatic potential of the encounter to be focused on the issues themselves rather than on the courtroom behavior of those involved. In
this directing of dramatic potential to the issues themselves, the Catonsville trial has, in our opinion, no equal.

On May 17, 1968 seven men and two women took 378 draft files
from Local Board 33 in Catonsville, Maryland and burned them.
Two of the men were well-known Catholic priests—Daniel and
Philip Berrigan. All nine were arrested at the scene of the burning,
where they had remained. They were promptly indicted by both a
federal and a Baltimore County grand jury on half a dozen charges
ranging from assault to conspiracy to damaging government property. Supporters of the nine would charge "legal overkill."

The defense team was large and headed by American Civil Liberties Union lawyer William Kunstler, now so well-known for his
work with radical defendants. Its other members were Harold Buchman, Harrop Freeman of the Cornell Law School, and William C.
Cunningham, lawyer and Jesuit priest. Originally the team included
Robert Drinan, dean of the Boston College Law School, also a lawyer and also a Jesuit priest, and now a congressman from Massachusetts. Conflicting commitments prevented his actual participation at
the trial.

The prosecution had its own way of contributing to the drama. It placed the government's case in the hands of men who would have to be identified with minorities often held to be oppressed by it: First Assistant U.S. Attorney Arthur Murphy, a black, and Assistant U.S. Attorney Barnet Skolnik, a Jew.

The drama extended into the streets as well. At the invitation of defendants through various media a large number of supporters came to Baltimore for the trial. Some would testify as character witnesses. Others would speak at rallies which took place every evening after the court sessions. Among the prominent persons who came were Dorothy Day, Bishop James Pike, Abraham Heschel, Noam Chomsky, Harvey Cox, Howard Zinn, Gordon Zahn, Marvin Gettleman, Eqbal Ahmad. Demonstrations took place outside the Post Office Building while the court was in session. Policemen in riot gear surrounded the building during these periods and entrance required clearance by United States marshals as the government countered defense's street theatre with one of its own.

Early in the trial, Attorney Kunstler introduced the Catonsville Nine:

Daniel Berrigan, 47 years old, priest, Jesuit, well-known poet and author. A few months earlier he had gone to North Vietnam at the invitation of that nation's government and had helped negotiate the release of three American prisoners.

Philip Berrigan, Daniel's brother, three years younger and also a priest. Philip was a member of the Josephites, an order of priests whose efforts have been directed toward helping blacks. He came to the trial from Allenwood Federal Prison, where he was serving a six-year sentence for having poured blood over draft files in Baltimore a few months earlier.

Thomas Lewis, an artist and art teacher. He had been convicted with Philip Berrigan and two others, James Mengel and David Eberhardt, for the Baltimore action.

David Darst, a Christian Brother and high school teacher in St. Louis. (He would die in an automobile accident shortly after the trial.)

Marjorie and Thomas Melville, wife and husband, formerly a nun and a priest in the Maryknoll order—a Catholic mission society.

They had served in Guatemala, from which they had been expelled because of their sympathy for the peasant movement there.

John Hogan, also a former member of the Maryknoll order. Like the Melvilles, he had served in and had been expelled from Guatemala.

George Mische, once attached to the government Alliance for Progress program in Latin America and then a peace movement organizer.

Mary Moylan, nurse and midwife, former lay missioner in Africa.

The Catholic character of the group was obvious: six of the nine either were or had been members of Catholic religious congregations and the other three were lay Catholics. While this did not become an issue in the trial, it is, we think, worth noting for the light which it casts on the peace movement. Not only were those involved Catholic but they had done what many in the movement were beginning to consider a "Catholic thing": raid a draft board. Similar actions taken later in Milwaukee and Chicago by Catholic religious and laymen also come to mind. In fact, there was an estimated twenty-five to thirty major raids on draft boards during the years of the Vietnam war. It is, of course, not true that only Catholics were involved; non-Catholics were also members of raiding parties. But as far as can be determined, about one hundred fifty priests, nuns, and lay Catholics took part in raids which resulted in some fifty-five convictions. Thirty were to serve prison terms. Eleven persons went underground to escape prison sentences.[2]

THE TRIAL

Presiding at the trial was Roszel C. Thomsen, Chief Judge in the United States District Court for the District of Maryland.

On October 4, 1968, a Friday, the attorneys for both sides met with Judge Thomsen for pretrial arguments. With Harold Buchman arguing, the defense addressed the "legal overkill" by attacking the multiplicity of charges generated by the federal grand jury. There were four:

1) damaging the property of the United States,
2) unlawfully obliterating records of the Selective Service System,

3) interfering with the administration of the Selective Service System, and

4) conspiring to commit the infractions in the other three counts.[3]

The conspiracy charge, Buchman said, was vague. As for "obliterating Selective Service records," it simply duplicated "damaging government property" in the case at hand. The government should elect one charge or the other. Without conceding the defense argument, the government dropped the conspiracy charge. They contended that "damaging" and "obliterating" were distinguishable, however, and Judge Thomsen agreed with them; he denied a defense motion to force the prosecution to elect.

On the following Monday, Chief Counsel William M. Kunstler took up the defense assault on the government's plans for the nine. He attacked the prospect of two trials on two sets of charges growing out of the same act. He petitioned to have the proceedings against his clients in the Circuit Court of Baltimore remanded to federal court. As things stood at the time, he argued, the two trials would place the defendants in double jeopardy. He also maintained that they were being charged under state laws for acts belonging to the jurisdiction of the federal courts (which would violate the Sixth Amendment), that they were being prevented by officials of the State of Maryland from adequately preparing for their trial under the federal charges, and that a state trial under the circumstances would deny them First Amendment rights.

Three of these four grounds had to do with which court would assume jurisdiction, while one—the third—related to the availability of the defendants. The latter became a petition for reduced bail for Daniel Berrigan, George Mische, and Thomas Melville—who had been arrested during the weekend before the trial by the state authorities. Here Judge Thomsen obliged by setting bail at $2500, down significantly from the $15,000 set by the state court. For the rest, however, there was less satisfaction for the defense. The federal court would not assume all jurisdiction, but would simply try its case first. After the federal trial the defendants would have to surrender to state authorities.

The defense declined to participate in jury selection. They neither submitted *voir dire* questions nor exercised their privilege of peremptory strikes: "The first twelve in the box is satisfactory as far as they are concerned," said Attorney Kunstler for his clients. The transcript of the trial does not indicate the reasons for this gesture. In private interviews, however, the defendants attributed it to a lack of confidence in the selection process and to the desire for a speedy trial.

When the trial proper began—on Tuesday morning—Attorney Arthur Murphy opened the case for the prosecution. He told the jury that what faced them was not "in a sense, the usual type of criminal case because of its ramifications." But he didn't say just what these ramifications were, and the rest of his opening statement indicated that he would proceed as if it were the usual criminal case. The trial, he said, did not involve the nation's participation in the Vietnam war, nor the defendants' right to protest this. Neither did it involve the defendants' social, political, or moral views. What it did involve was the indictment with its three accusations, as well as the evidence which would prove them guilty.

When William Kunstler opened for the defense, he asserted that none of the defendants would dispute the facts as the government had stated them. "Indeed, they are proud of it, and they think it is one of the shining moments in their personal lives."[4] This would not, then, be a case of judging facts:

> However the case is not as simple as Mr. Murphy says, any more than the trials of Socrates or Jesus were simple trials. On the facts they were guilty, too; but we have in this courtroom today, and for the continuation of this trial, we have what the defendants consider an historic moment: a moment when a jury may, as the law empowers it, decide the case on the principal issues involved.
>
> The Judge will instruct you as to this aspect when he gives you the law.[5]

Kunstler had in mind the principle of criminal law according to which "the jury has undisputed power to acquit, even if its verdict is contrary to law as given by judge and contrary to evidence."[6] This is known as the jury's power of nullification. Judge Thomsen interrupted Kunstler immediately to speak for himself:

> The court will instruct the jury, Mr. Kunstler, to decide the case on the facts as they appear from the evidence and upon the law as it may be given to them by the Court.[7]

He was determined that yet another principle of criminal law be maintained: "Jury should not be told that they may disregard law and decide according to their prejudices and consciences."[8] The jury may acquit in the circumstances described, but the jury must not be told that they can do so. This is truly a fascinating—and classic— paradox in criminal law.

If Kunstler was not allowed to suggest to the jury their power of nullification, he would prompt them to look beyond the facts. Beyond the facts in a simple physical sense—and yet part of the facts in the broad sense that it is one of the things that the jury must judge —lies intent. Kunstler said:

> . . . we are hopeful that, since intent is an essential requirement of any criminal prosecution, that you will find that they were not guilty of criminal intent.[9]

Judge Thomsen seemed willing to leave some latitude there, telling the jury:

> the issues before you are two: whether they did the things with which they are charged . . . (and whether) each act was done with the intent which the particular statute and the rules of law require.[10]

What the law requires as regards intent is rather limited and specific in comparison with what is ordinarily understood as intent. It would be Judge Thomsen's disposition to accept for the record virtually everything defendants wished to say in describing their state of mind, and then to limit its applicability by instruction to the jury.

The prosecution placed four witnesses on the stand, and they reconstructed the raid. A television newsman, who had been alerted to the action by a peace movement source, testified that a three-car caravan of reporters arrived at the parking lot outside the draft board headquarters in Catonsville at about 12:50 P.M. on May 17. They were just in time to find nine people, some in clerical garb, standing around wire baskets filled with files. Someone lit a match and the contents went up in flames. The news film taken at the time and placed in evidence at the trial recorded the burning, as well as the sound of prayers spoken by the participants. It also showed county police, summoned by draft board employees, taking the nine into custody.

After an FBI agent described the physical evidence gathered in the parking lot—the wire trash containers, the gasoline cans, and the burned files—two members of the draft board staff told of what had gone on in the office itself during the raid. When the group entered and began to take the files, the chief clerk, Mrs. Mary Murphy, first pleaded with them to stop. Then she tried to grab away from George Mische the wire basket into which the files had been dumped. In the scuffle she cut her hand and leg. Mrs. Phyllis Morsberger, a clerk-typist, testified that she had attempted to phone for help but had been prevented from doing so by Mary Moylan, with whom she scuffled. She also said that the third member of the office staff had been prevented from leaving her desk by Marjorie Melville.

These witnesses added that the defendants told them that they did not wish to harm them. "I am sure that Father Philip Berrigan told me that he didn't want to hurt me, and I am sure he meant it,"[11] Mrs. Murphy said. She added that the extent of physical harm to herself was "superficial." But psychologically it was otherwise: "I was very very much upset. Mental anguish, I had."[12] The spirited defense of the files against impressive odds revealed a strong identification on the part of the draft board staff with their roles. When Defense Attorney William Cunningham asked Mrs. Murphy, "Would you concede that the prime purpose of the work you do is to serve the government?" she responded "Yes, Sir. The Army of Defense. I am part of the Army of Defense."[13]

All nine of the defendants testified. On direct examination by members of their own defense team, they would speak of their backgrounds, the symbolism of their act, and, above all, their intent. To the prosecution on cross-examination they would admit the facts of the raid.

Brother Darst was the first to take the witness stand. Like those who would follow him, he regarded what he had done as a protest against the excesses of American foreign policy: the squandering of resources to promote death and destruction in Vietnam with the attendant neglect of human resources at home. Focusing directly on the action itself, he described the substance which had been used to burn the files, a crude napalm made according to a recipe contained in the United States Service Forces Handbook, and added:

We felt it was symbolic; we felt that it was fitting that this agent, which had burned so much human flesh in the war in Vietnam and in many United States Military interventions throughout the world, we felt that this was a fitting substance to use on these instruments of death.[14]

But it was the discussion of intentions which dominated defense testimony, and on this the nine were quite eloquent. David Darst:

Basically, . . . the two intentions would be, first of all, to raise a cry, an outcry, over what I saw as a very, very clear crime—a very clear unnecessary suffering; a very clear wanton slaughter . . .[15]

Philip Berrigan:

Well, once again, I saw no point to my life, if it continued in a rather normal fashion in this society. . . .

But the issue was not my life or my future. The issue was the deepening involvement of America around the world, not only in Vietnam, but in Latin America. . . . I was interested in doing all that I could to manifest my horror and outrage at what my country had become, you see, and so I had to do it again.[16]

Thomas Melville:

So we participated in the action, hoping to bring the attention of the peace movement to Guatemala, and, in that way, avoid another Vietnam.[17]

Defense Attorney Buchman:

Was the state of your mind limited only to Guatemala, when you went to Catonsville?

Melville:

No: the state of my mind is limited only by the military capacity of the United States Government, and that is infinite.[18]

Marjorie Melville:

. . . So I wanted to do something. I know that burning draft files is not an effective way of stopping a war, but I certainly can't find any other way of stopping this war. I have really racked my brain, and I have talked to all kinds of people. I can't face the military power of this country.[19]

John Hogan:

I just wanted to let people live. That is all.[20]

George Mische:

> The intent was to follow the higher law that all of us have, as hu-
> man beings, and as Americans, and as whatever we consider our-
> selves: humanists, Christians, Jews, Buddhists, or what not.

> That was our responsibility: that was our intent. The double intent
> was to save American lives, Vietnamese, North and South, Ameri-
> can lives, everybody, to stop the madness. That was the intent.[21]

Mary Moylan:

> . . . What we are saying by pouring napalm on draft files, is that I
> wish to celebrate life, not to engage in a dance of death that the
> American Government seems intent on.[22]

Tom Lewis:

> It was . . . the response of a man, a man standing for humanity; a
> man as a Christian, as a human being, seeing what was happening,
> not only in Vietnam, but beyond Vietnam.[23]

The testimony of each witness included the influences which had led him or her to Catonsville. Pursued in some detail with each, it was explored further in Daniel Berrigan's testimony than in others. Berrigan testified last, his presence reserved for the moment when it would have the greatest impact. Harrop Freeman led Berrigan through a description of the stages of his development as a radical. It had begun shortly after his ordination in 1952 with a year in France. This was France at the time of the Worker Priests and Dien Bien Phu. It included a brief period as auxiliary chaplain to Ameri-can soldiers in Germany and then six years as a professor at Le-moyne College in Syracuse, where he met David Miller. In 1963 he went again to France and then traveled in Eastern Europe, Russia, and South Africa.

Berrigan had returned in 1964 and at that time began writing and speaking against the Vietnam war. This earned him a brief exile in South America, something approved by Cardinal Spellman and Ber-rigan's own religious superiors. His experience with Third World poverty in the nation's hemispheric neighbor—then object of the expensive and apparently futile efforts of the Alliance for Progress —left him more determined than ever to challenge the course of his country's policy. Then there was the visit to North Vietnam, where he was presented with the impact of American bombing—on the nation and its people:

> We saw parts of human bodies preserved in alcohol. The bodies of children . . . women, teachers, workers, peasants who had been destroyed in the fields and destroyed in churches and in schools . . . and in hospitals by our saturation bombing . . .[24]

Under Freeman's questioning the issue of Berrigan's intentions was raised several times, and he expressed himself at length and in brief. At length he said:

> I did not wish that innocent people be subject to death by fire.
>
> I did not wish that my flag be dishonored by my military and by my men of power and by my President. I did not wish that the American flag be steeped in the blood of the innocent across the world.
>
> I was trying to save the flag for decent people. That was very much on my mind.
>
> I was trying to save the lives of the poor, who are mainly being charged with the fighting and the dying of this war on behalf of the white rich, and the white men of power.
>
> In that sense, it might be true. I don't know whether it is literally true to say that I was at that time pouring napalm on behalf of Mr. Murphy. . . .[25]

Berrigan continued:

> So I am trying to suggest that my decision to go to Catonsville was not taken in a vacuum. It was taken as a result of this enormous moral push that was on me, because of what I had seen in Hanoi, because of what my brother had done previously in the pouring of blood, and because I was realizing also at Cornell that one simply could not announce the gospel from his passbook, and not be allowed, let's say, to speak or to act as a Christian, when he was not down there sharing the risks and the burdens and the anguish of his students, whose own lives were placed in the breech by us, by this generation that I and others belong to.
>
> I saw suddenly—and it struck me with the force of lightning—that my position was false. That I was threatened with verbalizing my moral substance out of existence. That, I, too, was placing upon young shoulders the filthy burden of the original sin of war. That, I, too, was asking them to become men in a ceremony of death.[26]

In brief: "I did not want the children or the grandchildren of the jury burned with napalm."[27]

Berrigan's wide-ranging testimony revealed two other dimensions of his thinking—those of the political planner and of the poet. Referring to conversations between himself and Berrigan which occurred prior to the Catonsville action, Freeman asked:

Q. Did we discuss . . . the theory of the intention to present a test case to courts in order to raise Constitutional and International law issues that could not be raised in any other way?

A. This question came up. . . . The offering of a test case similar to the one we are engaged in is exactly the way a man who might have some vision of the future would operate.[28]

At the other extreme of his thinking he offered a poem drawn from the visit to North Vietnam. It concluded his testimony under direct examination:

> Imagine; three of them
> As though survival
> were a rat's word,
> and a rat's end
> waited there at the end
> and I must have
> in the century's boneyard
> heft of flesh and bone in my arms
> I picked up the littlest
> a boy, his face
> breaded with rice (his sister
>   calmly feeding him
> as we climbed down)
> In my arms fathered
> in a moment's grace, the messiah
> of all my tears, I bore, reborn
> A Hiroshima child from hell.[29]

"Your Honor," said Prosecutor Murphy as he began cross-examination, "I think I am going to be kind of brief."[30] He was. Freeman's direct examination of Berrigan occupies sixty-seven pages in the court transcript. Murphy's cross-examination occupies one. The government team had an excellent sense of the value of contrast. With four questions, Murphy focused the proceedings in the direction of the indictments: Did Berrigan understand that the trial was a test case? Did he know, at the time of the Catonsville trial, that the law forbade what he and his colleagues did there? Did he know that what they did would disrupt the functioning of the local board? Did he know that what they did would affect the administration of the Selective Service System? To each question the answer was unequivocal: "Yes." The prosecution had no further questions.[31]

The prosecution, it will be recalled, has the last word in summing up for the jury; this presumably helps compensate for the disadvantages of bearing the entire burden of proof. Barnet Skolnik would actually make the last remarks, in rebuttal to Kunstler. But Arthur Murphy began the government summary—before the defense spoke. He carefully reviewed evidence and the testimony which bore directly on the charges, and then turned to what he termed "the crux of the case."

> Are the beliefs of these defendants . . . the kind recognized by the laws of the United States, so as to excuse their conduct, and, therefore, justify their acquittal on the three charges about which I have spoken to you?[32]

They are not, of course. Deliberate law violation cannot be excused by any exalted motive or degree of belief, sincerity, or the like:

> . . . if you allow this kind of law to develop in the United States, each individual can then, for his own motive or for his own purpose, select the law which he chooses to violate, irrespective of how sincere he may be, and know that he will be excused.

> No society . . . can exist without laws, and this is why those persons who sincerely believe . . . cannot be excused when they transcend these boundaries set up by law.[33]

Kunstler took sharp exception to this argument with its inflation of the jury's burden of responsibility when his turn came to summarize. It was the jury's responsibility to decide this case and this case alone: "You are not to be frightened by the argument used often that, if you decide one way here, you affect someone else over there."[34] Again conceding the facts of the government's case, he associated the Catonsville action with the First Amendment: it was a matter of free speech: "I think that that is an element of free speech: to try, when all else fails, to reach the community."[35]

"All else fails"—the defendants had attempted everything imaginable to influence the nation's war policy prior to deciding to burn the Catonsville records. Philip Berrigan had even met with Secretary of State Rusk. But no one listened—it was the Catonsville venture or nothing. If this sort of thing could not be done, "good men must lie down when the routine, normal efforts fail; and evil goes unchecked in the world."[36] The free speech reference led to his repeating Andrew Hamilton's exhortation to the jury in the Zenger case, to "make use of their consciences" in judging their fellow men.[37] This brought Judge Thomsen into the picture with considerably more emphasis than usual. It is the duty of the jury, he said, "to follow the instructions of the court as to the law, *as we do, and should do in each and every case if our system is to survive.*"[38] Survival of the system: a rather surprising estimate of the stakes in the action taking place before him.

Kunstler closed with quotes from Senator Fulbright ("To criticize one's country is to do it a service and pay it a compliment"), from Albert Camus speaking to a German friend ("You were satisfied to serve the power of your nation and we dreamed of giving ours her truth"), and from Daniel Berrigan—repeating the poem from Hanoi.

When Barnet Skolnik took up the task of rebutting Kunstler, he charged directly at the key defense theme that prior to Catonsville everything had been tried, but no one listened.

> Ladies and Gentlemen, I suggest that they do not mean that no one listened. You have listened, and we have listened, and I suspect that the people to whom they write and to whom they spoke and with whom they pled listened. . . . People listened and then said, "I have listened and I do not agree."[39]

Catonsville was an attempt to force on people a position which they rejected. "There is, to the government's mind, a fantastic arrogance that goes along with the sincerity of these nine people."[40] The people have listened and then they have responded: "This prosecution is the government's response, the law's response, *the people's response,* for what the defendants did."[41]

Judge Thomsen's instructions to the jury were extensive and, in the matter of intent, structured to leave a most enduring impression. After a number of conventional instructions, he read each of the counts of the indictment to explain its meaning. And as part of the explanation of each count—three times in all—he said: "The only bad purpose the government is required to prove in this case is the intent and purpose to disobey, to do something that the statute forbids."[42] If, then, the defendants went to Catonsville to deliberately destroy files, obliterate records, and interfere with the administration of the Selective Service System, "then it is no defense that he or she also had one or more other intentions, such as to make an outcry or a protest against the Vietnam war."[43]

All nine were found guilty on all three charges. A voice from the audience cried: "Members of the jury you have just found Jesus Christ guilty."[44] Others stood and agreed. The courtroom was cleared.

THE APPEAL

The appeal before the United States Court of Appeals for the Fourth Circuit attacked Judge Thomsen's handling of the jury from two angles. According to the first, he had been wrong in the way in which he defined criminal intent for them, because of his very restrictive description of *wilfully* as it applied to this case. According to the second, he should have told them—or allowed the defense to tell them—that they could acquit the accused even if the latter were guilty. These two contentions strike out against two of the more deeply rooted tendencies of the legal system. The attack on *wilfully* urged the inclusion of worthy motives in the notion of intent, and as for the power of the jury—nothing less than the doctrine of jury nullification was urged. The brief advancing this was lengthy and detailed, at times resembling a scholarly monograph. It was presented by the four lawyers who had been in court for the trial plus Father Drinan and Fred Weisgal.[45] The government's brief, short— some would say cursory—was presented by Steven Sachs and Barnet Skolnik.

The appellants argued that the term *wilfully* should have been defined by the judge in a way that included evil purpose, rather than by reference to the intention of breaking the law alone. At the trial they had asked for instructions to the jury which would have broadened *wilfully* as follows: "honest belief in the invalidity or illegality of the war, or absence of evil motive or bad purpose to disobey or disregard the law;" the use of this definition could justify acquittal. They introduced a series of cases where convictions had been reversed because the jury had not been instructed that intent meant evil motive. Typical was *Morissette* v. *United States,* where the accused had been convicted of taking shell casings from an Air Force bombing range under the impression that they had been abandoned. Morissette's conviction was reversed even though he intended to do what the law forbids—intended to take them—because he did not know they had not been abandoned, and therefore had not intended what was illegal.

The government brief responded that in every case cited there was a question of whether the defendants really *knew* that the law forbade what they were doing. But the Catonsville defendants admitted that they did know this. They were attempting to relate the question of intent to the further considerations of exalted moral purpose. Taking up the *Morissette* case specifically, the government said:

> . . . Morissette as applied to the facts of the instant case supports only the unremarkable proposition that appellants would stand wrongly convicted had the evidence indicated that they burned the Selective Service files thinking them to be abandoned waste paper.[46]

Circuit Judge Sobeloff, writing for Circuit Judge Winter, Chief Judge Haynesworth, and himself, agreed with the government that the defendants' knowledge rendered their arguments inapplicable in this matter.

Turning to this second point, the appellants' brief notes that defendants in war resistance cases "have begun to assert, in new dress the time honored doctrine of jury nullification." "Their argument," the brief continues, "is a simple one."

> If the jury is, ideally, a representative cross-section of the community, and the defendant is willing to admit that he is indeed guilty of the acts in question, why, then, may he not be acquitted if the community, represented by the panel, approves of their commission? The only fly in the ointment—. . . is that jurors, almost without exception have no idea of and, thus far cannot be sufficiently enlightened as to the extent of their power in this respect.[47]

The argument in support of this view began with the history of jurisprudence and in this with the position of Littleton, an English jurist of the fifteenth century, on the power of the jury. He felt that the jury was entitled to take upon itself judgment of law. So did a series of renowned American constitutional and political figures extending from John Adams, Andrew Hamilton, John Marshall, to Learned Hand, who said, in 1926, that jurors, if they will, "may set at defiance law and reason and refuse to find the accused person guilty. When they do he escapes, however plain his guilt."[48]

Yet the development of jurisprudence over the years has made this a minority view. Indeed the prevailing and controlling position has been that the jury's function is to apply to the facts the law which the judge gives them. This seems to have been established in the case of *Sparf and Hansen* v. *the United States* in 1895, the majority opinion for which was written by Mr. Justice Harlan. The decision had its dissenters—Justices Gray and Shiras, the latter of whom the brief quotes—and it has its expert opposition today.

The brief cites two contemporary proponents of jury nullification —Paul Freund, well known expert on constitutional law, and Joseph L. Sax, of the University of Michigan Law School, author of an article on the prosecution of war resisters. Freund had remarked that in conscience cases "a jury should be allowed to acquit people who act in a measured way for reasons of conscience." He added:

> There ought to be some new doctrine which would permit a judge to tell a jury that they were to decide in the light of all the circumstances. After the law has been explained to them, the judge might add that the defendants can be acquitted and that the jury does not have to give reasons.[49]

The sense of Freund's comments is that the legal system ought to expand to accommodate this conscience phenomenon. This is also the theme of Sax's article, which treats the issue in more of its detail and which the brief quotes at great length. Sax underscored heavily the nature of the jury as community representative. The refusal to inform the jury of its power, he feels, has the effect of curtailing the accused's appeal to the community's sense of justice. This is particularly serious in the case of vigorous political dissent because what may be at issue in such instances is "a difference between the citizen's obligation to the demands of the individuals who hold public office at a particular time, and to the principles upon which this nation was founded."[50] Where such differences occur, protest can help restore proper alignment.

Sax reviewed the issue of unjust acquittal to note that (1) it sometimes occurs even now as in the trial of some accused of crimes against civil rights workers, but (2) nothing in the history of the periods when jury nullification was accepted suggests that the government was impeded in getting criminal convictions. He added that the fear of unjust acquittals related primarily to violent and seriously antisocial conduct, while the unlawful acts of protestors are normally quite trivial.

The extensive quoting of Sax was climaxed and rounded out with his recapitulation of the question:

> . . . it is probably not even appropriate to view the issues as whether we should recognize the justness of permitting the law to be violated, rather, it is whether the legal system ought to expand somewhat to recognize a broader spectrum of rights through which citizens can protest against allegedly unjust laws, rights which go beyond the confines of free speech. . . .[51]

"Those who think resisters are tearing at the fabric of society," he added,

> might wish to consider the possibility that a society is best able to survive if it permits a means for taking an issue back to the public over the heads of public officialdom when it recognizes that a government may have so implicated itself in a wretched policy that it needs to be extricated by popular repudiation in a forum more immediately available and less politically compromised than a ballot box.[52]

The authors of the brief expressed the same theme in their own words:

> . . . the jury is, both by original design and the nature of its inherent structure, the safety valve that must exist if this society is to be able to accommodate itself to its own internal stresses and strains.[53]

The government responded that

> . . . The essential flaw in the argument consists in its failure to recognize that the jury's power to disregard the law, to act contrary to law from motives of sympathy, or fear, or prejudices, or "con-

science," is one the exercise of which in a modern democracy per-
verts our system of government under law. . . .[54]

As for the arguments of Freund and Sax, the government said that
if they were speaking of laws which shock conscience or offend the
community, then their arguments simply did not apply in the present
instance. To the extent that Freund and Sax intended their view to
apply to cases like the one at hand, "the government strongly urges
that they are wrong."[55]

Here too, the appellate court declared for the prevailing view.
Judge Sobeloff too reviewed the history of the jury nullification issue,
but he concluded by quoting the Harlan opinion in the *Sparf* case.

> But upon principle, where the matter is not controlled by express
> constitutional or statutory provisions, it cannot be regarded as the
> right of counsel to dispute before the jury the law as declared by the
> court. . . . We must hold firmly to the doctrine that in the Courts of
> the United States it is the duty of juries in criminal cases to take the
> law from the court and apply that law to the facts as they find them
> to be from the evidence.[56]

This opinion, Sobeloff said, has "carried the day," which means that
the government has judicial history—precedent—on its side on the
matter, and their alliance would triumph.

Sobeloff acknowledged the morality of the defendants but also
the principle that it did not constitute a defense. He concluded on the
ever-present theme that "No legal system could long survive if it
gave every individual the opportunity of disregarding with impunity
any law which by his personal standard was judged morally untenable."[57] The verdict which had been reached in the U. S. District
Court for the District of Maryland was affirmed.

The appeal to the Supreme Court was briefed by Kunstler and
Buchman. They dropped the question of intention to concentrate on
jury nullification, reminding the Justices that

> For the first time since *Sparf and Hansen* v. *United States,* 156 US
> 51 (1895), this Court is confronted with the claim that the right to
> a jury trial embraces the right to appeal to the conscience of the jury
> to acquit.[58]

The argument was basically that of the appellate court brief, though
in much shortened form. They added to Hamilton, Freund, and Sax

only a complaint about the undue and growing influence of an article by Justice Fortas on civil disobedience, in which the latter insists that every violation of law no matter how well motivated must be punished.

The government brief—Griswold, Wilson, Monahan—limited its argument to a paragraph listing cases decided according to the pattern set by *Sparf* and a second which observed that despite the rulings by the judge, defense counsel had informed the jury that it need answer to no one for what it did. "Thus, the defendants were allowed to notify the jury of its power and precluded only from expressly encouraging the jury to exercise it."[59]

Certiorari was denied. The judge continues to dominate.

COLLOQUY FOLLOWING THE TRIAL OF THE CATONSVILLE NINE

Let us return briefly to the district courtroom of Judge Thomsen as the trial neared its end. When the testimony was finished, the case summarized, and the jury had withdrawn to deliberate, there was an exchange between the judge and the defendants which captures to a remarkable degree the status of the entire encounter between the peace militant and the law at the level of the courtroom. We find that it expresses the poignancy evident in all of the trials which we considered. It was civil, yet at the same time passionate. It revealed both parties at their most typical, struggling with the assets and liabilities of the positions to which they were committed. We can think of no better way to summarize our description of this series of trials than to offer important parts of it in the words of the participants themselves:

> MR. MELVILLE: Your Honor, we feel that the overriding issue in the case has been somewhat obscured by the treatment given, in the sense that, if our intention or intent was to destroy Government records, we could have done that very easily by going in at nighttime and taking them out and burning them.
>
> As it was, we went in the middle of the day; and after burning them, waited around for fifteen minutes until the police came, to give testimony to what we did.
>
> Our intention was to speak to our country, to the conscience of our people.
>
> We feel that we have not been able to get through to the leaders of our Government.

Now, today and during these last few days we have been in this Court in this same attempt to speak to the conscience of the American people. We feel that those 12 jurors are the representatives of the conscience of the American people.

They have been brought here now, and they have heard all kinds of legal arguments, which I suppose they must hear. But we feel that, still, the overriding issue has been obscured, in the sense that, they are going in there now to judge whether we committed the acts that we said right from the very beginning that we committed.

THE COURT: With the intention of doing it. I understand your point perfectly. It is simply that I have the responsibility of deciding what the law is. The jury are not the representatives of the American people. You have spoken to the American people through the people who are here in the courtroom and the press from all over the country.

Nobody has cut you down on the evidence that you wanted to present. You have made your case. You have been given an opportunity to make your case in public.

The jury's function is not, as I understand the law, to do what you think their function is. . . . it was immaterial how sincere you were and how right you may ultimately be judged by history.

I am not questioning the morality of what you did; but I am simply ruling that under the law, as I understand it, and which I am duty bound to enforce and instruct the jury on, I disagree with the theory of law which you are presenting, and which was argued very eloquently by your counsel as far as I would permit him to do it. Because I cannot allow and I cannot rule that somebody may argue something which is entirely contrary to the law, as I understand it, and, therefore, asking the jury to disregard their oath. I cannot allow that. . . .

. . . .

I simply say that, however noble the motive is—I am not questioning in any way the highness of the motive, and I think that anybody must admire a person who is willing to suffer for his beliefs—people who are going to violate the law in order to make a point must expect to be convicted. . . .

. . . .

MR. MELVILLE: The thing is, Your Honor, we are not arguing from a purely legal standpoint. We are arguing to you as an American, with your obligations to American society; to those jurors as Americans, and their obligations to American Society.

If it is just a question of whether we committed this particular act or we did not, then we feel that perhaps it would be better if the jury is just dismissed; and we can save ourselves a lot of time and money by just you deciding on what our sentence will be.

THE COURT: If any defendants wish to change their plea from "not guilty" to "guilty," the Court will consider whether such a plea is voluntarily given.

MR. MELVILLE: We recognize no crime in what we did, Your Honor.

. . . .

MR. MISCHE: The question I have, Your Honor, concerns conscience. Since we had acted out of conscience, I was confused. Maybe I did not understand you right. When Mr. Kunstler was giving the summation and was referring to that Zenger–Andrew Hamilton case, I thought I heard you say—I am not sure, but I wanted to find out before the jury went out—did you tell the jury they could not act according to their conscience in the box?

THE COURT: I did not mention it.

MR. MISCHE: I thought you did, and that is why I ask.

THE COURT: I did not talk about the conscience point, because I did not want to emphasize the fact that I had to rap Mr. Kunstler down.

He told me last night that he wanted to argue conscience, and so forth, as a defense. I told him I would let him know this morning what my ruling would be.

I do not mind saying that this is the first time that question has been raised in this Court, and I made some examination of the law and consulted the other Judges of this Court. The Judges of this Court were unanimous in their feeling that that could not be permitted.

I did not come to that conclusion because I had talked to them. I came to that conclusion myself first and consulted my associates to see if they thought I was wrong. . . .

. . . .

FATHER DANIEL BERRIGAN: Your Honor, we are having great difficulty, I think, in trying to adjust to the atmosphere of a courtroom in which the world is excluded, and the events that brought us here are excluded deliberately by the charges to the jury.

THE COURT: They were not excluded. The question—

FATHER DANIEL BERRIGAN: May I continue, Your Honor?

THE COURT: Well, you say they were excluded.

FATHER DANIEL BERRIGAN: They were. The moral passion was excluded.

THE COURT: They were excluded only if the jury found—

FATHER DANIEL BERRIGAN: It is just as though we were in an autopsy, and we were being dismembered by people who were wondering whether or not we had a soul. We are sure that we have a soul. It is our soul that brought us here. It is our soul that got us in trouble. It is our conception of man.

We really cannot be dismembered in such a way that it can be found eventually that our cadavers are here, and our soul is elsewhere, and our moral passion is outside the consideration of this Court, as though the legal process is an autopsy upon us.

THE COURT: Well, I cannot match your poetic language.

(*Applause*)

THE COURT: Any further demonstration and the courtroom will be cleared, and I mean that, the whole crowd.

You made your points in front of the jury, on the stand, very persuasively. I admire you as a poet. . . . I have no doubt of your complete sincerity. . . .

. . . .

But I think that you all for some reason, either because your lawyers have not gotten it over to you or for some other reason, simply do not understand the functions of a court.

FATHER DANIEL BERRIGAN: I am sure that is true, Your Honor.

THE COURT: And the limitations of a court. I must tell the jury what it is. You admitted that you went there with the purpose which requires your conviction on each of the counts.

You wrote it out in advance, which covers almost, in effect, both of them.

Your counsel stood up and boasted of it.

You took the stand and, in answer to Mr. Murphy's short cross-examination, which the Government gave in each case, made it perfectly clear what one of your intents was.

FATHER DANIEL BERRIGAN: One of our intents.

THE COURT: That is right.

And if you have the wrong intent, I told the jury that it did not matter how many good intents you had. And I told them that because I believe that that is the law which I am required to tell them.

Now, you have a great feeling of vocation for the young people, the young men and the young women of this world, and for other people. I admire your feeling of vocation.

I happen to have a job in which I am bound not only by an oath of office, but by a long tradition of which we are proud in this country.

FATHER DANIEL BERRIGAN: Yes, sir.

THE COURT: We are proud of the Constitution of the United States. We are proud of the rights that people have under it.

If this had happened in many countries of the world, you would not have been sitting here. You would have been in your coffins long ago.

We have the Constitution of the United States that protects your rights to make many of these protests, which could not be made elsewhere, without any penalty; that is, without any legal penalties—

FATHER DANIEL BERRIGAN: Yes, Your Honor.

THE COURT: (Continuing)—although it may hurt your advancement in certain societies, or something like that. I cannot help that.

But the Constitution protects many rights that you have. And the Constitution, as I understand it—and I will be corrected if I am wrong—requires you also to obey legally what the law is, or else to take whatever consequences may be visited upon you as a result of it.

Now, nobody is going to draw and quarter you. You may be convicted by the jury and found guilty; and, if you are, I have already said what I propose to do. I certainly propose to give you every opportunity to say what you want. . . .

. . . .

FATHER DANIEL BERRIGAN: Your Honor, may I ask just one more question, and then I will be silent?

THE COURT: Yes, indeed.

FATHER DANIEL BERRIGAN: I think you spoke again very movingly of your conception of your vocation, and I wish merely to ask whether or not one's reverence for his tradition of law or his tradition of religion or his tradition of any worthwhile, let's say, human inheritance does not also require us constantly to reinterpret this and to adjust it to the needs of the people here and now, to the point where this does not remain a mere inheritance which is deadening us, but a living inheritance which we, ourselves, offer to the living here and now.

So that it may be possible, even though the law has excluded certain very enormous questions of conscience, that we, ourselves, admit them for the first time and, thereby, rewrite the tradition for the sake of our people.

THE COURT: Well, I think that there are two answers to that:

You speak to me as a man and to me as a judge. To me as a man, I would be a very funny sort of man if I had not been moved by your sincerity on the stand and by your views.

I have not attempted to cut off any of these reasons so that you can spread it to the people as a whole. I have done that as a judge. I think many people will be inspired.

I doubt if any one of these jurors has any great enthusiasm for the Vietnam war. It seems to me that most of the people of the United

States now want to terminate the war. The question is how best to do it.

I frankly say that, although I think I am as anxious to terminate it as the average man, let us say, perhaps more than the average man, one thing I know is that I do not have enough information; I do not have the background information to know how to do it; and I propose to vote in the elections for people who, I think, may be able to do it.

Because I agree completely with you, as a person, that we can never accomplish what we all would like to accomplish in the way of giving a better life to people in this country, if we are going to keep on spending that much money. We certainly are not going to do it. We have not done it, and I do not believe that we will be able to do it, or will do it, whatever it is.

And the answer to that, it seems to me, has to be that you work on your Congressman; you organize and try to get elected the people who will do it. . . .

. . . .

The point we have to see is that in this country we say, or it is the basic principle, I think, of our country—and I know it is the basic principle of our law—that we try to have the majority control; that they do it through orderly fashions; and people cannot take the law into their own hands. I did not give this charge to the jury here, because I thought it would hurt you more than it would help you, but people simply cannot take the law into their own hands. . . .

. . . .

Now we either have a rule of law or we do not.

FATHER DANIEL BERRIGAN: You are including our President in that assertion also?

MR. MISCHE: And the Supreme Court?

FATHER DANIEL BERRIGAN: That he must obey the law?

THE COURT: Of course, he must obey the law.

MR. LEWIS: He hasn't, though.

. . . .

THE COURT: If the President has not obeyed the law, there is very little that can be done about the President, except not to re-elect him.

MR. MISCHE: That is where it is all about.

THE COURT: Well, he is not up for re-election.

I am not passing on whether the question of the Vietnam war, the legality of it, is a matter which can be decided by the courts or not. That question is before the Supreme Court now and will, no doubt, be decided by the Supreme Court sometime soon, whether they can pass on it and what the answer is.

Certainly, I do know—and all I have held in this case and what I was bound to hold—is that it cannot be passed on in this case.

. . . .

FATHER DANIEL BERRIGAN: Your Honor, could I ask why couldn't the legality of the Vietnam war be argued in this court?

THE COURT: If it is a political question—this is for the Supreme Court to say; some things are political questions; some things are legal questions—if it is a political question, it cannot be argued in court under our system of government, as I understand it.

If it is a legal question, it can be argued in the courts in an appropriate case. But all I have held here is that this is not an appropriate case in which to raise the question in the way you seek to have it raised.

. . . .

FATHER DANIEL BERRIGAN: Your Honor, you have referred to the war question as a question which may be either political or legal. Suppose it were to be considered as a question of life and death. Would that be appropriate here?

THE COURT: Well, again, that is a poetic way of saying—I am not sure what the legal proposition is. I understand why it seems a matter of life and death to you. Of course, the existence of the war is a matter of life and death to all boys who are in it. It is a matter of life and death to some people in Vietnam.

The one thing that was conspicuously absent, I found, from the recitation of horrors were the attacks by the Viet Cong and North Vietnam on perfectly peaceful villages in South Vietnam.

If you do not recognize that as a problem, I am curious to know why. It is not appropriate to ask the question with the jury here; but, if you are convicted, I am going to be curious to know why.

FATHER DANIEL BERRIGAN: I think for two reasons, Your Honor: No. 1, I was not an eyewitness of anything in South Vietnam. I was not there. And, No. 2, I believe there is a quality of difference between the hand-to-hand or person-to-person violence, which I in no way condone and which I condemn, of the Viet Cong and the technologically introduced, massive violence that we have exercised in North Vietnam.

I call these two very different human situations. But I believe with Camus that, wherever men are being killed, we must say we condemn it and say no to it. But I think there are different stages, different qualities, different ways of dealing with individuals and masses of people.

We have certainly introduced something new, beyond the Vietnamese capacity to deal with their enemies.

THE COURT: Well, I certainly feel we have to do something, but I do not think that breaking the law is the way to do it.

I have more personal and less altruistic reasons for hoping the war is over. I have a group of grandsons who, before long, will be of age to go. I certainly want to get rid of war. That may be a selfish, personal reason; but it puts me on your side in wanting to get rid of the war, if I had no other reason.

. . . .

MR. MISCHE: If we have people from the peace movement here, Your Honor, and if this is not the case, will you, then, allow them next week to file in your Court, calling into question the entire Vietnam war; and you will be willing to review it in its entirety? Whatever decision you have, then, can be submitted to the Supreme Court.

I am sure that, with all of the Americans sitting here today, we will get lawyers next week; we will file the case with you, personally.

THE COURT: But you have to have a case—

MR. MISCHE: You have to break a law first.

THE COURT: (Continuing)—that can be brought in court.

MR. MISCHE: You have to break a law. It seems that, before we can get a Judge to face the situation, you have to break a law, as Dr. King found.

THE COURT: I think I can answer that for you.

If the question arises in this Court in a case in which it is properly raised—and that is something that the lawyers know about—no Judge of this Court is going to duck it.

I do not know whether it would come to me or to some other Judge. We have various assignments.

If the question is properly raised, nobody in this Court is going to duck deciding any question, however difficult. We may decide that it is a political question. We may decide, under the separation of powers, that we have nothing to do about it.

PEACE MILITANTS
AND JUDGES SPEAK OUT

Chapter Eight

The Career of
Civil Disobedience

The peace movement has been in fact what it has called itself: a *movement*. What that term conveys in the rhetoric of today's political activity is that the peace movement has not been an *organization*. This, in turn, means that it has not had an established structure, central leadership, agreed upon spokesmen, or a commonly accepted ideology, features normally attributed to organizations. What it has claimed by calling itself a movement is spontaneity, both of impulse and of direction, and the ability to tolerate remarkable diversity in ideology and practical approach among its adherents. Still, the movement was a coherent phenomenon in the 1960s, and this was due to certain things which peace militants did have in common. These were (1) a clear, practical, and urgent goal: end the Vietnam war; (2) a distinctive historical situation: that of an articulate and committed minority; and (3) a moral ideal with which the nation at large identified them and in terms of which they understood themselves. This ideal was civil disobedience.

Civil disobedience was the legacy of the preceding generations of peace militancy, for whom it meant moral witness. The non-violence of pacificism certainly recommended itself to the movement of the 1960s because of the latter's minority status and its lack of the conventional apparatus of political power. *Witness* was also appropriate in an age which acted out its problems before television cameras. Yet civil disobedience had its disadvantages. For one thing, the moral and psychological demands which it made on its practitioners were enormous. For another, there was constant concern about whether moral witness was equal to the urgency of the wartime situation. It was always in danger of dissolving into its own symbolism, of becoming a kind of theatre which satisfied the desire of the conscientious to feel that they were doing *something,* but which had little discernible impact on a very real war producing very real casualties in ever lengthening lists. In the face of urgent pressure for real results, moral witness became legal confrontation and even defensive violence. The career of the ideal of civil disobedience in the 1960s is the history of these pressures and these transformations.

From 1968 to 1970, one of the authors interviewed many peace militants and discussed civil disobedience with them.[1] Some of the peace militants who were interviewed had been defendants in the trials which we have described. Others had taken part in demonstrations but had never been prosecuted. The latter include Reverend George H. Williams of Harvard Divinity School, who had collected cards at the Arlington Street Church ceremony with Reverend William Sloane Coffin; Reverend Robert McAfee Brown, a theologian from Stanford University; sociologist Gordon Zahn and the late social critic Paul Goodman. Zahn and Goodman had been pacifists during World War II. Like Brown and Williams, they had received draft cards at demonstrations.

We will devote the first part of this chapter to the ideal of civil disobedience as it was discussed and debated by those who had to decide if and how to live by it. The history of the period, upon which we touched briefly in our first chapter, will be viewed again here, somewhat less briefly, and from within the movement. In the second part of the chapter, we will consider the way the public has viewed the peace movement, and the response from the movement to that view.

We asked the peace militants a series of questions—seven in all—designed to elicit their defense of the movement against criticisms frequently made about its behavior. These questions took up such issues as the reasons for choosing civil disobedience as a mode of protest, the appropriateness of acting through the courts rather than

through Congress, and the unintended consequences of civil disobedience as these relate to disrespect for law, criminal conduct,
and treason.

THE IDEAL

For the peace movement the sixties began as a time for moral
witness. The perspective of the radical pacifist dominated, and what
that perspective meant above all else was non-violence. The commitment to non-violence was carried into the peace movement by
such veteran radical pacifists as Dorothy Day, A. J. Muste, and
David Dellinger, who had kept it alive during the preceding decade.
They had maintained their opposition to war even during World War
II, when so many withdrew from the peace movement to support the
nation's military effort.[2] After that war the radical pacifist perspective
continued in such organizations as the Catholic Worker and The
Committee on Non-Violence, the latter founded by A. J. Muste and
others. It continued in the protest action of such younger colleagues
of Muste as Bradford Lyttle, Marjorie Swann, and Barbara Deming.

To the radical pacifist, non-violence means the refusal to hurt,
condemn, hate, or attempt to humiliate one's opponent. Stated posi-
tively, it is an attempt to elicit the resources of his humanity, to make
him aware of the coercive and otherwise inhumane character of the
institutions in which he is—usually unwittingly—involved. Pacifists
attempted to reach the electrical workers who help build nuclear
submarines, the draft board clerks and prison guards, as well as the
public at large. Their civil disobedience was part of a strategy of
sensitization. In Bradford Lyttle's words,

> Coercive techniques involve regarding people as objects and push-
> ing them around—manipulating them by money or by violence—
> and you can demand and expect immediate changes on that basis,
> just as you can demand changes in the physical world when you
> push it around. But with non-violence you reject this concept of in-
> fluencing people—you don't push them around—you don't bribe
> them—you attempt to influence them by other ways, and ultimately
> these ways have to rely upon their own thought process and their
> own ability to perceive truth.[3]

Radical pacifists recognize that a particular act of civil disobedience is not likely to yield immediate results. People need time to
think. Where there are deeply rooted attitudes to be changed, more

than one experience is usually necessary. Patience, as well as tenacity, attends the convictions of the radical pacifist, and where such convictions control, there is little likelihood that the lack of obvious success in a given series of protests will prompt a slide toward last resort violence.

Along with the patience that resists violence, there is also a distinctive purity in the radical pacifist. This mitigated against their accepting even the appeal to the courts as a tactic. Such an appeal attempts to invoke coercion and is, therefore, a kind of violence. As we have already noticed, the destructive symbolism in draft card burning and the breaking and entering necessary in draft board raids distressed the radical pacifist.

From the onset of atmospheric testing of the hydrogen bomb in 1945, the nuclear pacifists entered the peace movement. By and large, they adopted the radical pacifist commitment to moral witness. Many were clergymen or professionals like Reverend Robert McAfee Brown, Dr. Benjamin Spock, Reverend William Sloane Coffin, Mitchell Goodman, Reverend James Mengel, Kay Boyle, and Howard Zinn. Typically, they had served in or supported American military operations during the Second World War, but had been brought up short after the bombing of Hiroshima and Nagasaki. They were responding to technological violence by promoting an ethics of survival. Like so many of the radical pacifists, these people had records of protest action and service in human rights movements prior to the 1960s.

The entry of the nuclear pacifists into the peace movement occasioned no major changes in the latter's commitment to the civil disobedience of the radical pacifists. But those who joined it during the 1960s and in opposition to the Vietnam war did cause a change. This group included David Henry Mitchell III, David Harris, David J. Miller, Michael Ferber, Terrence Cannon, and David Eberhardt. With the experience of the civil rights movement before them, they took the peace movement from moral witness to the legal confrontation to which we have devoted most of these pages. David Mitchell, speaking of his own case, expresses this point of view:

> I went to court and said, I believe this war is wrong, not just for me, but it is wrong in itself—legally—and I am not arguing civil

liberties or rights of conscience, but I want to prove that the war is wrong.[4]

This was less pure, less patient, and much more committed to proximate results than the civil disobedience of the radical pacifist. Mitchell said that it was not civil disobedience at all, agreeing in this instance with the strict legal definition of the phenomenon, the definition which turns on whether or not the laws challenged are valid.

Like many of the others whom we have mentioned, Mitchell was very clear about his aims. But civil disobedience is a very complex phenomenon. In the highly charged atmosphere of the 1960s, it was easy for a peace militant to lose his way. David Harris, one of the organizers of Resistance, criticized an emphasis on getting arrested, which had come to take the focus off the real goals of civil disobedience. He said,

> . . . my feeling was people had the attitude, "well, take us to jail, please take us to jail," and that the purpose was they were going there to be arrested rather than . . . to sit in the door ways and block it.[5]

He noted the contrast with his own group. "Our attitude was, if you get busted, you get busted and do your time. But the point is not to focus on whether you get arrested or not."[6]

If the sense of Harris's complaint was that the goals of pacifist action were being lost sight of by many who adopted the ideal, the Oakland Seven offered an example of a group of peace militants who rejected the ideal itself. They moved beyond moral witness and beyond legal confrontation to defensive violence. The interviews with four of the Oakland Seven reveal that they had been formerly committed to the radical pacifist ideal. Terry Cannon, for example, had been raised a Quaker, did alternative service as a conscientious objector, and was active in the civil rights movement in the South. Like so many others, his thinking changed as a result of many experiences in protest action. He felt a need to reevaluate the effectiveness of the tactics used in the past. "We had to break out of the bonds of the pacifists," he said. Their style of symbolic demonstration was beginning to "fossilize" at a certain level:

> We thought that the sight of young people being beaten and jailed in the South would cause moral revulsion in the United States. It

didn't—it caused a little bit—then it subsided. . . . I tend to feel the
same way with the peace movement, that for a certain period it did
have an enormous effect.[7]

For the Oakland Seven it was a case of raising the "symbolic ante."
This meant that they would not only reject the traditional intention
to submit to arrest, they also advanced the idea of "defensive violence" while planning to shut down the Bay Area induction center on
successive days. Defensive violence was not only alien to the traditional notion of civil disobedience, it was rejected by Resistance.
David Harris speaks from his observation of early planning: "They
were engaging in a rhetoric around violence—a vicarious kind of
violence."[8]

Bob Mandel (Oakland Seven) described the intention of the campus organizers to interfere more realistically with the Selective
Service System at its most basic level:

> We had no illusion that we were going to be able to do it very
> successfully. Nonetheless, our intention was to make them use as
> many police as possible. . . . What we wanted to try to do was in-
> stead of getting arrested, we wanted to see if we could shut it down
> and shut it down as long as possible. And actually wage a sort of
> guerilla warfare on a very limited, very primitive scale.[9]

By the appeal to "collective self-defense" the Oakland Seven
hoped, among other things, to generate a sense of solidarity between
blacks and working-class whites on one hand and a largely middle
class pacifist movement on the other. In retrospect, Terry Cannon
felt that they had achieved a degree of success in this:

> We wanted to create a situation for people to go a step beyond the
> pacifist non-violent demonstration. . . . We also felt that when it
> was shown that whites were willing to fight—physically fight—for
> their rights, the cause, that would make it easier to have political
> relationship with non-middle class white student types . . . we were
> able to talk with Black Panthers on an equal level. We were able to
> hold our heads up. Basically, people discovered a new pride in them-
> selves. . . .[10]

David Harris did not share this satisfaction about the results of the
demonstration. The tactic was one of "traditional Marxist logic,
making the contradictions clear. . . . They made sure the policemen

had to act like policemen." The result was that this approach did not help to focus the attention of people on the war. He continued:

> They really believed that if you got people out in the streets and put them in a confrontation with the police and precipitated having the police beat these people, that those people would be educated in the process. . . . I thought getting them out there to get them beaten only confused (people) more. It really made them pick false targets like the police. . . . I thought they were as guilty of the beatings as the police.[11]

Dennis Mora, one of the Fort Hood Three, also rejected the traditional designation of civil disobedience:

> My act was not civil disobedience . . . it was an act of conscience —but more importantly it was a method, the only means of political struggle at the time for me, as a soldier in the army. I used it only as an instrumentality . . . the only way to put content into any kind of a law.[12]

Mora, a Marxist, rejected the traditional concept of civil disobedience because of its pacifist orientation, its middle class composition, and the fact that "it just takes moral stands." It was a "luxury indulged in for the most part among white middle class people." "The greatest fault with the peace movement is that it hasn't catalyzed the peace sentiment of the masses of the American working class." Like the Oakland Seven, the Fort Hood Three hoped to generate a sense of empathy between the ethnic minorities in this country and the Vietnamese, based on the oppression they both experienced from capitalist and imperialist governments. Only the prospect that this appeal to the working class might develop into a mass movement justified conscientious law violation as far as Mora was concerned. As a Marxist, he said, "the individual responses or acts of heroism or moral courage are absolutely meaningless unless they can be tied into a mass movement."[13]

The charge that middle class pacifists took civil disobedience to be an end in itself is not altogether justified. Some law resisters did acknowledge that civil disobedience sometimes did more to satisfy personal integrity and to promote group solidarity than to end the war, but they hoped that it would go beyond this. While this sentiment might be observed more frequently among those whose civil disobedience constituted misdemeanor forms of law violation, it was not evident among those who were prosecuted for felonies. All of the prosecutions in this study were of the latter sort. We turn now to the challenges to the peace movement's tactics.

THE CHALLENGES

Challenge Number One

Civil disobedience is not necessary in a democracy such as ours. The Constitution protects the rights of protest and dissent within broad limits. It generously protects the rights to organize people for protest as well as the right to assemble, picket, stage freedom walks or mass demonstrations. There is really no need to break the law.

Everyone interviewed disputed the assumption that what they did was illegal. Though it was widely called disobedience, though it by-passed the more familiar political methods protected by the Constitution, and though it climaxed in arrest and prosecution, what they were doing was on the side of law and not against it. Many added that they considered what they did a last resort, and some justified it in view of the criminality of the government.

Occasionally, an interviewee gave the impression that the law with which he sided was basically a religious matter. Thus Reverend James Mengel, one of the Baltimore Four, convicted for pouring blood on draft files, said,

> . . . ultimately one feels that one has to do this—there is no other way. There is no turning back and that this is the Lord's will for me—I must do this. If I don't do this I will be disobedient to my Lord and to myself.[14]

This was relatively rare, however, and though prosecutors and judges sometimes acted as if they were dealing with a personal version of higher law and with individual conscience, most resisters disavowed this in favor of the formally promulgated laws of men and of nations. They would agree with Dr. Spock's remarks at his trial:

> I never felt that I had to differentiate between law and conscience or fall back on conscience, because I always believed that a citizen must work against a war that he believes in good conscience to be against international law. This is the Nuremberg principle which I believe is part of the United States Law.[15]

David H. Mitchell's position was the same: "I feel that I wasn't violating a just law, but I was rather coming to court with justice in terms of law also on my side and an attempt to enforce that law in the courts."[16] So too with David Eberhardt of the Baltimore Four: ". . . the kind of actions we take are really following a law—and not just a higher law but in some cases, international law."[17]

Rev. William Sloane Coffin took the idea of attempting to enforce law by civil disobedience to the best conclusion that most peace militants could conceive.

> In this case what I have in mind is civil disobedience which tests the legality of the law which I do not accept as being constitutional. It could follow the pattern set when the civil rights people challenged the constitutionality of segregation laws in the South. It was apparent civil disobedience, but it turned out that I was not civilly disobedient at all.[18]

Not only was civil disobedience legal then, but "One does this only as a last resort." Theologian Robert McAfee Brown said this during his interview. His response was typical. Every person interviewed had tried some if not most of the conventional means of reaching the public and the government. But despite their efforts, the war was being escalated, the draft extended, and by 1968 the number of American combat deaths had risen as high as 1,000 per month.

Brown had gone from a ministerial conscientious objector status prior to World War II to a military (naval) chaplaincy during that conflict. He had supported the government's military policy during the Korean War, and at first supported it in Vietnam. After reading and thinking through such issues as anti-ballistic missiles, he changed his position to what he describes as "nuclear-era pacifist." Speaking of his decision to collect draft cards in violation of the Selective Service Act, he said:

> I acknowledge that there is a legitimacy to a system of law in this country, and that as a citizen one places himself within the framework of a pattern in which, for the sake of the total society, individuals agree that there are certain things in a society that they will not do. . . . I don't drive on the left hand side of the road etc. . . . But then the point may come when for me to submit to the rule or the custom or the law of the society poses for me a very important question of conscience. Can I do this which society asks of me,

without violating the commitments which seem to me of ultimate
importance? . . . in most cases one can combine ultimate loyalties
with his provisional but very important loyalties to the state. But a
point of conflict may come. It has come to me very clearly in terms
of issues of the war and support of those who feel they cannot accept the provisions of the draft. . . . One works as much as possible
within the framework of the law, and therefore, in this perspective, I,
in engaging in civil disobedience against the Selective Service Act,
am willing to commit myself to the procedures of the courts. . . . I
came myself to a conscious decision toward the end of that summer
after the revisions of the Selective Service Act were put into effect.
. . . Up to that point, my main concern had been to try to get
revisions of the Selective Service Act to take account of the right
to conscientious objection of those who had no religious ground and
also for selective conscientious objection. Up to that point, that was
my vehicle to try to bring about the change in the law. Then, when
it was clear that no change would come, we had this law for another four years, then I felt I must move to this further step. . . .[19]

The last resort theme was strong in the testimony of Philip Berrigan
and Mary Moylan of the Catonsville Nine, it will be remembered,
and was also a part of the picture at the trial of David Mitchell, who
had begun with street protest against nuclear weapons testing. Berrigan spoke of the heavy price which peace militants pay for what
they do.

> . . . it is enormously frustrating and taxing to us psychologically
> and emotionally. And yet, at the same time, we could think of no
> other substitute as good as this process . . . a substitute that would
> hope to accomplish the aims that we looked for.

But for alternatives to action like his own he saw society paying another, higher price:

> . . . the only alternative to civil disobedience, besides apathy and
> immobility, of course, is violence . . . unless people are capable of
> civil disobedience and thereby forcing this country to come to
> terms with its own life and its own history and culture and its dec-
> laration of itself, then violence is going to be a certainty—in fact
> violence is such a definite probability at the present time one can
> look upon it as a . . . future certainty.[20]

Mitchell Goodman, speaking of the Justice Department demonstration during Stop The Draft Week in 1967, also mentioned last

resort, but added another consideration: the criminality of the state. He said of those preparing to demonstrate: "We were taking a last chance with the democratic system—the democratic process and essentially seeking redress to grievances including redress of being forced to participate in war crimes."[21] Virtually all of the interviewees took up this theme. Marcus Raskin said, for example, "the issue of civil disobedience to me is not terribly relevant in all these matters. The issue is far more criminality of the state."[22]

How can it be considered criminal to resist crime non-violently or to refuse complicity in a crime? In his speech at the Arlington Street Church, Rev. William Sloane Coffin struck this note forcefully:

> To us the war in Vietnam is a crime. And if we are correct, if the war is a crime, then is it criminal to refuse to have anything to do with it? Is it we who are demoralizing our boys in Vietnam, or the Administration which is asking them to do immoral things?[23]

In his remarks at the Justice Department demonstration in October 1967, Coffin made the following observation:

> This week once again high government officials described protesters against the war as "naive," wild-eyed idealists. But in our view it is not wild-eyed idealism but clear-eyed revulsion that brings us here. For as one of our number put it: "If what the United States is doing in Vietnam is right, what is there left to be called wrong?"[24]

But high government officials were not the only ones who entertained questions about the soundness of the peace militant understanding of the war situation. Many asked, perhaps only to seek reassurance, "Do you really know enough about this complex international situation to make the very serious judgments that you make?" In order that we might explore this issue we posed the following challenge to the interviewees:

Challenge Number Two

Criticism of current (1967) United States policy in Vietnam is essentially a function of ignorance; first-hand knowledge of the President's reasons for his policies in Vietnam would change the mind of the protester. Indeed, it has been said that there is an inverse relation between militancy and hostility, and first-hand knowledge of President Johnson's policies in Vietnam would change the protester.

The general sense of the peace militant response to this claim is that information on which to ground a rational decision to oppose the war was always readily available and required none of the privileged access to which the objection alludes. The response of virtually every peace militant interviewed was oriented to some extent by the *illegality* of the American military presence in Vietnam. Beyond the fact that there was such a presence and that it had been established by presidential action, the material needed to decide upon resistance (or support) consisted of such things as the United Nations Charter, the Treaty of London, the Geneva Accords, and the United States Constitution. There was no problem getting information here. A great number of books (usually in paperback) and articles entered the market describing the conflict, American involvement in it, and the various documents upon which the challenges to the legitimacy of that involvement were based. The anti-war activists may well have been the best informed protesters in history.

The other dimensions of the protest attitude, rooted primarily in the conviction that the war was immoral, rested on information about the impact of the military operation on the Vietnamese and on the way in which the government justified it to the American people. Information on the way in which the war was being conducted and on the enormity of its impact on the Vietnamese was available in impressive quantity and from a variety of sources. For one thing, a number of peace movement activists had actually visited the war theatre, particularly North Vietnam. These included Barbara Deming, David Dellinger, Kay Boyle, Daniel Berrigan, Howard Zinn, and Dagmar Wilson. Ms. Wilson, who helped found the Women's Strike for Peace in 1961, spoke of her own experience in North Vietnam:

> I stood with them beside their children when our bombers came. . . .
> I was standing there with children and they were not my children
> but they were children. Children look to adults to protect them
> and when an adult cannot protect children, that is a moment when
> you really are frustrated to the point of exasperation. My feeling
> was, here I am, the bombs are starting here, the American women
> can do no less . . . and I made up my mind then, really at the very
> last moment, that I would go as far as necessary in this protest.[25]

Books and articles by these visitors and by reporters like Bernard Fall, Wilfred Burchette, and Felix Greene, as well as the accounts of disillusioned soldiers like Green Berets' Donald Duncan and Gary Rader, were all published. Their views were disseminated in the foreign and the underground press and also in the above-ground vociferous journals of dissent like *I.F. Stone's Weekly, Ramparts,* and *Liberation.*

In fact, the American news media were more of a resource than one might think to hear radical criticism of them. The war was fascinating news, and in reporting it certain themes came through very clearly to add to the plausibility of resistance. The self-immolation of Buddhist monks and nuns held out to any reader and viewer an overpowering witness against the regime which the American effort was supporting. From early 1965 onward, the American press —particularly papers like the *New York Times*—devoted regular news space to the very high level of civilian casualties and to the vast number of refugees and their misery. This, of course, raised the serious question of whether what we might accomplish in Vietnam could possibly be worth this cost. (The report of the International War Crimes Tribunal held in Stockholm and Copenhagen in 1969 includes a rather large list of persons—Europeans, Asians, and some Americans—who had visited North Vietnam to study the effect of one or another aspect of the war.)

The sense that something was seriously wrong in the American war effort was also communicated by the behavior of government figures. There were, of course, outspoken congressional opponents to the war like Wayne Morse and William Fulbright, who had no difficulty in getting their views publicized. But more than this, there were the now famous predictions of a quick end of the conflict (predictions which left the impression that its scope was to be restricted), which were contradicted not only by the later course of events but also by the fact that the war effort was being escalated at the time they were made. Secretary of Defense McNamara in January 1964 made his famous prediction of withdrawal by the end of 1965.[26] McGeorge Bundy and Vice President Humphrey added similar predictions during the following months. Add to this the questionable circumstances —now widely admitted—of the Tonkin Gulf Resolution and you have a plausible basis for mistrusting the government's own descriptions of its behavior.

The revelation of the Pentagon Papers[27] by Daniel Ellsberg disclosed a sequence of government decision-making and justification which tends to verify in retrospect the convictions of the peace militants about the intentions of the government and its duplicity in handling the news. The papers revealed no significant facts known only to government and justifying its decisions.

Challenge Number Three

No matter how carefully the act of civil disobedience is planned and acted out, it is still an infringement on another's right if it inflicts pressure or loss of convenience on members of the public who are not directly responsible for the wrongs being protested. This is particularly so if the law violated is a valid law, because it communicates undisciplined activism and defiance of authority rather than a confrontation of social ills.

The response of the civil disobedient to the complaint about inconvenience asserted, first of all, that one could not absolve the public of all responsibility. The second major aspect of their reaction to this challenge dwelt upon the nature of civil disobedience as a technique of sensitization and on the responsibility of the protester.

James Mengel (Baltimore Four) stated the case for collective guilt:

> I think we are all guilty of what is happening in Vietnam and I don't see anyone as innocent of that . . . all of us should be inconvenienced because we are inconveniencing some other people.[28]

David Dellinger added, in the same vein,

> To go about life as usual as if this catastrophe has not taken place has to be challenged somehow. . . . The war and the racial situation in America today is considered to be in the nature of a national emergency under which people have a right to challenge the convenience and tranquility of their fellow citizens.[29]

It would admittedly be better not to infringe on the rights of others except for unusual reasons, they felt. Inconvenience was considered justified as a temporary symbolic measure to sensitize people who did not seem to appreciate the dimensions of the emergency. Barbara Deming, a veteran of many protest experiences in both civil rights and peace movements, spoke of the inconveniences and of turning them into sensitization:

> You make it impossible for people just to live their daily lives as they have before . . . particularly to wage their wars and their oppression as they have before. You shake things up enough so that they have to make some adjustment in the situation or life is impossible.[30]

Once things are shaken up, people who are inconvenienced may ask why, and it is incumbent on the civil disobedient to make the "why" clear. As Miss Deming continued:

> . . . by behaving civilly—that is, by behaving with respect for their human rights—you are in control of how they respond to you. You make it harder for them to justify themselves and for other people just eliminating you instead of changing themselves. . . . You make them . . . look at the issues.[31]

"This can be construed as a gift of consciousness," said Daniel Berrigan, "when a person in some way is made aware of reality as opposed to his American Dream."[32]

None of the peace militants interviewed denied that civil disobedience could communicate defiance of authority. This prospect did not make them particularly uneasy, chiefly because of their attitude toward institutions. Radical pacifist ideology contains an important proposition to which many peace militants would adhere and with which most of the others would sympathize. Paul Goodman states it in an article:

> . . . valuable behavior occurs only by the free and direct response of individuals or voluntary groups to the conditions presented by the historical environment. It claims that in most human affairs, whether political, economic, military, religious, moral, pedagogic, or cultural, more harm than good results from coercion, top down direction, central authority, bureaucracy, jails, conscription, states pre-ordained standardization, excessive planning etc. Anarchists want to increase intrinsic functioning and diminish extrinsic power.[33]

Most peace militants felt that there was need to question authority, that people have to develop the habit of responding first with their own consciences and then working out the relationship with authority. Where the civil disobedient has been effective, according to

Goodman, is "in the sense of making people feel that you don't have to obey . . . these authorities are not divine. . . ." This was, also according to Goodman, analogous to the concept of Jeffersonian anarchism, which held "that the concept of apparently constituting authorities deciding something is not the last word, because the Constitution of those authorities really depends on the people . . . the last word is never said. . . ."[34]

This defiance of authority was viewed as rational, disciplined, humane, and ultimately constructive. *Anarchism,* the intrinsic functioning of individuals, is not *anarchy,* the dark menace cited by so many proponents of law and order. "It cannot lead to anarchy," said Barbara Deming, "since it is protesting anarchy. The question of law and order has been set precisely upside down in their minds, law and order which we are told to respect is actually a masking of what is a gross disorder."[35]

As we noted earlier, for pacifist anarchists like Goodman and Day, the questioning of centralized authority is law respecting. It also respects authority, which, it maintains, must not be abused:

> I don't think anybody has authority unless they show by their lives that they are worthy of authority. . . . I think the breakdown of authority has come about because there is such corruption . . . and great inequalities in the whole legal system. . . . Decentralized authority which non-violent anarchism would espouse would be a source of strength since it places much greater responsibility on each person. . . . This is the way it operates at the Catholic Worker.[36]

But pacifists like Dorothy Day shared the concern of critics of the peace movement that non-violent protest could be provocative. She had discussed this with the late Martin Luther King, and reminisced:

> He said they [the responsible public] do not realize what is in them until it is brought out by a pilgrimage, a procession, a picket line, or a protest march. And then when it is brought out, acts of violence occur, but the shock may be an awakening.[37]

The peace activists were ready to acknowledge that their acts of civil disobedience could communicate unanticipated, negative interpretations. "If they want to read them as undisciplined activism, they will," said the late David Darst (Catonsville Nine). But if civil disobedients planned their action carefully, those who were open-minded would see the rationality of their acts, "that they are not just anarchic, adolescent acts of rebellion against authority."[38] There was uncertainty in the minds of some about the effectiveness of acts of civil disobedience, but not about the need to follow their consciences:

> The pacifism I espoused, the draft non-cooperation and the card burning itself were all part of a personal moral imperative. . . . [David Miller][39]

> I think we have to follow our consciences and do the work we have set ourselves out to do and to accept it sometimes as small. Yet, I have a great confidence that it has affected people's thinking and their interests tremendously. [Dorothy Day][40]

Daniel Berrigan also commented on the possible limitations of the action of the Catonsville Nine: "Even if there isn't this public effectiveness about objectives, I think there was a deeper question of our own lives and how we live as men."[41] As for the overall effectiveness of acts of protest, Howard Zinn commented: "I agree effectiveness is limited. But I argue that our effectiveness would be even more limited if we didn't engage in those acts."[42]

Challenge Number Four

Civil disobedience is subversive to the principle of majority rule. In addition, it leads to indiscriminate law violation and violence. In this it is no different than ordinary criminal behavior.

"We don't have majority rule now . . . it is a minority rule, and the majority apathetically goes along or abstains."[43] Most respondents agreed with this sentiment of Marjorie Swann's, one of the leaders of the Committee on Non-Violence. Many also added that in the case of Vietnam the majority was not consulted in the decision to wage war. Even if it had been consulted and had agreed, majority rule is not supposed to exclude the legitimate activity of a minority.

But the question of majority rule is admittedly a complicated one. Barbara Deming pointed to situations existing today where those in control of this country can make a decision not simply for the majority in this country but for people everywhere. Nuclear weapons testing where fallout could damage people around the world was a case in point. The issue is no longer limited to majority assent of the people in any one country if what is involved is the welfare of the majority of people around the world. "It is possible for a minority to act," she continues, "in the name of the great international majority . . . if you throw your weight against the majority, as well as authorities in the name of all kinds of people and their basic rights," this is something different from gaining "something for yourself, some privilege."[44]

Respondents conceded no particular relationship between civil disobedience and indiscriminate law violation. Daniel Berrigan, in particular, pointed out that genuine acts of civil disobedience are not going to happen frequently because they demand too much. The ideal action of the civil disobedient differs qualitatively from indiscriminate law violation in its demands upon the person. It requires a spiritual purity, a willingness to suffer and to stand in jeopardy of the law, unselfishness, and absence of personal ambition. On the other hand, "indiscriminate law violation is already a fact—and not because of acts like civil disobedience."[45] Respondents tended to echo Berrigan's final remark when this subject came up, turning the question toward the criminality of government.

When the question of violence was introduced into the issue of law violation, respondents answered with a combination of principle, compassion, and a sense of the practical. Howard Zinn, one of the writers on these issues who the peace militants took seriously, made some instructive remarks regarding violence. He notes that the difficulty is not one of establishing a principle of non-violence and then not wavering from it. Rather, the difficulty is in applying it in a complicated situation, since it is almost never simply a case of whether you are for or against violence.

> It gets complicated when you are dealing with a violent situation which you are already in like a war and where the question of the violence of an act of civil disobedience can't be measured in the abstract, but has to be measured against the violence of the ongoing war. And so, while you can argue that burning draft records or let's say blowing up Dow Chemical Company is a violent act, *as it is* [emphasis added], in relation to the violence of the war I would certainly argue that burning draft records is justifiable. Because

the morality of non-violence has to be seen not in the narrow context of the act itself, but in the broader context of what is the
situation that you are in. . . .[46]

What several of the respondents saw in the "broad context" was a
"subtle, threatening violence of institutions," which had to be ex-
posed even at the risks of overreaction and of the temptation to defensive violence. They endorsed the sentiment that "the violence of
the oppressed is never equal to the violence of the oppressor," and in
their general comments on violence tended to temporize with violence of the oppressed. Thomas Melville (of the Catonsville Nine)
commented on the basis of his experience in Guatemala:

> Violence to us means . . . violating human life. Not just physical
> but intellectual—moral life—economic life—political life. You can
> do this by different types of force and I think not necessarily phy-
> sical. . . . The economic forces being used against blacks . . . they
> have no economic force to counteract that so that the only force
> that they have is physical. If they defend themselves you do not
> term that violence. . . .[47]

This sympathy for violence by the oppressed of different cultures as
they seek relief through extraordinary processes was also manifest
in George Mische's (Catonsville Nine) remarks:

> When everything else fails they may turn to things that often would
> be defined as violence, namely armed rebellion, revolution, what
> not. But, in the mind of the man who is revolting it might not be
> violence at all. It's self-defense. His human life and rights are being
> violated.[48]

All this, we must make clear, is in respondent's discussion of the
oppressed, not of themselves. If they refused to condemn this violence, they declined also to adopt it for themselves. Whatever violence occurred within the peace movement was "inevitably on the
fringes," according to Paul Goodman, and since it was not the
"essence" of the movement, its occurrence was "sad" but "no big
deal."[49]

It was particularly important to Daniel Berrigan that the peace
militants maintain their non-violence. "Once this thing has lost the
particular lucidity of non-violence," he said, "we might just as well
step over the line and put on a helmet and join the military or the

para-military."[50] For Berrigan and others, however, there was a difference between violence to persons and violence to property. He and they distinguished further between private property and public property, particularly public property—like draft files.

> The government use of common property . . . has become a point of enmity against social change and against the social and the personal needs of people . . . the only way to vindicate the rights of men against this misuse of property is to bring the property under a symbol that will be both inhibiting, practical, and symbolic.[51]

The raiders of the Catonsville draft board, who saw the files as "death certificates," felt that any sense of threat to normal private property could be dispelled by the protestors' remaining on the scene and interpreting the symbolism of their acts.

> At the first stages people might be frightened away because they're confused, but once people have the opportunity to hear from the people themselves, why they act in such a way, they can interpret it and usually I find that many people who were unreachable other ways now can be reached.[52]

Yet some in the peace movement itself were repelled by this type of action. As we noted earlier, for radical pacifists, breaking, entering, secrecy, fire, and destruction are simply extensions of violence.

All of the peace militants at their trials, as well as the others whom we interviewed, rejected the designation *criminal* to describe their acts of law violation. David Harris spoke of an attitudinal difference between his act of draft refusal and that of a criminal. "I was obviously much more conscious of what I was doing . . . than any criminal I've met." He noted another difference:

> I hadn't accepted the role of defendant or as criminal, and virtually all the so-called criminal cases I've seen were the cases of people who . . . did accept themselves as criminal. They didn't like the fact they were caught . . . or really feel that they had broken the law. . . .
>
> I really saw myself as someone engaged in a conflict. What I tried to do in the trial, and I think I was fairly successful at, was not accepting the logic of the courtroom and the judicial process. But trying to go into the courtroom and make the contest not between two different legal cases, but between two different logics. Two wholly different ways of making decisions and perceiving the world. And

> I think that's the difference between us and the rest of the people
> who break the law. . . .[53]

At certain points, Harris was willing to admit similarities between civil disobedients and criminals. So was David Dellinger, who said: "Most criminals are as moral as I am." The "common criminal" is often a "rebel without cause bearing witness to deprivation." Criminals and civil disobedients are challenging the same system, only the former are seen as doing it blindly, helplessly, and hopelessly. This affinity is strengthened by the jail experience that so many civil disobedients have had, and they view jails with a revulsion that demands that they be abolished as they currently exist for they in no way rehabilitate the people they absorb.

Barbara Deming saw a salutary effect that conscientious law violation could have on these non-political prisoners.

> If they can be shown ways in which they can protest in a disciplined
> way when they become more conscious of what is making them feel
> this way, what is acting upon their lives, then their protest can be
> turned into a different, constructive, conscious direction. Witness the
> reported decline in general lawbreaking during the periods of or-
> ganized protest of Martin Luther King and the Montgomery bus
> boycott.[54]

Challenge Number Five

The courts are not the proper forum for challenging foreign policy and executive war making powers. Congress, as representative of majority rule, is the appropriate forum. This was certainly the case with the labor movement. Why not the peace movement?

No one agreed that the analogy of the labor movement could be applied to the peace movement. Not only were the historical and geographical settings different, the implications of their success were dissimilar. The gains of the labor movement were purely national and ultimately tied to the American Dream. The peace movement is totally other. Daniel Berrigan commented:

> The labor movement has actually joined throughout the world
> in support of war and support of State Department policy and in
> support of subversion in Latin America. . . . Success by the peace
> movement . . . would concretely mean that we could not continue

to bleed the world for the economy of a warring society . . . the achievement of peace in the world is by no means connected with the American Dream or with the American self-image or with American economic primacy in the world.[55]

Some respondents took exception to the implication that they regarded the court as the *only* forum. The court was one way among many to reach the people and to promote institutional and policy change. But the effort was being carried out at many levels which the challenge did not appreciate. There were, for example, the education and lobbying activities by peace organizations in Washington like the Women's International League for Peace and Freedom, the Friends Committee on National Legislation, the Methodist Board of Missions. Some organizations like the Unitarian Universalist Service Committee had had offices in Washington for thirty-five years. There were in addition to these the newly formed organizations initiated by clergymen, G.I.'s, women, students, etc. Howard Zinn commented: "the problem is to make all branches of government responsive to popular activity and to commotion in the country."[56]

Certain things pointed to the courts, however, as particularly appropriate in the circumstances. One was the failure of various other efforts to change government policy, the failure which made the courts the last resort. Another thing pointing to the courts was the conviction that only they could check the presidential pre-emption of congressional war-making powers. "Congress has become powerless," observed Paul Goodman, "and the executive has become overwhelmingly powerful. . . . It is possible that the courts are a more powerful check on the executive than Congress."[57] There was also the constitutional assumption that the President should systematically and conscientiously enforce the laws of the land. This too required judicial attention, as Philip Berrigan observed:

> We're operating out of the bankruptcy of the executive branch, which has refused to face its responsibility in regard to this war in defending the Constitution. But we had no other way than to go to the courts.[58]

Berrigan saw little hope for reliance on normal parliamentary procedures in effecting any kind of change, particularly since he saw parliamentary processes controlled by "the circles in power."

> There is quite literally no hope for parliamentary process in the time that we need to get change in this society. . . . There is a need to see grass roots make a move for power they do not possess. The ultimate question is how are we going to redistribute the power.[59]

There was among respondents the basic conviction that the courts are where one ought to be able to find justice; this conviction was coupled with considerable disillusionment on this very score. Thus Rev. James Mengel:

> The courts should be concerned with everything regarding the case. . . . They give the impression that they are and they talk about the truth, the whole truth and nothing but the truth. But, as a matter of fact, and certainly this was true in our case and I assume it is true in other cases, they don't want to hear the whole truth. They limit one from giving the whole truth. This is a terrible thing. . . .[60]

George Mische:

> I think that all three branches, the executive, the legislative, and the judicial, are all immune to the forces of social change. I think that this has been proven in the past. The President has said that he didn't care what public opinion felt . . . he was going to see it through his way. Congress had enormous amounts of pressure put on it by society to legislate new laws—to change the draft system, to declare this war unconstitutional . . . and has refused to do it. The court itself has refused to even rule on the constitutionality. So I think they all three are in the same position.[61]

David Harris did not think the courts could "functionally" be concerned with conscience. But he saw the problem as more related to the society:

> Society relies on the courts for justice, and at this point to rely upon your laws to give justice means you've lost justice. . . . Justice is obviously something that happens throughout society, not just in the courts. It takes a just society to have just laws.[62]

Challenge Number Six

When the peace militant does choose the court as focus of his action, he asks it to take personal motive and individual conscience into account. But personal conscience can lead men to good or evil, even assuming that society could distinguish elevated from base mo-

tivation. To allow distinctions on the basis of motive would change
the nation from one governed by law to one governed by personal
impulse.

There are courts in which the defense can present witnesses and
arguments which testify to why, ultimately, a defendant broke a law.
In the state courts of California, for example, a jury can hear such
testimony and take it into account in deciding guilt or innocence.
The trial of the Oakland Seven provided an example of this. But
such courts are rare. In federal courts and in most other states, prosecutors challenge such testimony as irrelevant and are usually sustained. Thus, as we saw in the Catonsville Nine trial, a distinction
was eventually insisted upon between the defendant's *motive*—why
they broke the law—and their *intent*—did they know that they were
breaking the law and did they do so intentionally? While the judge
allowed testimony on the former matter in the interest of completeness, he forbade the jury to consider it in deciding guilt or innocence.

Reaction on the part of the peace militants interviewed as to the
way in which courts dealt with the question of motive, or of *conscience,* as it is more often put, was quite varied. That the courts do
not allow conscientious motive to be considered as a defense did not
appear to be a fatal flaw for those civil disobedients to whom the
issue of morality was paramount and legality a mere technicality. It
was enough for them that the process reached those involved as
individuals.

> Civil disodedience [said Bradford Lyttle] gnaws at the soul of
> every judge in the country who is not a gross political appointee and
> a very coarse person. . . . They recognize that civil disobedience
> raises the most profound criticisms and questions about the whole
> system of coercive law that can be raised.[63]

Among those intent on the legal confrontation, some viewed the
courts' handling of testimony with suspicion. Marjorie Melville felt
that the judge at her trial (Catonsville) refused to admit a concern
which the court actually felt.

> I think the court is concerned with why we did it—the very fact that
> every time the question of morality or immorality of the Vietnam
> war was even hinted at, it was gaveled closed—don't even mention

this—we are not discussing the immorality of the war. . . . If it weren't relevant in their mind they wouldn't be so concerned with striking it out.[64]

David Mitchell felt that the courts at each level used testimony about his motivation to misrepresent his case. He said that "they were willing to have me testify to motivation, lack of criminal intent, in fact they sort of welcome that—to get them off the hook."[65] The "hook" was the need to take his case as a legal challenge to draft-related issues. Testimony as to motive was apparently enough identified with cases of conscientious objection that, in Mitchell's opinion, it was used to treat him as a conscientious objector. But:

> This wasn't a selective conscientious objector case. It was having to do with the application of law and nothing to do with rights of conscience or civil liberty, but a legal challenge of the application of the draft.[66]

The chief problem to be faced was not misrepresentation but the basic nonrecognition. It led Philip Berrigan to comment that "legal justice is not necessarily human justice" and Robert McAfee Brown to say:

> I don't know any way to deal with this problem except to keep pressing for it particularly in the name of those young men who are willing to pay the very high price for not having it taken into account. . . . I've got to support them in this kind of concern.[67]

The very least that would be accomplished would be an historical record of accumulated effort.

Daniel Berrigan conceded the difficulty of the problem but insisted upon its constitutional and historical importance. Others then took up the prospect for development in the legal system. First Berrigan:

> We have placed in a sense a very great burden on the courts in forcing them into this question. But, if somebody isn't going to enter this question, what is going to happen with regard to everything this question brings up—that is to say, the very existence of constitutional rights and indeed the Constitution itself. . . . The law, especially the higher court, has not been particularly courageous in confronting these things which war always brings to the front. The rights of conscience are always a crucial issue in times of war.[68]

Howard Zinn adds:

> There is a need to break down in the consciousness of people the
> fixation with the law which doesn't allow them to make an easy
> transition from the immorality of the war to the morality of breaking
> the law to oppose war.[69]

Sociologist and veteran pacifist Gordon Zahn observed:

> I think this whole pattern of trials is going to be reviewed in the
> historical perspective as a rather low period in American judicial
> history precisely for this reason, that there was this artificial separa-
> tion of motive from act.[70]

The review which Zahn anticipates could make for progress in law.
Berrigan points out a pattern of nonconsideration, which the civil
disobedient finds extremely frustrating:

> The courts have refused to look at these things seriously—as in the
> case of draft card burning and other crucial questions—because
> the war is on. . . . you are left entirely without recourse, because in
> peace time they don't arise and at war time they won't consider
> them.[71]

But occasionally damage done during a war is repaired afterward.
The Supreme Court after World War II, for example, held martial
law as declared in Hawaii to have been illegal. George H. Williams
was optimistic about the ability of the legal system to accommodate
conscience, once the system can come to grips with the problem
without inhibition:

> if any society can give legal status to conscience ours can—it is
> pluralistic. We have learned to live a long time with quite diverse
> expressions of conscience, and I hope the time will come when our
> lawyers or jurists, as well as our ethicists and constitutional theorists,
> can safeguard this principle. . . .

Williams continues, touching, among other things, the "privateness"
of conscience:

> I feel that this conscience is not entirely private in the end. It is the
> locus where something more universal becomes incandescent, and
> I am willing to see our courts have difficulty with ascertaining
> whether this is really prudential or selfish or deceitful or whether it

is a true illumination of conscience. Because I think it should be
recognized; it is quite difficult. I think it is the last really new terrain
into which the courts and the jurists are going to penetrate.[72]

One would like to hear more, and also something less vague than
"the locus where something more universal becomes incandescent."
But at least Williams senses that there must be some alternative to
the conviction that personal conscience is the domain of radical
idiosyncrasy. This conviction seems almost universal in the rhetoric
of the judges, who seem to think that the introduction of private conscience would open a floodgate to an unimaginable array of asocial
impulses posing as unchallengeable personal convictions. But the
conviction that the war was illegal and immoral did not rest on
someone's inscrutable interior life. It was not a personal quirk of this
or that resister eager to pick and choose the laws that he would
obey, but was defensible on the basis of quite verifiable—public—
evidence.

Howard Zinn and others note that group consensus had already
developed in this country regarding two issues: the morality of the
war in Vietnam, and segregation. These two issues could be treated
with confidence by the courts because of this crystallization of
opinion:

> ... there is a set of norms which develop in history and around which
> there grows a kind of consensus of opinion. . . . There is a consensus
> about immorality of war which we pay obedience to when we are not
> in the courts. . . . There is a morality about poverty which we recog-
> nize. . . . But as soon as we get into the courts, we cut off what we
> have said . . . and begin to apply law in a rigid way . . . the courts
> don't take morality into consideration even though there is a con-
> sensus of morality on a question. . . . I don't think there is a great
> problem in deciding what's right and wrong; the real problem is try-
> ing to adjust the law to that rather than adjusting our notions of
> morality to the law.[73]

George Mische saw the support for including conscience in a
court of law in the precedent set at Nuremberg. There we told the
German people that

> they had a responsibility to break the law, if the law that they were
> following violated the rights of other people, nations, humanity.
> Our own government in its very basis of the Boston Tea Party and

the Declaration of Independence demands people to live according to their conscience.[74]

According to Mische, how well this conscience is developed is the major concern of the legal system:

> . . . what the court and the community have to decide is whether the person breaking the law fully understands the whole picture of what's happening and therefore probably justify that this law has to be broken. This is probably the biggest challenge before the courts.[75]

For the individuals in this study (many of whom have been designated by critics as "moral imperialists"), there was no insurmountable problem in telling a good conscience from a bad one. Daniel Berrigan said:

> If the law is really a kind of flesh and blood instrument or embodiment of the life of man, then it will know the Ross Barnetts from the Martin Kings, as I know them. I have no difficulty with that because I am a man and I'm in society.[76]

Zinn saw acts of civil disobedience contributing to the emergence of such moral agreement:

> People who engage in civil disobedience are really thinking about building up a moral agreement in the society about a particular act, but they believe that until that moral agreement is built up, they should not desist from their actions.[77]

Challenge Number Seven

Draft card burnings, blocking induction centers, destruction of draft files, carrying a Vietnam flag, speaking of "our friends the North Vietnamese," all of these acts constitute treasonous forms of behavior.

The charge of treason has always followed peace movement activists. Their loyalty was challenged particularly during World War II, when few would justify the actions of Hitler. Later during the nuclear testing period the choice between the threat of Communism and human survival generated ambivalence, and whatever advantage operated was in the direction of anti-Communism. The promulgators of Vietnam policy advanced the containment of Communism as the single most important reason for sending troops to Southeast Asia. The early polls indicate that the public generally supported this policy at the time.

The association of peace militants at peace rallies with other radicals of the far left, particularly Communists, threatened to dissipate their intended moral focus and consequently the support of the public they were trying to reach. Rev. Robert McAfee Brown reported that as a minister he feared losing the middle group—but he noted that an unwillingess to associate with groups further to the left who were expressing these concerns would leave a vacuum which would be filled only by those with positions more radical:

> I did not have the moral luxury of being involved with those whose ideological presupposition I totally shared. It was necessary where inflammatory and violent rhetoric was presented that other dimensions be represented.[78]

If there was some indecisiveness over the question of association, there was none about the direct charge of treason. "To me, people who charge that draft card burning and blocking of induction centers are treasonous forms of behavior don't really understand what America is supposed to be," said Mary Moylan.[79] George Mische's response was similar:

> . . . some people may not understand that some things they would consider treasonous might really be the best thing for the country . . . there were Tories and many people who thought what early Americans were doing was very treasonous to England—even to the colony that they were living in. . . . They don't have the full perspective. . . .[80]

Howard Zinn introduced another qualification: "I don't define patriotism as loyalty to the government. I define patriotism as a concern for the people."[81]

Others dismissed the challenge:

> If this be treason then make the most of it. [David Dellinger][82]

> Of course, I think it's absurd. Because if treason is going to enter into it at all, it's the betrayal of sworn duty of office by those who hold office. [Daniel Berrigan][83]

Definitely not. No, they are quite—very patriotic—they are responsible acts in an effort to help and to heal, to save. They appear outwardly to be otherwise but essentially, basically, they are great, beautiful, helpful acts. [Rev. Mengel][84]

The United States is committing treason to humanity as it is in Vietnam. [David Dellinger][85]

This remark by Dellinger turns attention to the broadened perspective of the civil disobedient in the matter of loyalty. He has a sense of loyalty to humanity: the death of American soldiers could not be separated from the death of Vietnamese. This perspective was evident in Rev. William Sloane Coffin's choice of a quote from Thoreau during his trial: "I am first of all a citizen of the world, and of this country only at a much later and convenient hour."[86]

I don't even recognize the matter of treason [said Marjorie Swann], because I don't feel that the most important loyalty a person has is to the nation-state which he happens to be born in. I think his most important loyalty is to his fellow human beings.[87]

Kay Boyle, speaking of a remarkable meeting between herself and Madame Binh of the North Vietnamese delegation in Paris, described the combination of loyalties to humanity and nation. After she had been introduced to Madame Binh as "a lady who has been to jail several times in protest against the war in Vietnam," Ms. Boyle said:

. . . she looked up at me—and tears poured down her cheeks, and we just held each other like that for a moment. . . . But this didn't mean I wanted the Communists to win . . . everything that we expressed was what women express about the horror of what is taking place to our American youth, to her North Vietnamese children. I think it is ridiculous to say it is because you say "our friends the North Vietnamese" that you necessarily want the Communists to take over the world.[88]

There was widespread belief among the respondents that they were acting out of a sense of responsibility which did not compromise their loyalty. Barbara Deming remarked:

> Nothing could be further from treason than the effort to try and prevent your country from doing evil. It would be very disloyal not to try to change it.[89]

Rev. Robert McAfee Brown shared this attitude and noted its propriety:

> It's an attempt to be extremely loyal to what the country ought to be and now does not seem to be. . . . A democracy ought to take account of the conscientious concerns of its citizens.[90]

There was historical justification for these actions as long as they were "aboveboard, acclaimed by manifestos and public statements, are not intentionally conspiratorial," as Rev. George H. Williams commented. He continued:

> . . . the legal mind and the prophetic mind are in conflict, and I introduce then the corporate terms that are entirely political in origin but have a legal and religious, moral status in the Anglo-American world: namely, the loyal opposition.

He insisted that peace movement actions had a positive effect:

> This has been a heroic moral period in American history . . . it stretched the possibilities for acceptable critical behavior until finally . . . churches, universities, youth, armed services are aware that something is wrong with this war.[91]

There was the confidence then that at least the attempt to sensitize the public met with some success. According to George Mische:

> There's a new awakening in this country to compassion. Civil disobedience has done a lot to soften people, to make them a little bit more human, restore some of their humanity because they can see that there are other people who are so concerned about these things that they would lay themselves on the line and not worry about the consequences. Naturally, when we see this kind of thing even the most hard-hearted person has got to be moved by it. He has got to try to relate to it. He's got to try to understand—find out why this guy did this—because he certainly can understand that, well look if this guy would not have done it he could play it cool the rest of his life and not count any severe consequences.[92]

Chapter Nine

A Response from Ordinary Men

Remember it just happens now that the courts are ahead of the Congress. This very rarely happens in our history. Suppose we were back in the old days like when Roosevelt was trying to do something. He had a court that was absolutely opposed to everything he was doing. I don't want to trust it to the courts. I have great reservations. The longer I'm a judge the more reservations I have. We are ordinary, confused human beings. [Judge C][1]

Judge C, as we shall see in what follows, favored a good deal of initiative on the part of the judiciary. Still, as the interviewer explored the theme of judicial initiative with him, he uttered the caution quoted above. Like all of the judges interviewed, Judge C was sensitive to the limitations of the legal system and apprehensive over its having to face an issue which might be beyond its capacity.

But the peace movement had thrust the question of the war upon the courts as a claim for justice, and to this the judges had to react. As they discussed their responses, the judges revealed a surprising diversity of positions on the nature of the legal system and of their own responsibilities. We will focus on their positions on three basic issues: (1) the relation of the legal to the moral dimensions of the civil disobedience phenomenon; (2) the relation of judge with jury in deciding civil disobedience cases; and (3) the relation of the law to the political issues involved. At each of these points questions arise which bear on the most basic concepts of the legal system.

Some of the material that follows is from books, articles, and

transcripts. By far the greater amount, however, has been gathered
in direct interviews. In some instances the judges interviewed are
those who have tried civil disobedience cases. In others they are not.
All acknowledge, however, that the issues raised are of the greatest
professional importance.

I. JUDICIAL RESPONSE—THE LEGAL AND THE MORAL

None of the judges whose position on the matter is known to the
authors maintained that the courts could treat civil disobedience as
something legal. Liberal or conservative, they acknowledged what
seems to be in the very nature of the situation: civil disobedience is
by definition the breaking of law, and the courts, no less by definition, must treat the breaking of the law as just that. According to a
judge generally considered to be liberal, "the judicial function within
the legal structure has to be carried out within the framework of
justifying the legal structure" (Judge X). A more conservative judge,
asked if there could be a legal right to civil disobedience, said that
the whole idea was contradictory. Since in a legal system what is
a right is defined by law, the claim that one can legally disobey the law
amounts to having the law command and release at the same time:
you must . . . but you need not. This judge concluded: "civil disobedience is not a civil 'right' in the sense that it creates any
corresponding duty of a democratic state or society to recognize and
allow it."[2]

The legal vindication of a number of civil rights protesters does
not constitute an exception to this viewpoint. According to Judge X,

> Typically, the sit-ins to desegregate public accommodations in
> the South involved a violation of statutes in southern states, but
> since the statutes themselves were held unconstitutional, those de-
> fendants who carried their appeals high enough were ultimately
> found not guilty because the statute they were charged with violat-
> ing was itself unconstitutional and therefore annulled. So, in that
> sense what is often thought of as civil disobedience can be legal, but
> if the ultimate ruling is that the statute which was violated is a valid
> statute, and it was violated, then necessarily the conduct was illegal
> and the civil disobedience was illegal.

Because these civil rights episodes introduced instances where the
law was at odds with the law—something upon which peace militants

also sought to capitalize—vindication still took place within the legal structure. It was by appeal to yet another *law,* usually the Constitution, which took precedence. Judge Sweigert, whose article we quoted above on the question of right to civil disobedience, said that civil disobedience should be judged according to the standards by which one judges rebellion. It is

> a form of violence with all the risks and dangers that such acts imply and generate—an act, the worth of which cannot be evaluated in terms of "right" but only in pragmatic terms of its ultimate success or failure in imposing their will upon the state and others in society.[3]

If it is true that successful rebellions terminate in new sets of laws, then even here vindication would be in the only terms recognizable by the legal structure: by law.

Civil disobedience cannot be considered legal, then. But can it be considered moral? Here there is definite disagreement among judges. At one extreme there are some who hold it to be immoral as well as illegal. Others feel that it can be moral, but even these differ about whether or not the courts can accommodate its morality.

Let us consider first the position of the judges who regard civil disobedience as immoral. Judge Sweigert, in his article, confronts the civil disobedient at that point where most would feel his greatest claim to morality lies: his non-violence. Sweigert says of this:

> Although no physical violence may be involved, such a "violation" of law is itself (as the common derivation of the word suggests) a form of "violence" directed at the state and others in the society.[4]

Another judge made the same point, though less categorically and without the appeal to etymology: "in almost all acts of civil disobedience, there is usually some injury to others" (Judge B). Obviously the law on one hand and the welfare of other persons and of the state on the other hand hang so closely together that a threat to the former is a threat to the latter. Where moral and legal values fuse in this way, there is no room for the moral to become a basis of appeal against the legal. This seems to be the view of the two judges who made the following remarks during interviews:

> My own feeling is that you cannot have moral justification, because it's entirely a subjective judgment that that person makes. And

if we permitted that to go on, then anyone could have a subjective judgment in reference to whether he would violate the law, a given law, or not. For example, a person could say that he felt that he shouldn't stop at a stop sign, because he felt, morally, it was ridiculous for him to stop at that particular stop sign. By failing to stop, of course, he not only endangers lives of others, but his own. So I don't think that there can be any justification—moral justification —because of the fact that it calls for a subjective judgment of an individual, and I feel that we cannot exist in a compact civilization with a person being permitted to pick and choose those laws he would obey. [Judge A]

What if someone should say, "I have the right to rob somebody physically," and believe it. Do you think that should be the defense to robbery? I mean, that's the question I would pose to these people who say, "I'm opposed to war in any form." They certainly have the right to be opposed to war in any form; I suppose a person has the right to say he has the right to commit robbery if he wants to, but he is completely anti-social when he does it. [Judge B]

Here again we have the threat to moral values from civil disobedience. To read the examples, these values would be in the lives (in the first instance) or the property (in the second) of others. The remarks also suggest unequivocally that these lives and this property are inserted in a social order, which is itself a moral value and the disruption of which is immoral and illegal.

The nature of the threat is stated differently here, however. Now it is "subjective judgment," the sort of thing which would permit a person "to pick and choose the laws he would obey," which is the threat. How often we have heard this during the trials! The judges usually do not give this attitude the name that it bears in the lexicons of morality, but that name is *pride*. They feel that the description fits, however, anyone who, in the words of another conservative judge, "takes it upon himself to . . . set himself above the law . . ." (Judge Z).

As we have noted, there is in this position an identification of law and morality which undercuts any prospect of the civil disobedient's justifying himself before a court by appeal to extra-legal values. He emerges an individual deviant, legally and morally idiosyncratic. Conscience is not a locus where, in Rev. George Williams' terms, "something more universal becomes incandescent," and there is no room for the idea that he might be advancing a value which is quite genuine but heretofore unacknowledged. Critics of this position point to the fact that the values advanced by the civil disobedient may not be strictly a function of his private perspective. They may in fact be affirmed by a significant minority. They may even be the view of a majority which had not yet had time to turn them into law. Where conservative judges complain that a defendant "sets himself above the law," their critics counter that these judges take the law as an end in itself.

The response of the conservative judges is that there is no room for moral considerations *in court*. It is up to another institution—the legislature—to reckon with such values. The judge who had offered the robbery example quoted above answered in this way when the interviewer explored the possibility of judicial accommodation with him.

> INTERVIEWER: The distinction that they would make is that they are not being anti-social, that they would not harm another person, that they are rather taking a stand to protect the lives of other men.
>
> JUDGE B: The point is, who makes that distinction? The statute which sets up the standards is enacted by the lawmaking body, not by the courts.

Another judge repeated the opposition between subjective judgment and law:

> There are those who claim that there is a moral justification for civil disobedience. I don't happen to be one of those who subscribe to that. The difficulty as I see it is that the moral justification rests on theses that are too uncertain, that are too subjective; they're subject to as many interpretations as there are people engaged in it. I've heard arguments going further than that, with which I have considerable sympathy, and that is that it's not moral for anyone to violate the law, even though he is willing to pay the penalties, because he is taking it upon himself to sort of set himself above the law and that that law applies for most people but not to him, for reasons that he asserts himself. That subjective element is subject to a great deal of abuse. [Judge Z]

This jurist specifies that even the willingness to accept the penalties does not redeem the behavior of the civil disobedient morally. Here he disagrees with many judges who feel that such redemption is possible. For most of the latter, redemption would not occur in court, however. Here the prescribed punishment would be assigned, usually with an acknowledgment of the moral character of the defendant and of the possibility that history might well justify him. Judge Thomsen, who presided at the trial of the Catonsville Nine, was particularly strong in assertions of this sort, as were Judges Clarie (Mitchell) and Tyler (Miller). All adopted approximately that position which was asserted by Supreme Court Justice Fortas, whose writing on civil disobedience began to circulate in 1968. Fortas said:

> It is only in respect to such laws—laws that are basically offensive to fundamental values of life or the Constitution—that a moral (although not a legal) defense of law violation can be possibly urged. Anyone assuming to make the judgment that a law is in this category assumes a terrible burden. He has undertaken a fearful moral as well as legal responsibility. He should be prepared to submit to prosecution by the state for the violation of the law and the imposition of punishment if he is wrong or unsuccessful. He should even admit the correctness of the state's action in seeking to enforce its laws, and he should acquiesce in the ultimate judgment to the courts.[5]

But some judges conceded that the civil disobedients not only might be morally correct, but that they need not necessarily wait (in prison) for history to justify them. The courts themselves could find accommodation. As one might expect, the general philosophical outlook supporting this position was quite different from that supporting the conservative view. Commenting generally on the legitimacy of civil disobedience, Judge X said:

> I think that we have to keep in mind law and government are not ends in themselves. They are a means by which people try to order their interpersonal relationships to achieve the best kind of status and interpersonal relationships that can be achieved. So, the sanctity of the law has to be defended on some basis other than the law as an end in itself, and similarly the sanctity of established governmental processes. So, within that framework of philosophical reference, shall we say, I would see a place, at least theoretically, in which no law would be completely immune from violation as a means of seeking redress for evils which spring from some other law than the law being violated.

Judge X had also said:

> I think that philosophically, a good case can be made for the propo-
> sition that in a democratic government, and particularly in an Amer-
> ican Democracy historically, there is a philosophic role for protest
> that goes to the point of disobedience. Many of our historical heroes
> became heroes because they defied the law in obedience to a higher
> law.

If the more conservative judges did not necessarily defend the
proposition that the law is an end in itself, they maintained a relation
between it and moral ends such that the courts could not accommodate civil disobedients, however authentic their motivation. Judge X,
on the other hand, believes that the courts could accommodate such
persons, for whom he saw a role in the developing of value.

> The person who sticks his neck out for his conscience occasionally
> does acquire ultimately the role of a hero because in either a con-
> temporary or historical judgment he has expressed values which
> other people generally respect or love. He may be doing something
> that simply needs to be called to the attention of the public or he
> may be enough ahead of the times so that it's going to take a little
> perspective for the public generally to appreciate that he was right.

He might not even be prosecuted, but if he is, there is considerable
discretionary power available to judges. He continues:

> Even though you have criminal acts, there is still so much that's dis-
> cretionary in connection with the case that everything that relates to
> motivation and intent is relevant and so I couldn't rule out civil dis-
> obedience simply because the conduct is illegal and something has
> to be done to vindicate the law. . . . Whatever they call it—dictates
> of their conscience, a higher moral law, however we define it—I
> don't think that we should ignore this, and it may be that we should
> make a place for the person who, through his disobedience and his
> incurring a criminal violation and a conviction, should be given
> credit for having called attention to some things which need correc-
> tion.
> INTERVIEWER: How could you give them credit?
> JUDGE X: It would have to be in terms of public appreciation, and
> recognition ultimately, perhaps within the judicial function—I can
> conceive of cases in which a judge might very properly say you are
> guilty and one of the collateral effects of your conduct which results
> in your conviction is that a great evil is going to be rectified and for

this the community owes you some thanks. So, I am sending you out of here with a penny fine.

INTERVIEWER: Sort of a symbolic sentence?

JUDGE X: Yes, and I'm recommending to the governor or the President, as the case might be, that he issue a pardon for you in appreciation of the fact that what you have done has brought about such a desirable result. Now, I don't mean this is a frequent kind of thing, but philosophically I can see a place for this on some rare occasion.

Some judges who conceded that the law and morality might at times collide spoke about the personal position in which they might find themselves in such a situation.

I took an oath to uphold the Constitution and the laws of the United States. I didn't take an oath to be a good man and do what I thought was right. [Judge C]

This judge, who clearly had sympathy for protest, disassociated himself from his official role to comment on the question of violence in civil disobedience.

This is a completely personal reaction and not as a trial judge who has to follow the law; not what I think it ought to be. I have to do what I think the law says . . . as a person I feel that there are times when there is justification for violence in civil disobedience to the limited extent that there is unlawful or unreasonable force being used by the police, then the right of self-defense comes up and the demonstrator has the right to protect himself. All you have to do is watch the T.V. and you can see that occurring. In Chicago, there were times when under California law, under the new decision that came down, it holds specifically that a police officer cannot use excessive force to arrest, and when he does so he is as unlawful as the demonstrators, and the demonstrator has the right to protect himself.

When he was asked if this sort of disassociation of personal from professional life might not chip away at personal integrity, Judge C replied:

I can't see it that way. You shouldn't be a judge or you shouldn't be in public office. You're taking an oath to uphold the office and whatever the oath is. Our duty is to interpret the law the way it is, to follow the supreme law of the land and the laws of the state. When there's a void we have to interpret them. They didn't makes us judges to make our own law, but as I say, there is a growing edge to the law all the time. It is just evolving changes all the time. We're involved in that process. Every decision you make is making law.

Another judge, admitting that he disagrees with certain laws but goes on living with his disagreement and enforcing the laws, focused his answer at a point where the tension between morality and law might be great:

> I may be a little bit ambivalent in my approach to this question. In other words, I don't think that I've ever faced myself with the moral challenge in that respect—when I thought war was wrong, what would I do? Well, I've always said to myself, if I thought it was, I just wouldn't do it, period, and I wouldn't hesitate to say so. And if I felt that way, I'd step up and be counted. And if I were—if it happened to be at this job, I'd resign from the job and take the consequences of what I'd had to face. But I would not attempt to enforce the law and be against it at the same time. That's—I don't mean to say that I have to agree with every law that is before me, because there are a number of laws that I have to interpret or have to enforce with which I don't agree, or at least, I think, ought to be modified to some extent. [Judge B]

Judge X, one of the most liberal, spoke of the individual position of judges in terms of the sort which have often been applied to the "subjective judgment" of the civil disobedients:

> I don't think anybody can do this with ease, but I don't think judges are significantly different from other people. I don't think they're greatly different after they go on the bench than they were before. Some of the peripheral things may change, but I don't think that the basic man changes simply by reason of going on the bench. I think that the answer to your question has to be rooted in the fact that *everybody has to assign a considerable degree of humility to his own judgments and convictions, particularly in a democracy, to the extent that the evidence for persuading other people to change are relatively open.* So, I think that the area in which the individual can derive the judgment of society as a whole on the basis of his own personal convictions has to be pretty narrow; and so there are many things where he disagrees, but which he has to accept in order to make existence tolerable for himself and the people with whom he lives. The alternative approach would be anarchy. So, he has to make this kind of judgment, and as I say, essentially, he has to have enough humility in him to realize that no matter how strongly he

> may feel on a variety of things, with rare exceptions he has to accept
> the collective judgment of others. [Emphasis added]

If the civil disobedient must not set himself above the law by defiance, the judge must not set himself above it by claiming it to be coextensive with his own convictions. Pride becomes him no more than it does the defendant.

II. JUDICIAL RESPONSE——THE JUDGE AND THE JURY

> One of the problems which every judge has is to tell a jury from time to time that I am going to give you the law—and you must accept it as I give it to you—even if you don't like it—even if you think it's wrong and should be changed—even if you think I misstated it. Because sometimes I tell the jury that the law is thus and so when I don't think it should be thus and so—but it is, and it is not my responsibility to change it. [Judge D]

This remark echoes a theme which we heard often during the trials, and most recently from Judge Thomsen as he instructed the jury at the trial of the Catonsville Nine:

> It is your duty to accept without question for the purpose of the case the statements which I make to you about the law. . . .
>   If I make a mistake in what I tell you, it will be reversed by a higher court that sets the matter straight. That is the rule of law in this country.[6]

Accepting the law as the judge gives it means several interconnected things, as one observes the behavior of jurists and juries. It means that the law which the judge introduces must be taken to mean what he says it means. Juries must not depart from his interpretation of it. Neither may juries adopt for the case a law which the judge does not declare relevant. We saw several instances of attempts by civil disobedients to introduce treaties and even articles of the Constitution. These certainly have a claim to status as law, but they were refused. Neither can the jury depart from the law—and the evidence —to introduce items from the area of motivation. This usually means that they cannot introduce issues of morality. This series of limitations on what the jury can do in regard to the law and to the judge's instruction on it, contains a certain amount of ambiguity. One reason is that there is disagreement among judges and even from state to state on some of the items in this allegiance of jury to judge. Another is the article of criminal justice according to which the jury can reject law and evidence in making its decision—though they cannot be instructed on this.

When most of the judges responded to questions about their relation with the jury, they had in mind the prospect that the jury might venture into the moral dimensions of the issues. One judge held this would be highly undesirable. According to him, the jury functions as it should when

> The question becomes . . . has the defendant violated that law, or hasn't he, by his conduct? And this, of course, by its very process avoids a great many of the arguments the defendants attempt to raise which go to the legality of the Vietnam war for one or the other questions concerning the moralities of the law—the adoption of the law, and I think it misplaces the jury functions to attempt to have the jury pass upon that morality. I don't think that is what our form of government was ever intended to set up, that there should be—whenever there is a jury trial—that the question of the morality of law would come into play. [Judge B]

Another judge agrees, first underscoring the difference between the legal and the moral:

> The jury looks to the courts for instruction as to what constitutes guidance for the determination of what is lawful and what is unlawful. It doesn't look to the judge for guidance to determine what is moral and what is immoral. It doesn't look to the judge to determine what is in violation of conscience of the individual and what isn't in violation of the conscience of the individual. [Judge A]

Apparently, the distinction between law and morality must be preserved for at least two reasons. One is very familiar: the prospect of chaos which is seen as the consequence of any departure from strict observance of the law and particularly any departure into morality. Judge A continues:

> We would have every conceivable definition of morality and every conceivable definition of conscience under the sun and you would have utter chaos. I could argue, and I could see too, that the man

who has the eloquence and the philosophical ability to promote a philosophical point of view could defeat almost any kind of prosecution, particularly if the areas involved become social or political in character as they relate to the government and they relate to the necessity of law to bring about complaints. We'd have real chaos.

To the chaos which would follow from the sheer multiplicity of views, Judge Z adds a rather sinister note:

> If we depart from the standards which are prescribed in the law—I can think of no more dangerous instrumentality than a jury of twelve people, authorized in some way to express the judgments of the court and still not be bound by the rules of the court, anymore than an army, which is not subjected to discipline, internal discipline, would be a safe instrument to have abroad. A court which was not circumscribed by legal requirements would be a dangerous instrumentality. Think of the power that a court exercises; if that power can be exercised arbitrarily, according to whim or fancy, or according to my own personal moral judgments—it's a dangerous instrumentality to let loose. It would be better not to have any courts than to have courts which function at the whim of the judge or jury.

But beyond chaos and the danger of arbitrary power, still another reservation on the jury's responding to the moral demands of the situation surfaces.

> If this was allowed . . . you would have twelve untried people, unelected, that don't go through any of the process of facing the public, stating their position, have none of those safeguards which are set up for the election of representatives of the people in the legislative body, would be making these decisions. This, in my opinion, is just inconsistent with the notion that we are an ordered form of government and that we deal in ordered bodies and have an ordered society. [Judge B]

Judge B restates the view that the legislature is the proper place to accommodate moral issues, but to that adds reasons why this is so. It is a matter of safeguards which promote responsibility: the process of election involves the need to account to the public; the process of jury selection does not. Consequently, there is too little assurance that the position taken by a juror would really be that of the community. Jurors have not had the public testing that politics brings. Their formal irresponsibility contrasts with the responsibility delegated to legislators.

Another judge took up the issue of the jury's qualification, but in another direction.

> Sometimes it seems to me that the jury runs far afield, in arriving at its verdict or its inability to arrive at a verdict, as a result of somebody running beyond the scope of the law and the evidence. They start theorizing as to why the person was injured or why the defendant did the conduct and not with the conduct itself. Because they are not trained, they are all different degrees of experience and backgrounds and education and intelligence and what have you from which they are selected, so the court has to try to guide them within this channel. You are dealing with laymen; I think that they have to be guided, of course, within the bounds of what the law says. [Judge Y]

The jury is untrained. The court—the judge, that is,—must guide them. In this case the jury is contrasted not with the legislator and on the basis of responsibility but with the judge and on the basis of training. Judge Y is certainly expressing the prevailing contemporary view of judge-jury relations, a view which is very sensitive to the importance of legal training—and of its lack—in the courtroom. The issue arose for us in the case of the Catonsville Nine. The opinion written by Judge Sobeloff for the Appellate court in this case was treated at length. He noted that in the early history of the American colonies juries nearly always had the power to decide the law as well as the facts and that they continued to have it until approximately fifty years after the Revolution. "However, the judges in America, just as in England after the Revolution of 1688, gradually asserted themselves increasingly through their instructions on the law."[7]

Thereupon the judges gradually asserted their authority as the law was increasingly professionalized. This reflected the growth in the law's complexity as well as the extension and refinement of legal training which took place in response to it. There is little doubt that this professionalization of the law has had its impact on the judge-jury relationship and upon the determination to keep the law in the hands of the judge.

Still, the legal system is genuinely committed to the jury and troubled at any threat to its function. Thus the doctrine of jury nullification remains, and Sobeloff in his opinion recognized

> . . . the undisputed power of the jury to acquit, even if its verdict is contrary to the law as given by the judge and contrary to the evidence. This power must exist as long as we adhere to the general verdict in criminal cases, for the courts cannot search the minds of jurors to find the basis upon which they judge.[8]

Judge Aldrich, writing the majority opinion for the appeals court in the Spock case, noted that the pressure from the bench on the jury had been excessive. Having taken exception to Judge Ford's demanding special findings from the jury, Judge Aldrich invoked the latter's role of representing the community conscience—something with which some judges would simply not agree:

> Here, whereas, as we have pointed out, some defendants could be found to have exceeded the bounds of free speech, the issue was peculiarly one to which a community standard or conscience was, in the jury's discretion, to be applied.[9]

Judge Aldrich, writing in 1967, cited at length a work on the jury trial written by Wigmore and published in 1929. Wigmore argues in a rather compelling way for the role of the jury to bridge an inevitable gap between general rules of law and justice in a particular case. The jury, he maintains, provides the necessary flexibility in the legal process. Law and justice are very often in conflict, Wigmore notes, because law is a general rule (even the stated exceptions), while justice is the fairness of this precise case under all its circumstances. Law and justice then very often do not coincide:

> Everybody knows this, and can supply instances. But the trouble is that law cannot concede it. Law—the rule—must be enforced—the exact terms of the rule, justice or no justice. . . .
> So that the judge must apply the law as he finds it alike for all. And not even the general exceptions that the law itself may concede will enable the judge to get down to the justice of the particular case, in extreme instances. The whole basis of our general confidence in the judge rests on our experience that we can rely on him for the law as it is. . . .
>
> . . . .

> Now this is where the jury comes in. The jury, in the privacy of
> its retirement, adjusts the general rule of law to the justice of the
> particular case. Thus the odium of inflexible rules of law is avoided,
> and popular satisfaction is preserved.[10]

What the jury actually takes into account in the privacy of its de-
liberations isn't clearly evident, even to the jury itself. It is certainly
doubtful that it can always be counted upon to maintain an indifference to issues like motive when these are obviously a major feature
of the defendant's outlook. Perhaps it was with this in mind, or perhaps it was the result simply of an expanded and flexible understanding of relevance, but the state of California allows juries to consider
motive if they wish to do so. As one judge quoted it to the interviewer:

> This is the Standard Criminal Jury Instructions for the state of Cali-
> fornia. It is 35 revised and reads as follows:
>
> Motive is not an element of a crime charged and need not be shown.
> However, you may consider motive or lack of motive as a circum-
> stance in this case. Presence of motive may tend to establish guilt,
> absence of motive may tend to establish innocence. You will there-
> fore give its presence or absence as the case may be, the weight to
> which you find it to be entitled.

This provision was clearly operating in the case of the Oakland
Seven, where it was included in the judge's instructions. It has not,
apparently, ushered chaos into the legal system of the state of California. Juries find the additional consideration manageable. An important reason for this is, we believe, that there simply are *not* as
many positions as there are people in the realm of morality. There
are, in fact, clearly a limited number, judicial and prosecution rhetoric to the contrary notwithstanding.

To return to the nullification question, Judge Sobeloff notes that
the power of the jury to acquit in exigent circumstances contrary to
the law as given by the judge and to the evidence is not always contrary to the interest of justice. However, to encourage the jury either
by defense argument or by judicial instruction (as the appellant had
urged) would, he feels, be to negate the rule of law in favor of the
rule of lawlessness.[11]

The ultimate resource of jury power is supposed to remain un-

known to the jurors. The defense attorneys know and can only hope
that the realization will dawn on jurors as they deliberate. But at the
trial there is a great deal working against the growth of that awareness. More than anything else the judge works against it. Judge A
said:

> I do not think a juror has the right to vote his conscience, so to
> speak, in reference to his attitude toward the law. And when he is
> sworn in as a juror he affirms, or makes such an oath at the time, to
> follow the instructions of the judge.

This oath is then reinforced when the judge instructs the jury: "It is
your duty to accept without question for the purpose of the case the
statements which I make to you about the law."[12] At the very least
such instructions impede the discovery process. Equally important,
they are in substance untrue, a fact which must continue to generate
tension around them.

III. JUDICIAL RESPONSE—THE POLITICAL QUESTION DOCTRINE

> Although no nation in the past has ever engaged in such a critical
> act of self-judgment, we must set the moral precedent of judging
> ourselves today by standards at least as rigorous as those we em-
> ployed against our enemies a quarter of a century ago. Unless we do
> so, we will compound the consequences of our guilt by failing to ac-
> knowledge it.[13]

It was in an attempt to mount the challenge of which Robert
McAfee Brown spoke that opponents of the Vietnam war engaged
the legal system during the 1960s. Civil disobedience was the most
familiar tactic, and it is to this that we have given most of our attention. We should recall, however, that there were also attempts at
legal challenge which did not take the form of civil disobedience.
There were suits against the government and against government
officials seeking to prevent them from sending this or that person to
Vietnam on the grounds that the orders were illegal. We saw one
instance of this in the case of the Fort Hood Three, who attempted
such a suit against Secretary of Defense McNamara. They, like the
civil disobedients—whose ranks they soon joined—encountered the
government claim that the issue was non-justiciable because it was a
political question. To call a question political is to claim that, al-

though a constitutional issue may be involved, resolution of the issue is appropriate not to the judiciary but to another government agency —the legislature or the executive. We want to review this reference to the "political question" now.

The suit by the Fort Hood Three was rejected by the appeals court because, as the judge said, "it is not the function of the judiciary to entertain such litigation which challenges the validity, the wisdom or the propriety of the Commander in Chief of our Armed Forces abroad."[14] As we noted when we discussed the Fort Hood Three case, Justice Douglas affirmed quite definitely that the exercise of executive power in foreign affairs could give rise to consequences which were justiciable. Dissenting from the majority in this case, he urged review, as did Justice Stewart. Their position that the question might be justiciable harmonizes with a rather deep-seated conviction that a person or persons whose life or property is endangered is entitled to legal recourse.

Among the judges whom we interviewed, Judge E answered at some length the following question:

> Couldn't some legal form be devised which could allow a group of citizens to take the government or the President to court to challenge this question of the morality/legality of the war?

> JUDGE E: Well, I think that is a good idea. I don't know just what it would be. It is a very complicated business. But as to the idea there ought to be some means whereby a group of responsible citizens, representing a substantial—say a third or more—segment of the population, or the views of such a segment of population, ought to have some means for getting an adjudication—for example, as to whether or not we can be in Vietnam as we are without there having been a declaration of war—I think this kind of thing is desirable. Now, you know, government is a kind of enigma in some ways. By and large, I think if you were to take a cross-section of all the human beings in the world, regardless of where they live or the color of their skin or their economic circumstances, I think they would be, almost to a man, honestly opposed to war. Yet we have war, and I think one reason we have war is because of some inability—and I am not blaming anyone—of the governments to give effective voice to the desire of the majority of the people for peace.

Judge E not only favors the establishing of this possibility, he relates it to the question of the proper respect for minority opinion.

This option which he endorses would certainly help relieve the judicial scene of the alternatives—so dear to both prosecutors and judges—of accepting the law as it stands or "setting oneself above the law" in some sort of ego-trip.

But this alternative does not yet exist, and the legal system during the 1960s could not be persuaded to tell the executive to cease and desist in Vietnam. The Fort Hood Three turned to civil disobedience along with so many others. Thereupon, as we have seen, the question became that of using treaties and other items of international law as defense. The range of disagreement among these judges on the appropriateness of such moves is very impressive. At one extreme we have Judge E, who, asked if he thought that principles of international law should be taken into account in U. S. courts, answered crisply, "No, I don't. . . . I do not think that international law should be a basis for a person disobeying the laws of the United States." National sovereignty was apparently what concerned this jurist most. Recall that he was quite willing that the courts provide the opportunity for *citizens* to challenge the President, but the prospect of the introduction of international law seemed like the incursion of something foreign.

Asked about the apparently legal status of treaties, Judge E said:

> They are not binding law upon the courts of the United States. If they are to be taken into account in such matters as litigation and sentencing, of course, they should be. . . . If we entered into a treaty in which those laws became like the Constitution, paramount to the draft laws, it would be a different thing, but we haven't. I am not saying this is good; I am just saying the way it is under our system. I do not know that I am wise enough to say one way or another.

Judge Northrop, who presided over the trial of the Baltimore Four, agrees with Judge E. In an opinion in that case, he said that the courts could not venture into the question of government behavior in the area of international law

> . . . even if the government's actions are contrary to valid treaties to which the government is a signatory. And the Supreme Court has held that Congress may constitutionally overrule treaties by later enactment of an inconsistent statute, even though the subsequent statute is in violation of international law.[15]

We have noted that Article VI paragraph 2 of the Constitution declares treaties to be part of the nation's law and that former Supreme Court Justice Goldberg insisted that they were legally binding. Justices Stewart and Douglas of the present Supreme Court certainly seem open to the prospect that they may be. While Judge E and Judge Northrop deny this, Judge C affirms it unequivocally:

> The Nuremberg trial is an issue. It's part of the supreme law of this land. There is no question. There are three types of activity condemned by agreement and treaty and punished at Nuremberg. They are first, crimes against peace, that is, waging wars of aggression; second, war crimes, that is, violation of the laws and customs of war; third, crimes against humanity, including torture, killings of civilians, deportations, and forced labor. Now that's the Nuremberg trial. These are recognized in our own military law. It is in the military orders given to every soldier, sailor, and marine corps man: he is told that he does not have to obey his officer if he makes him do one of these things. So, Nuremberg is part of the law of the land. How can you say it isn't? There is no question about it. It's part of the law of the land.

Few are as definite as Judge C on this matter however. Some speak at times as if it is only a matter of having the right case, which means, apparently, a case in which rights of the defendants spelled out in the international law in question are *directly* at issue. This seems to be Judge Northrop's point in a case where the defendants were tried for defacing government records:

> . . . these defendants do not have the standing to raise the validity of governmental actions, either under international law or constitutional law, on the grounds that the rights of parties not before this court are violated. Courts must deal with the case in hand, and not imaginary ones.[16]

Judge Thomsen seemed to be saying the same thing in the colloquy with the Catonsville Nine: If only this were a question of refusing to step forward for induction rather than the destruction and obliteration of draft records . . .

Remarks like these by Judge Northrop and Judge Thomsen, taken alone, suggest that a court just might proceed if the case were the right one. This implies no special need for action by agencies outside the legal system or even by the Supreme Court (though Judge Thomsen also feels the need of action from this quarter). Judge C has an even more definite and more enlarged conception of the role of the lower courts in this matter. Asked about a law-making role for lower courts ("Do you think that there is such a thing as judicial legislation?"), he said,

Oh sure there is, sure there is, and I think we all do it to some extent in the judiciary. And I think that we have to, . . . because if we didn't, then we wouldn't serve any purpose. You could just put the law in the slot and we could put the trangression in the slot and out would come an answer. I don't believe that the system is meant to be that way.

Most of the judges do not have the definite convictions of either Judge E or Judge C, nor do they see themselves deciding the matter. They are simply undecided, and they want to see the matter resolved either at another level of the judiciary than their own or by another agency than the judiciary. When he was asked if he would allow the introduction of principles of international law into a case before him, Judge B. said:

It is a difficult and complicated question, but it has to be. Each one of these claims has to be decided on its merit. All I would say to you is, however, every judge that I've heard of passing on this has always turned it down. I don't know why, but they always have.

Judge Y has similar feelings, and is interested in seeing the situation clarified:

Well, I don't think we can, at the present status of the law, you see. I think that maybe they should at some point. And I don't know who is going to take a lead on it. But I can't do it. I mean, I don't have that kind of power or authority. I don't think it was ever tried in any of the cases to speak of. It was generally agreed that they were not going to.

If the judges manifest confusion and inhibition, they also point in the direction which they think that development will take. Judge Y and Judge E, both rather conservative, have similar expectations. According to Judge Y,

We are dedicated to the idea that we have a rule of law and not a rule of men. I think that to that extent that we can adhere, maybe with limitations initially, adhere to principles of international law and applying some local laws, local United States law, whether they be actually local or federal; I think that we should do so, because I think that we've got to move in the direction of greater compliance or involvement with international law.

Judge E, who is, as we have seen, quite sensitive to issues of national sovereignty, nevertheless concedes that he is "pretty well convinced, and long have been, that we have to broaden law so that it reaches across national boundaries."

Asked who should supply the initiative to change the law in this way, some judges mention Congress:

That's up to the courts if the person violates the law. And if the law is improper, immoral, or illegal, then you have to change it elsewhere, in the legislature. [Judge Y]

And Judge W remarked that "It's not a justiciable question unless the Congress of the United States makes it so."

But Congress had itself given up its initiative in this matter, and this had far-reaching implications. For example, Nicholas D. Katzenbach, as undersecretary of state, was able to say in 1967, with a measure of historical support but without constitutional warrant, that declarations of war are "outmoded in the international arena." The implied corollary to this position was that the President can initiate hostilities at his own discretion without a declaration of war by Congress. After the session of the Senate Foreign Relations Committee at which Katzenbach said this, Senator William Fulbright, Committee Chairman, commented:

The fact that Congress has acquiesced in, or at the very least has failed to challenge, the transfer of the war power from itself to the executive is probably the most important single fact accounting for the speed and virtual completeness of the transfer.[17]

For most of the judges, however, it was to the Supreme Court that one must look for the change in law in question. Some conceded that the framework for adjudication of the legality of the war exists, but as Judge A said,

Until the majority of the Supreme Court say differently, we must follow the past decisions that it is not a justiciable question. . . . It certainly hasn't grown to proportions yet where it is recognized as a justiciable issue. Some lower court judges, a judge in Massachusetts a while back has strained the law a bit,[18] in my opinion, in connection with the so called subjective judgment of a person in reference to fighting in Vietnam, but outside that particular instance, it hasn't gone too far yet. The case is now before the United States Supreme Court.

It will be recalled that Judge Thomsen, in the colloquy after the Catonsville Trial, also anticipated Supreme Court determination of whether or not the legality of the Vietnam war was justiciable. Division of opinion in this direction extends, as we saw, to the Supreme Court itself, where Justices Stewart and Douglas had urged review. Judge C felt strongly with Douglas and Stewart and adopted the language of the former.

I think that the Supreme Court owes it to these people, who take this chance, in the words of Justice Douglas, not to duck the issue. It should be decided. . . . It's too important a problem, that if the war is illegal, and if he says I will not go and be willing to risk everything that you risk by doing that, I think he's entitled to have the Supreme Court of the United States quit ducking the issue and pass on it.

During the period which we have considered, the Supreme Court did continue to duck it.

CONCLUSIONS

Chapter Ten

As the Crisis Lifts

The peace movement did not succeed in getting the judiciary to declare the war illegal. The most dramatic hope which the movement held out for its policy of legal confrontation was not realized: the nation's military policy would not be dealt with as segregation had been. The peace militants paid a heavy price for their efforts. Most, though not all, were convicted. Furthermore in most, though not all, instances conviction followed a trial in which they were prevented from defending themselves on the basis of the issues which had actually prompted them to act. At this obvious level, the peace movement's policy of legal confrontation would have to be considered a failure.

During this period, the Supreme Court dealt with the key issue of the war's legality by refusing to decide and by refusing to say why it refused to decide. It was one thing for it to have reversed its previous course and to have taken a stand against state and local laws (in the matter of segregation). It was quite another to challenge the President and Congress during a time of national emergency.

On the same obvious level at which we saw the peace movement policy to be a legal failure, the behavior of the judiciary seems to have been a moral failure. To say this is to condemn the judiciary because the Supreme Court refused to take certain risks. But there is nothing intrinsically moral about risk-taking. In one instance it

may be heroic, in another quite foolish. In the case at hand, the
Court's behavior might be defended as a quite reasonable exercise
of prudence, dictated by the seriousness of its responsibility. It refused to risk a potentially destructive clash with executive and legislature, a clash which might have crippled the judiciary in the system
of checks and balances and humiliated it in the eyes of the public,
whose confidence it must have if it is to continue as the place where
justice is available. When the crisis eases, the issues which were
passed over in silence can be raised again.

This argument is attractive enough to merit close scrutiny. The
policy of refusal and silence, defended as a strategy for avoiding
risks, involved a series of risks of its own. If Professor Wechsler is
correct, the refusal to review the war-making decisions of the executive amounted to a decision in constitutional law to give up the power
to review them. Even if, as seems more likely, Wechsler is wrong, the
Court's abstaining at a time when the power to initiate military action was passing from Congress to the President compounded the
de facto distortion of the system of checks and balances in favor of
the executive. The Court's abstaining not only involved a risk, it
risked the very thing it was intended to protect: effectiveness in the
system of checks and balances.

By its silence on the reasons for abstention, the Court took a risk
with something else that it wanted to protect—public confidence.
The courtroom is the place where society makes its most deliberate
and explicit moral judgments. Because of this, it is traditionally—
even necessarily—a place of great articulation: an essential part of
the expectation of justice is the expectation of reasons, reasons why
the accused are found innocent or guilty. Professor Hughes has put
this well:

> A central plank in the concept of a just legal system is that, though
> there may be some exceptions, judgments shall generally be sup-
> ported by an opinion which is a public parade of the reasoning on
> which the judgment stands.[1]

Hughes recommends the explanation of the traditionally unex-
plained *certiorari denied,* by which the Supreme Court refuses review.

The Court's posture during the period of its encounter with the peace movement can scarcely be justified as effective risk-avoidance, since the risks were not avoided. If the judiciary is to be justified in terms of its own integrity and its place in the confidence of the public, then this will have to be on the basis of the other things which it did. As we turn to these, we should begin by noting that if the Supreme Court silently refused to rule the war illegal, it also silently refused to rule it legal, though there was ample occasion for it to do that if it had wished. The judiciary did not oppose the President and Congress as it might have, but neither did it rush into a monolithic unity with them.

There was also considerable differentiation of response within the legal system. On the part of the Supreme Court, there were some instances of important departures from the position of *certiorari denied* even in war-related questions. As we saw, the Court did speak to the First Amendment issues involved in draft card burning. In this it supported the government position. But toward the end of the period which we have considered, it was willing to enter the question of the way in which selective service laws were being administered. Here its decisions ran counter to the government policy of punitive reclassification.

Among the cases which we considered in detail there was also a variety in judicial response. There was one acquittal and one reversal on appeal. In one of the cases, the jury was allowed to take into account the beliefs of the defendants about the illegality of the war in deciding their guilt or innocence. There were judges, including two Supreme Court justices, who regarded the question of the war's legality as justiciable, and said so. The legal system had its own dissenting minority. In a time of crisis, the moral burden is often assumed by individuals who are at odds with their peers. Perhaps the era in which courts address the issues which those of the 1960s passed over will regard such individuals as moral—and legal—heroes.

One can, we believe, make a reasonable case for the moral justification of the judiciary in its encounter with the peace movement, on the basis of its secondary decisions and the actions of its dissenting minority. But if we look beyond explicit decisions and dissents formally given or refused and consider the legal process in a broader sense, we touch upon another of its dimensions with, we believe, real bearing on the legal system's discharge of its moral responsibility. The judiciary did not satisfy the best hope of the peace movement by declaring the war illegal, nor the best hope of the public for clear decisions effectively reasoned. But it did provide the peace movement with a powerful forum from which it could and did make its case, and this should be considered in connection with the public's expectation of justice.

There is no doubt that the trials like those which we have discussed did help arouse the conscience of the nation in a way which *eventually* made anti-war sentiment an important political current. If this status as a political current came too late as far as the peace militant was concerned, still, even as it was growing, it helped force Lyndon Johnson out of the presidential race and turned the community against the prevailing selective service practices.

For the peace movement, this use of the courts would have to be considered a success. As such, it contains a powerful irony. Legal confrontation was the policy of the peace militants who were not radical pacifists and who hoped to enlist the coercion of law in their cause. In this they failed. They did succeed in helping to arouse consciences and to generate the eventual anti-war political current. But their success in this was of the sort envisioned by radical pacifists: not by coercion, but by persuasion, example, witness. The policy of legal encounter, in short, proved to be a fairly acceptable strategy of sensitization.

Can the courts be regarded as anything other than an unwilling accomplice in this work of sensitization? Did they really do any more than provide stage setting for the peace militant as moral hero, whose impact on the public was really due to the press? The press *was* indispensable, but the drama itself was courtroom drama. The courts did not supply only the stage setting, they also provided the structure of the action. The clash of articulate positions and personalities in an encounter where the stakes involve both future victims of a distant war and the future freedom of the just men and women accused, the shaping of the whole event toward a climax of guilty or not guilty, it is to this that the sensitive respond. That drama has always belonged to the doing of justice in court. The press can report it well or badly, but the press cannot make it.

What is suggested here is that the community's expectation of justice, though it may be primarily oriented to the proper verdict, clearly explained, can draw some sustenance from such theatre. The case that it can rests on the notion that even the drama which terminates in the wrong decision may contain enough of the authentic sights and sounds of justice to be responsive to the public's hope. By the sights and sounds of justice we mean such things as the day in court, the attention of the prosecution, the usually adequate and often (in the cases which we considered, for example) eminently qualified defense, the articulation of the case from both sides, perhaps in front of the jury, perhaps only in an accompanying public commentary on it. A public with sufficient basic wisdom to realize that institutions, like persons, often perform poorly, that they need time to adjust to extraordinary demands and to reconcile inner conflict, can legitimately draw assurance from this.

If we add the sights and sounds of justice in the making to its secondary decisions and the actions of its dissenting minority, then the moral position of the judiciary during the latter half of the 1960s seems defensible, if not heroic. But it is defensible as a crisis behavior, itself pointing toward the period when the crisis lifts, a time when one imagines that cases will reach the jury in their own completeness and courts will handle all the decisions for which they are responsible with firmness and a public parade of reasons. That moment has yet to arrive, but in the interest of anticipating it, let us briefly consider some of the issues in which development can be expected and in which it may already be under way.

In the courtroom itself there seems to be a marked prospect for change in the relation of judge and jury. There appear, in fact, to be two aspects of the jury's position in relation to the judge which are open to development in the near future and whose development would mean a change in jury responsibility and a more meaningful "judgment by one's peers." One is in the area of what the jury can consider. As we noted in the case of the Oakland Seven, there are jurisdictions where the jury can consider motive, something which enlarges the range of their responsibility.

A second aspect of the judge-jury relationship in which changes can be anticipated is in the jury's awareness of its own power. The nullification issue is on highly unstable ground, resting as it does on the concealment from jurors of their own power at a time when education and communication threaten that concealment. It is interesting to speculate upon the effect that an advertising campaign, aimed at saturating the region of an important trial with the information that the jury can nullify, would have on jury selection. But even without this the word is getting out. The authors of this study have, along with millions of their fellow citizens, seen the nullification issue the subject of a prime-time television drama in which the lawyer-hero operated it successfully in favor of a sympathetic defendant. In the future the attempt to maintain the rule against jurors being informed about this might lead to the attempt to select less and less informed jurors and a *voir dire* aimed at ignorance. We do not pretend, of course, that a jury conscious of its power to nullify would be an unmixed blessing. Such juries may often act against the course of justice. We say only that the relation of such a group to the judge will be qualitatively different. In the long run it should be an improvement if it is true that responsibility is better served by those who understand it well than by those who do not.

And what of the prospects for the judiciary's reclaiming its place in the system of checks and balances? More than anything, this is a matter of its confronting the war-making power of the President, which in turn, means a change of posture on the issue of the justiciability of the war. As the decade of the 1970s opened and the Vietnam conflict wound its way through its increasingly unpopular final stages, the legal offensive against it continued. But the offensive no longer took the form of civil disobedience. The court challenges which have become most important are no longer government prosecutions of persons who refuse to be drafted or who burn their draft cards but suits by citizens who asserted that the war infringed upon their rights. Typically, they sought to have it declared unconstitutional for lack of congressional declaration. Among the important cases—cases which incidentally gave more judges an opportunity to speak on the matter—were *Mottola* v. *Nixon*,[2] *Berk* v. *Laird*,[3] and *Holtzman* v. *Richardson*.[4]

Judge William T. Sweigert of the Northern District of California ruled on the first of these in September 1970. We spoke of Judge Sweigert in the preceding chapter, where we characterized his outlook as conservative.[5] *Mottola* v. *Nixon* was a suit by three reservists and a draft registrant seeking to enjoin the government from conducting military operations in Cambodia and also seeking a declaration that the plaintiffs had the right to refuse to participate in what they regarded as an unconstitutional war. In a scholarly but forcefully written opinion Judge Sweigert reviewed the grounds on which the government most frequently defended itself against suits of this sort: lack of standing of the plaintiff, immunity of the President from suit, and the claim that the issue itself is a political question. His comment on the government challenge to the plaintiff's standing (the challenge which normally maintains that it cannot be demonstrated that the plaintiff actually will suffer the harm against which he seeks protection) is a good example of his outlook as this opinion expresses it.

> To argue that these three members of our armed forces reserves should have to wait until they are actually called and ordered to service in the Vietnam war before acquiring "standing" to raise the question of the validity of such an order, is such a thin, unworthy distinction that we decline to recognize it as ground for refusing "standing." To say that these three plaintiffs must wait until they are called up, perhaps suddenly, and ordered to the Vietnam area, perhaps quickly, and then file a court suit for a declaration of their legal rights, perhaps with too little time to do so, borders, we think, on the absurd.[6]

Turning to the ways in which he feels the judiciary usually responds to these challenges, Judge Sweigert says:

> Whatever the ultimate decision on the merits of the constitutional question may be, we are of the opinion that the courts, eschewing indecision, inaction or avoidance on such grounds as "no standing," "sovereign immunity" and "political question," should discharge their traditional responsibility for interpreting the Constitution of the United States.[7]

This comment about responsibility includes the Supreme Court, at which his final words are directed:

> Upon the foregoing considerations, this court has made its order, filed herewith, designed to further, so far as a District Court can appropriately do so, an ultimate ruling in our Ninth Circuit, and, hopefully, by the Supreme Court, upon all the important issues here considered.[8]

Judge Sweigert's comments place him in the dissenting minority along with Justice Douglas, whose remarks on such matters the opinion in *Mottola* v. *Nixon* brings to mind. Obviously, the determination to accept the responsibility for decision on the momentous issue of the war's legality can take root in the conservative as well as the liberal sense of judicial duty.

During the same month, September 1970, Judge Orrin G. Judd of the Eastern District of New York ruled in the case of an Army enlisted man who sought to enjoin the Secretary of Defense from sending him to Vietnam. In *Berk* v. *Laird* Judge Judd ruled against the plaintiff, holding the war to be constitutional because congressional acts of appropriation amounted to congressional authorization. This decision, which was affirmed on appeal, brought no joy to the peace movement. But it, no less than the opinion of Judge Sweigert, asserted the judiciary's claim to the issue of the war's legality and rejected the posture that it was a "political question."

Judge Judd would be heard from again. In June 1973 he refused to dismiss a suit by Congresswoman Elizabeth Holtzman alleging that the President's use of military forces in Cambodia usurped congressional war-making power. He maintained that the congresswoman's legislative responsibility gave her standing in the matter and reasserted his position that the political question doctrine did not render the issue nonjusticiable.

The Supreme Court denied certiorari in *Berk* v. *Laird*. Judge Sweigert was reversed on appeal in *Mottola* v. *Nixon,* but on the grounds of lack of standing, not political question. Though the dissenting minority which works on the conscience of the judiciary has acquired new members, it has yet to prevail.

Meanwhile, the development of the judiciary's position has been influenced from the outside by two series of events whose direct impact has been upon the executive and the effect of which has been to inhibit its power. The first of these has been the failure, since the beginning of the seventies, of Justice Department prosecutions for war-related crimes. The Harrisburg case which saw the Berrigan brothers and their associates in court once again, the trial of Daniel Ellsberg and Anthony Russo for having published the Pentagon Papers, and, most recently, the prosecution of the Gainsville Eight on charges that they conspired to disrupt by violence the Republican national convention of 1972 are all instances of this failure. These trials discredited the Justice Department, not so much because they did not result in convictions, but because of the character of the prosecutions. The government's reliance upon paid informers and electronic surveillance would have been repugnant to juries and the general public in any era. It was all the more so at a time when the Watergate scandal had begun to loom large in the nation's consciousness. It even offered a basis for the accusation that the Justice Department was pursuing weak or nonexistent cases for the purpose of harassment and intimidation.

The second influence was congressional action to restore its own initiative in the exercise of the war-making power and with it the legislature's place in the system of checks and balances. On the seventh of November, 1973, a war powers bill became law, requiring that the President inform the Congress within forty-eight hours of any commitment of United States' troops to hostilities abroad. Congress may, then, terminate the commitment after sixty days by refusing to approve it. The bill became law when Congress overrode a presidential veto, which clearly evidenced the determination of senators and representatives to recover ground which they felt had been lost.

During the Vietnam war, a large and daring peace movement confronted a judiciary disposed by prudence to a largely passive behavior of survival. But the war is over and the crisis activists have gone home. Neither by its size nor by its dramatic risk-taking does the peace movement command our attention now. It is quiet in the hands of dedicated caretakers.

The judiciary, however, shows signs of stirring from its relative passivity. Survival is less the issue now. After several years of debate, the question of the power to declare war has become familiar while the war itself has receded somewhat in the nation's consciousness. Judicial discretion, which once seemed to have tacitly declared that the judiciary's judgment was stifled by the strangeness of the war power issue and the momentousness of the war itself, is now in a position to acknowledge and embrace the reasons for self-assertion.

NOTES

Justice and Jeopardy

1. This term was proposed by Beverly Woodward in her "Nuremberg Law and the U.S. Courts," *Dissent,* March–April 1969, p.130.

2. The complete A.C.L.U. definition is as follows: "The wilful, non-violent and public violation of valid laws because the violator deems them to be unjust, or because their violation will focus public attention on other injustices in the society to which such laws may or may not be related." See A.C.L.U. News Release, New York, February 2, 1968.

3. Abe Fortas, *Concerning Dissent and Civil Disobedience,* New York: The New American Library Inc. 1968. This work distressed many peace militants because of the "hard line" which it took on the punishment of conscientious law violators.

4. Ibid., p.34.

5. Ibid., p.32. This use of the term owes nothing to the fact that the Fortas work is in a popular and nontechnical style. The same broad use is also found in technical journals. Thus Professor Graham Hughes in his "Civil Disobedience and the Political Question Doctrine" (*N.Y.U. Law Review* Vol 43, No.1, March 1968) also uses it for the non-violent breaking of both valid and invalid laws.

6. As the war "wound down" and then stopped in the early seventies, the pressure for solidarity lessened and Congress began to reassert itself. There were serious moves to legislate a halt to the bombing of North Vietnam, and to cut off money generally for military operations in Southeast Asia. As this volume goes to press, Congress has succeeded in passing a bill which limits presidential exercise of the war-making power by requiring approval of Congress within sixty days of any entry into hostilities. We return to this in our conclusions.

7. *New York Times,* February 6, 1966.

8. *Downdraft,* May 1965.

9. Colloquy—Court Transcript, p.33.

10. Ibid.

11. October 31, 1968.

12. United States Code, Title 28, Sec. 453.

13. We will also consider the case of David O'Brien, which led to an important Supreme Court decision on freedom of speech for dissenters and, more briefly, those of Oestereich and Gutknecht for their impact on the practice of punitive reclassification by the Selective Service System.

These trials have been selected because they were important events in the encounter to which this book is devoted and because in them the issues of morality v. legality are effectively posed. Obviously our selections do not exhaust the list of such trials, and other choices would be defensible in view of the same project. But no attempt has been made to be exhaustive. Our purpose has been to get at the fundamental character of the struggle, its essence if you wish, through particular instances in which this fundamental character is effectively revealed.

14. *Luftig* v. *McNamara*, 373, F2d 664 (D.C.D. of C. 1966).

15. *The Great Rights,* ed. Edmund Cahn (New York: Macmillan, 1963), p.134.

16. Ibid., p.137.

17. Herbert Wechsler, "Toward Neutral Principles of Constitutional Law," *Harvard Law Review,* Vol LXXVI, No.1 (Nov. 1959), p.9.

18. Graham Hughes, "Civil Disobedience and the Political Question Doctrine," p.15.

19. Alexander M. Bickel, *The Least Dangerous Branch* (New York: Bobbs Merrill, 1962) p.184.

2. The Trials of David Henry Mitchell III

1. *Downdraft,* May 1964.

2. In August, 1961, he was charged with disorderly conduct while protesting at the Polaris submarine site in New London, Connecticut. This arrest resulted in a conviction and a fine which Mitchell chose to work off with seventy-five days in prison. After nineteen days the sentence was nullified. In the following month, he was arrested while taking part in a vigil in front of the Soviet Mission to protest Russian hydrogen bomb tests. Charges were dismissed in this case.

3. Letter to Draft Board, December 3, 1961.

4. *Downdraft,* May 1964.

5. Actually, he characterized them as "utterly irrelevant" and as "spurious issues," in his Memorandum of Decision after Trial, pp.51–70.

6. Court Transcript, pp.360–365.

7. Ibid., p.ii.

8. Ibid., p.iii.

9. *Downdraft,* May 1964.

10. Ibid.

11. Memorandum, p.32.

12. Ibid., pp.65–66.

13. Ibid., p.66.
14. Ibid., p.68.
15. Ibid., p.70.
16. Brief for the Appellee, p.28, emphasis added.
17. Ibid., p.32. *United States* v. *Macintosh,* 283 U.S. 605 p.624 (1931).
18. Appellant's Reply Brief, p.9.
19. 354 F2d 767 (2d Cir. 1966).
20. Court Transcript, p.1000.
21. Ibid., 1001–1002. One of the many citations used by Mitchell to develop this aspect of his legal argument was the following: Article II, Sec. 2 of Control Council Law No.10

2. Any person, without regard to nationality or the capacity in which he acted, is deemed to have committed a crime as defined in paragraph 1 of this Article, if he

a) was a principal or
b) was an accessory to the commission of any such crime or ordered or abetted the same or
c) took a consenting part therein or
d) was connected with plans or enterprises involving its commission or
e) was a member of any organization or group connected with the commission of any such crime or
f) with reference to paragraph 1a) if he held a high political civil or military (including General Staff) position in Germany or in one of its Allies, co-belligerents or satellites or held high position in the financial, industrial or economic life of any such country.

22. Court Transcript II, p.5.
23. Ibid., p.18.
24. Ibid., p.8.
25. Ibid., pp.15–16.
26. Judicial Instructions, pp.1035–1036.
27. Court Transcript, p.1025.
28. Ibid., pp.1079–1080.
29. Ibid., p.1086.
30. Ibid., p.1085.
31. Ibid.
32. Appellant's Brief, p.8.
33. 369 F2d 324 (2d Cir. 1966).
34. Petition for a Writ of Certiorari, p.15.
35. Ibid.
36. Brief for U.S. in Opposition, p.2.
37. Ibid., p.3. A person has *legal standing* in this context when he is defending a legally protected right.
38. Ibid., p.4.
39. *Mitchell* v. *United States,* 386 U.S. 972 (1967).

40. Mitchell's five-year sentence may be compared with others for draft refusal at this time and in subsequent years; average sentence in 1967—32.1 months; 1968—37.3; 1969—36.3; 1970—33.5; 1971—29.1. Cf. Richard L. Killmer and Charles P. Lutz, *To Go or Not To Go: Conscience, War and The Draft* (Minneapolis, Augsburg, 1972).

3. David John Miller

1. House Report No.747, August 9, 1965.
2. *Congressional Record,* House, August 10, 1965, p.19135.
3. Ibid., p.19669.
4. Letter to the author of February 18, 1969. The demonstration against Niagara Mohawk protesting discriminatory hiring practices resulted in a trial on trespass charges. Miller was found guilty and served time in jail.
5. The Catholic Worker Movement consists of a small number of lay Catholics who live in voluntary poverty and serve the poor in the Bowery section of New York City. Since its inception, its ideological beliefs have included opposition to war in any form and to compulsory military service.
6. Received July 15, 1965.
7. Received August 24, 1965.
8. Court Transcript, pp.267–269.
9. Letter to author of February 18, 1969.
10. Court Transcript, p.308.
11. Government Memorandum in Opposition to Dismiss, p.53.
12. Court Transcript, p.281.
13. Emphasis in original. *Information for Whitehall Speakout Participants.*
14. Court Transcript, p.273.
15. Ibid., p.274.
16. Ibid.
17. *Stromberg* v. *California,* 283, U.S. 359 (1931).
18. *West Virginia State Board of Education et al.* v. *Barnette et al.,* 319 U.S. 624 (1943).
19. *Thornhill* v. *Alabama,* 310 U.S. 88 (1940).
20. When they first presented this motion, Karpatkin and Fraenkel added that Miller's rights to assembly and political freedom under the Ninth and Tenth Amendments had also been threatened.
21. Court Transcript, p.149.
22. Ibid., p.341.
23. Ibid., p.329.
24. Ibid.
25. Ibid., p.330.
26. Ibid., p.334.
27. Ibid., p.347.
28. Opinion of Tyler, D.J., March 7, 1966.

29. Ibid.

30. Minutes of Sentence, March 15, 1966, p.18.

31. 367 F2d 72, p.73 (2d Cir. 1966).

32. Ibid.

33. Appellant's Brief, p.11.

34. 367 F2d, p.77.

35. Appellant's Brief, p.33.

36. *Milk Wagon Drivers Union of Chicago Local 753, et al.* v. *Meadow-moor Dairies, Inc.*, 312 U.S. 287, p.293 (1941).

37. *Schenk* v. *United States*, 249 U.S. 47, p.52 (1919).

38. Court Transcript, p.106.

39. *David Miller* v. *United States*, 367 F2d 72, p.81 (DCSDNY 1966).

40. Ibid., p.82.

41. Ibid.

42. Petition for a Writ of Certiorari, p.18.

43. The brief noted that the Court of Appeals' weighing of the government interest side of the balance consisted chiefly of itemizing advantages which carrying a draft card might have for the *registrant*. Benefits of the *government* are far fewer and relate primarily to instances of national catastrophe. Emphasis in original.

44. Brief for the U.S. in Opposition, pp.4–5.

45. Ibid., p.8.

46. These included the questions: Did Congress intend to make every non-possession of a draft card a crime? Is the surrender of the card—to the Government itself—a form of protest protected by the First Amendment? Brief Amicus Curiae, p.3.

47. *United States* v. *David O'Brien*, 391 U.S. 367, p.375 (1968).

48. Ibid., pp.381–382.

49. Ibid.

50. Because the original judgment of the District Court was held to have been correct, there was no need to consider the Court of Appeals affirmation of a conviction for non-possession.

51. Court Transcript, p.22.

52. Ibid., p.33.

53. Miller had married while his case was in process.

54. Miller's lawyers objected to this on the grounds that he was sentenced for a crime other than the one for which he was convicted. While his status with the draft board would inevitably lead to another indictment, Karpatkin felt that the issues should be separated. This argument, as well as the charge that this sentence constituted "cruel and unusual punishment," was rejected as grounds for bond and appeal by Judge Tyler.

55. Ibid., pp.43–44.

56. Ibid., p.45.

57. Ibid., p.46.

4. The Fort Hood Three

1. Statement prepared jointly and read by Dennis Mora at the press conference, New York City, June 30, 1966.

2. Specifically: Article I, Section B, Clause 11, of the Charter of the United Nations of 1945; Southeast Asia Collective Defense Treaty 1954; The Geneva Agreement of 1954; The Nuremberg Judgment; and The Kellogg-Briand Pact of 1928. They maintained that the court had this jurisdiction under the United States Constitution (Article III, Section 2, Clause 1) and United States Code, Title 18, Sections 1331, 1361, and 2201.

3. Ruling of the Court, Civil Action 1733-66, July 11, 1966.

4. Record of Trial, p.3.

5. Ibid.

6. Ibid., p.41.

7. Ibid., p.65.

8. Ibid.

9. Ibid., p.66.

10. Ibid., p.9.

11. Ibid.

12. Ibid., p.10.

13. Ibid.

14. This request had previously been made to the Commanding General of the First United States Army, who convened the Court. He had denied it as unnecessary and immaterial.

15. Record of Trial, p.33.

16. Ibid., p.67.

17. Ibid.

18. Ibid.

19. Chapter XXVII, par.169, p.321 (emphasis added).

20. Brief of Accused submitted to Commanding General First U.S. Army (1966), p.4.

21. July 12, 1966, Defense Exhibit E.

22. Record of Trial, p.50.

23. Ibid., p.78.

24. Ibid., p.81.

25. Ibid., p.84.

26. Ibid., p.117.

27. Ibid., p.119.

28. Ibid., p.120.

29. *The Great Rights* (1960), p.136.

30. 273 U.S. 536, p.540 (1927).

31. 369 U.S. 186 (1962).

32. *Larson* v. *Domestic and Foreign Commerce Corp.*, 337 U.S. 682 (1949) citing *United States* v. *Lee*, 106 U.S. 196 (1882).

33. *The Great Rights* (1960), pp.134–135.

34. *Luftig* v. *McNamara,* 373 F2d 665–666 (1966).

35. Termed United States Army Court of Military Review since 1969. It is a three member panel of military officers who are lawyers.

36. Reply to Assignment of Errors, p.11.

37. Ibid., p.15.

38. Ibid., pp.20–21.

39. Board of Review, June 27, 1967, p.2.

40. *Wyatt Tee Walker et al.* v. *City of Birmingham,* 388 U.S. 307 (1967).

41. Petition for a Writ of Certiorari, p.10.

42. *New York Times,* November 14, 1967.

43. Ibid.

44. *Mora et al.* v. *McNamara Secretary of Defense, et al.,* 389 U.S. 934–935 (1967).

45. Ibid., p.936.

46. Ibid., p.937.

47. Ibid.

48. Ibid., p.935.

49. *New York Times,* November 6, 1967. These cases were *Ex Parte Milligan,* 71 U.S. (4 WALL.) 2 (1866) and *Duncan* v. *Kahanamoku,* 327 U.S. 304 (1946).

5. The Conspiracy of Dr. Spock et al.

1. For example, on December 16, 1968, the Supreme Court held illegal a draft board's use of delinquency proceedings to change a registrant's draft classification. This was *Oestereich* v. *Selective Service System Local Board No. 11, Cheyenne, Wyoming, et al.,* 393 U.S. 233 (1968). The Justice Department had submitted a brief which conceded that the registrant had been improperly classified, but claimed judicial review was unavailable. On January 19, 1970, in *Gutknecht* v. *United States,* 394 U.S. 997 (1970), the Supreme Court held that delinquency proceedings could not be used to move a registrant up in the order of induction thereby hastening his induction. In *Breen* v. *Selective Service System Local Board No. 16,* Bridgeport, Conn. 396 U.S. 460 (1970), the Court held both that a registrant could not be reclassified for turning in a draft card and that a registrant could take court action to challenge a reclassification. The Breen decision followed Gutknecht by a week —January 21, 1970.

2. 393 U.S. 233, p.237 (1968).

3. Ibid.

4. Ibid.

5. Court Transcript II, p.25.

6. Ibid., XVIII, p.123.

7. Ibid., XVIII, p.130.

8. Ibid., XVIII, p.126.

9. Ibid., XVIII, p.123.

10. Ibid., II, p.24.

11. Ibid., II, p.25.

12. Ibid., II, p.47.

13. There were at least three statements similar in intent to "The Call" circulating at the time. They were sponsored by groups of professionals, particularly those associated with young people on college campuses. A group known as Clergy and Laymen Concerned about the War in Vietnam also formulated a statement, "Conscience and Conscription," in support of conscientious objection to the war. Coffin and the Rev. Robert McAfee Brown were members of this group and had helped in drafting the statement. Now there was an attempt to coordinate these parallel efforts by relating them, at least through public announcement, to the events of Stop The Draft Week.

14. The activities of this group included counseling, legal and financial assistance, and in some instances a communal life style. One of its founders, David Harris, served a three-year sentence for refusing induction.

15. Ibid., II, p.71. Emphasis added.

16. Jessica Mitford, in her *The Trial of Dr. Spock* (New York: Alfred Knopf, 1969), devotes an interesting chapter to the lawyers involved in the case.

17. Ibid., XVIII, p.14.

18. Ibid., II, p.49.

19. Ibid., XIX, p.53.

20. Ibid., X, p.61.

21. Ibid., XVI, p.73.

22. Ibid., X, p.83.

23. Ibid., XII, p.35.

24. Ibid., IX, p.60.

25. Ibid.

26. Ibid., X, p.38.

27. Ibid., XVI, p.50.

28. Ibid., XII, p.71.

29. Ibid., XIII, p.139.

30. Ibid., XVI, p.112.

31. Ibid., XVIII, p.136.

32. Ibid., XVIII, pp.139–140.

33. Ibid., XVIII, p.141.

34. Ibid.

35. Ibid., XVIII, p.146.

36. Ibid., XIX, p.73.

37. Ibid., XIX, p.54.

38. Quoted by Judge Ford from Judge Gaston's address to a Princeton University audience in 1835.

39. Court Transcript, Vol. XX, pp.24–25.

40. *United States* v. *Spock et al.,* 416 F2d 185.

41. Ibid., p.186.

42. Instances of illegal acts cited were: seeking sanctuary in other countries, refusal to obey illegal and immoral orders in the armed services, unlawful refusal of induction.

43. *Scales* v. *United States,* 367 U.S. 203 (1961) and *Noto* v. *United States,* 367 U.S. 290 (1961).

44. Ibid., p.188.

45. Ibid., p.190.

46. Majority Section II, para.2–3, question no.1.

47. *United States* v. *Gernie,* 252 F2d 664 (2d Cir. 1958).

48. Ibid., p.182.

6. *The Oakland Seven Conspiracy*

1. *San Francisco Chronicle,* May 29, 1969.

2. Stop The Draft October 17, Stop The Draft Week Committee, Campus Stop The Draft Week.

3. Ibid.

4. Not all of the men finally indicted were ever students at the University, e.g. Jeff Segal and Terrence Cannon. They were, however, members of the campus organization.

5. Penal Code Section 602j provided that any person who entered upon any form of real property with the intention of interfering with, obstructing or injuring any lawful business is guilty of *trespass.* Penal Code Section 148 provides that every person who willfully resists, delays, or obstructs any public officer in the discharge of his duty is guilty of a crime (for brevity's sake) known as *resisting.* Penal Code Section 370 defines public nuisance as "anything which is injurious to health, or is indecent, or offensive to the senses, or an obstruction to the free use of property . . ." while Penal Code Section 372 provides that anyone maintaining public nuisance commits a misdemeanor. (All of the above are misdemeanor offenses.)

6. These were confiscated prior to the demonstration.

7. *San Francisco Chronicle,* February 12, 1969.

8. October 2 meeting.

9. Reporter's Partial Transcript, Charles Garry's closing argument, p.59.

10. Jensen intimated that Segal, from the National Office of Students for a Democratic Society, had been hired as an organizer and paid for his work preparing this demonstration. Reporter's Partial Transcript, Closing Argument on Behalf of the People, p.80.

11. Ibid., p.90.

12. Ibid., pp.139–140.

13. Reporter's Partial Transcript, Instructions to the Jury, p.34.

14. These instructions are further considered in the following pages.

15. All citations are taken from the Court Reporter's Transcript, Vol. XIX, June 14, 1968.

16. All citations are taken from the Court Reporter's Partial Transcript, Wednesday, March 26, 1969.

17. Jessica Mitford, *The Trial of Dr. Spock,* p.234.

18. Ibid., p.232. Emphasis in the original.

19. Interview, April 19, 1969.

7. *The Catonsville Nine*

1. The defendants in this trial resulting from U.S. Grand Jury indictment following the 1968 Democratic Convention in Chicago included: Abbie Hoffman, David Dellinger, Gerry Rubin, John Froines. Lee Weiner, Rennie Davis, Tom Hayden and, initially, Bobby Seale. Judge Julius Hoffman presided.

2. This type of radicalism among Catholics had a number of sources. One of these was a kind of belated recognition of the model of the Catholic Workers and one of their founders Dorothy Day. David Miller (see Chapter 3), David O'Brien, James Forest, and James Cornell were examplars of draft resistance from within this movement. To these may be added the impact of the self-immolation of Roger La Porte, a high school student who burned himself to death. There was some ambiguity in their relation to the raiders, however. If the Catholic Workers inspired resistance, they were themselves totally non-violent. They did not encourage actions like the burning of draft files however much the proponents of the latter might distinguish attacks on property from attacks on persons. (James Forest, a Worker who took part in the Milwaukee draft board raid, was an exception.) If the attitude of the Catholic Workers could be called supportive, it did not consist of approval of the character of the actions. It was "non-judgmental" as one Worker interviewed said.

3. The Baltimore County Grand Jury had added counts of assault and robbery.

4. Court Transcript, pp.224–225.

5. Ibid., p.225.

6. See *United States* v. *Moylan* 417 F2d 1002 (4th Cir. 1969).

7. Court Transcript, p.225.

8. Criminal Law 768 (1).

9. Court Transcript, p.231.

10. Ibid., p.33.

11. Ibid., p.322.

12. Ibid., p.324.

13. Ibid., p.327.

14. Ibid., p.393.

15. Ibid., p.400.

16. Ibid., pp.461–462.

17. Ibid., p.533.

18. Ibid., p.538.

19. Ibid., pp.634–635.

20. Ibid., p.619.

21. Ibid., p.509.

22. Ibid., p.556.

23. Ibid., p.590.

24. Ibid., p.663.

25. Ibid., p.684.

26. Ibid., p.667.

27. Ibid., p.601.

28. Ibid., p.678.

29. Ibid., p.703.

30. Ibid.

31. At this point, the defense had intended to present a group of expert and character witnesses. But during the questioning of Philip Berrigan, the prosecution stated that it did not deny that the view that the Vietnam war was illegal was a reasonable one that could be held by reasonable men. Since this was at the heart of what the character witnesses—all obviously reasonable persons who regarded the war as illegal—would say, the defense decided to excuse them. This move was surrounded by a good deal of argument during which the government made it clear that its "concession" on this point was grounded in their contention that the question of the war's legality was irrelevant in the first place. In any event, the defense simply introduced its witnesses to the court with the jury absent, after which time the court adjourned.

32. Court Transcript, p.755.

33. Ibid., p.762.

34. Ibid., p.779.

35. Ibid., p.782.

36. Ibid., p.783.

37. In 1735, Hamilton defended John Peter Zenger before a Colonial court on charges of seditious libel. Though his client was guilty according to evidence and law, Hamilton persuaded the jury to acquit. The Zenger case is constantly cited as precedent for jury nullification.

38. Ibid., p.783, emphasis added.

39. Ibid., pp.795–796.

40. Ibid., p.798.

41. Ibid., p.797, emphasis added.

42. Ibid., pp.832–833.

43. Ibid., p.832.

44. Ibid., p.873.

45. The latter was Philip Berrigan's lawyer during his trial for pouring blood on draft files.

46. *Morissette* v. *United States* 342 U.S. 246 (1952), Appellee's Brief, p.4.

47. Appellant's Brief, pp.53–54.

48. Ibid., p.62.

49. *New York Times,* September 19, 1968.

50. Joseph L. Sax, "Conscience and Anarchy: The Prosecution of War Resisters," *Yale Law Review,* LVII (June 1968), p.491.

51. Ibid., p.493.

52. Ibid., p.494.

53. Appellant's Brief, p.76.

54. Appellee's Brief, p.5.

55. Ibid., pp. 5–6.

56. 417 Fed. Reporter 1002.

57. Ibid., p.1009.

58. Petition for Writ of Certiorari, p.7.

59. Brief for the United States in Opposition, p.5.

8. The Career of Civil Disobedience

1. All of the interviews in the preparation of this study were conducted by Rosemary Bannan.

2. See Lawrence Wittner's *Rebels Against the War* (New York: Columbia University Press, 1969) for an account of this.

3. Interview, July 20, 1969.

4. Interview, July 24, 1969.

5. Interview, April 24, 1969.

6. Ibid.

7. Interview, April 27, 1969.

8. Interview, April 24, 1969.

9. Interview, April 22, 1969.

10. Interview, April 27, 1969.

11. Interview, April 24, 1969.

12. Interview, July 19, 1969.

13. Ibid.

14. Interview, May 15, 1968.

15. Court Transcript of Trial, Vol.XVI, p.112.

16. Interview, July 24, 1969.

17. Interview, May 14, 1968.

18. Court Transcript of Trial, Vol. IX, p.97.

19. Interview, April 26, 1969.

20. Interview, May 14, 1968.

21. Interview, April 21, 1969.

22. Interview, May 1, 1969.

23. Reported in Court Transcript of Trial, Vol. VIII, p.155.

24. Statement at the Justice Department, October 20, 1967.

25. Interview, May 26, 1969.

26. *New York Times,* January 19, 1964.

27. *New York Times,* June 13, 1971.

28. Interview, May 15, 1968.

29. Interview, February 20, 1969.

30. Interviews, May 18, 1969.
31. Ibid.
32. Interview, October 31, 1968.
33. "The Anarchists," *Liberation,* June 1967, p.47.
34. Interview, February 19, 1969.
35. Interview, May 18, 1969.
36. Dorothy Day interview, September 22, 1969.
37. Ibid.
38. Interview, October 8, 1968.
39. Letter to the author, November 18, 1969.
40. Interview, September 22, 1969.
41. Interview, October 31, 1968.
42. Interview, February 11, 1970.
43. Interview, July 20, 1969.
44. Interview, February 18, 1969.
45. Interview, October 31, 1968.
46. Interview, February 11, 1970.
47. Interview, May 26, 1969.
48. Interview, October 8, 1968.
49. Interview, February 19, 1969.
50. Interview, October 31, 1968.
51. Ibid.
52. Interview with George Mische, October 8, 1968.
53. Interview, April 24, 1969.
54. Interview, February 18, 1969.
55. Interview, October 31, 1968.
56. Interview, February 11, 1970.
57. Interview, February 19, 1969.
58. Interview, May 14, 1968.
59. Ibid.
60. Interview, May 15, 1968.
61. Interview, October 8, 1968.
62. Interview, April 24, 1969.
63. Interview, July 20, 1969.
64. Interview, May 26, 1969.
65. Interview, July 24, 1969.
66. Ibid.
67. Interview, April 26, 1969.
68. Interview, October 31, 1968.
69. Interview, February 11, 1970.
70. Interview, February 10, 1970.
71. Interview, October 31, 1968.
72. Interview, February 10, 1970.
73. Interview, February 11, 1970.

74. Interview, October 8, 1968.
75. Ibid.
76. Daniel Berrigan interview, October 31, 1968.
77. Interview, February 11, 1970.
78. Interview, April 26, 1969.
79. Interview, October 9, 1968.
80. Interview, October 8, 1968.
81. Interview, February 11, 1970.
82. Interview, February 20, 1969.
83. Interview, October 31, 1968.
84. Interview, May 15, 1968.
85. Interview, February 20, 1969.
86. Court Transcript of the Trial, Vol. VIII, p.54.
87. Interview, July 20, 1969.
88. Interview, April 27, 1969.
89. Interview, February 18, 1969.
90. Interview, April 26, 1969.
91. Interview, February 10, 1970.
92. Interview, October 8, 1968.

9. A Response From Ordinary Men

1. The judges interviewed wished to remain anonymous. All interviews were conducted between May 1968 and December 1969.

2. Judge William T. Sweigert, "Moral Preemption: Part III Claims of *Right* under Positive Law," *The Hastings Law Journal,* Vol. XVII March 1966, p.466. In July 1962 Judge Sweigert sentenced three pacifists to thirty days in jail for attempting to sail their light craft *Everyman* into the atomic testing area near Christmas Island (a U.S. government restricted area) in defiance of a federal court injunction.

3. Ibid., p.470.

4. Ibid., p.464.

5. *Concerning Dissent and Civil Disobedience,* Signet 1968, p.63.

6. Instructions to the Jury (Catonsville Nine), Court Transcript, pp.818–819.

7. *Mary Moylan et al.* v. *United States,* Q 417 F2d 1006 (4th Cir., 1969).

8. Ibid., p.1006.

9. *U.S.* v. *Spock et al.,* 416 F2d 182 (1st Cir., 1967).

10. "A Program for the Trial of Jury Trial," *Am. Jud. Soc. J.,* Vol. XII (1929), pp.170–171.

11. 417 F2d 1006 (4th Cir., 1969).

12. Judge R. Thomsen, Instructions to the Jury, Catonsville Nine Trial, p.818.

13. Rev. Robert McAfee Brown, "War Crimes," Clergy-Laymen Concerned.

14. Court Transcript, Civil Action No. 1733–66. July 11, 1966, p.2.

15. Opinion delivered, April 19, 1968, p.10.

16. Ibid., p.11.

17. *Chicago Sun Times,* July 11, 1972.

18. See *United States* v. *Sisson,* 297 F. Supp. 902 (D. Mass., 1969).

10. As the Crisis Lifts

1. Graham Hughes, "Civil Disobedience and the Political Question Doctrine," *N.Y. Law Review,* Vol. 43, No.1, March 1968, p.12. Professor Hughes, who is quite concerned about Court silence, adds: "But to deny certiorari, to dismiss suits without a reasoned opinion has a tendency to arouse suspicion that the court is simply shrinking from making pronouncements about the basic norms of the system. . . . If courts cannot decide questions about the legality of government action, then they have a public duty to give acceptable legal reasons for their inability to seize the issue." P.18.

2. *Mottola* v. *Nixon,* No.70943 (N.D. Cal., 1970), 3SSLR3312.

3. *Berk* v. *Laird,* 317 F. Supp. 715 (E.D.N.Y., 1970).

4. *Holtzman* v. *Richardson* (E.D.N.Y., 1973), 4LW2015.

5. cf above p.185–86.

6. *Mottola* v. *Nixon* (N.D. Cal., 1970), 3SSLR3315, n.12.

7. Ibid., p.3318.

8. Ibid.

INDEX